Y0-DTI-854

My Fun with Learning

2

The Earth and the Stars

•

Adventures in Science and Discovery

•

Fact Book

The Southwestern Company

Nashville, Tennessee

PRINTED ON RECYCLED PAPER

Contents
The Earth and the Stars

The Earth and the Sky	4
Earth—Our Home	7
The Continents	12
Asia—The Largest Continent	16
Antarctica—The Frozen Continent	20
Europe—Land of the Explorers	24
North America—Our Continent	28
South America—Our Neighbor Continent	32
Africa—A Large and Varied Land	36
Australia—The Island Continent	40
Natural Forces at Work	44
Wind, Water, and Rocks	49
Weather	54
Earth and Space	60
Our Star—The Sun	63
The Moon	68
The Planets	72
The Stars	80
Rockets and Space Travel	84
Life on Other Planets	88
The Final Frontier	91

ACKNOWLEDGMENTS:

The Earth and the Stars

ABOUT THE AUTHOR

Raymond V. Hand, Jr. is a writer and editor specializing in reference and other nonfiction books. He is joint author with Eugene Ehrlich of *The NBC Handbook of Pronunciation*. Among the books to which he has contributed are *The Oxford Illustrated Literary Guide to the United States, The Macmillan Concise Dictionary of World History,* and *The Harper Book of American Quotations*.

ILLUSTRATIONS

Lloyd Birmingham pp. 16, 20, 24, 28, 30–32, 36, 40, 42–43, 54–59, 80–83
Ric Del Rossi/The Ivy League of Artists, Inc. pp. 17–18, 25, 27, 34–35
Dennis O'Brien/The Ivy League of Artists, Inc. pp. 44, 46–48, 60, 68, 70–71, 88–89
Joel Snyder/Publishers' Graphics, Inc. pp. 12–13, 15, 22–23, 37, 39, 63–65, 67, 84, 86–87
James Watling/Publishers' Graphics, Inc. pp. 4–7, 9–11, 49–50, 53, 72, 74–75, 77, 79, 91–92, 94–96

Copyright 1994, 1993, 1992, 1991, 1990, 1989, 1987, 1984, 1982, 1979, 1973, 1968
by the Southwestern Company
Printed in the United States of America

Produced by The Hudson Group, Inc.
Art Direction by Pam Forde Graphics

Adventures in Science and Discovery

Early Ways of Counting	98
Pythagoras—The Father of Mathematics	104
Archimedes' Bathtub	110
The Search for the Philosopher's Stone	117
Copernicus, Galileo, and the Stars	122
The Apple and Isaac Newton	127
Leeuwenhoek's "Little Beasties"	131
Mr. Watt's Steam Engine	135
John Dalton, Atoms, and Molecules	140
Michael Faraday's Candle	144
The Germ Theory	149
George Eastman's Little Brownie	155
The Age of Radio Begins	161
Alexander Fleming Discovers Penicillin	166
Bits, Bytes, and Binary Numbers	170
The Magic Helix	177
Voices on a Beam of Light	181
You, Scientist	186

Adventures in Science and Discovery

ABOUT THE AUTHOR

For the past 20 years *Barbara A. Branca* has worked in the field of science education as an author, editor, and teacher. She has written eight books for young readers, including activity books entitled *Animals and Plants, The Earth, What Makes Things Work,* and *Great Americans,* contributed to several science textbook series, and written numerous articles for science almanacs and encyclopedias. She has taught courses in science and environmental education and helped to found a community science museum.

ILLUSTRATIONS

Gary Lippincott/Publishers' Graphics, Inc. pp. 117, 119, 131, 133, 161–165, 177–179
John Rice/The Ivy League of Artists, Inc. pp. 104, 106–109, 149–150, 152–153, 166–167, 169, 186–187, 189
David Rickman/Publishers' Graphics, Inc. pp. 98–102, 122, 125, 144, 147–148, 181–183, 185
Joel Snyder/Publishers' Graphics, Inc. pp. 110–115, 135–137, 139, 170, 172–175
James Watling/Publishers' Graphics, Inc. pp. 127–130, 140, 142–143, 155–159

Fact Book

Facts About Our Earth   **192**
      The Earth • Continents • Oceans • Deserts • Seas
      Islands • Countries • Mountains • Lakes • Waterfalls
      Rivers • Rainfall • Temperature Records

People and Their Ways   **201**
      The Story of Man • Populations • Languages
      Young People's Organizations

What Mankind Has Done   **218**
      The Seven Wonders of the World • Buildings • Dams
      Waterways • Bridges • Satellites • Space Probes
      Nobel Peace Prize Awards

Numbers Tell Us Many Things   **227**
      Numerals • Weights and Measures
      U.S. Coins and Currency • Foreign Money

Our United States   **235**
      The Indians • Signers of the Declaration of Independence
      The Thirteen Colonies • How the United States Grew
      The Civil War States • Growth of American Railroads
      Presidents • The Fifty States • The U.S. Government

Sports   **250**
      Baseball • Football • Basketball • Soccer
      Professional Sports Champions

Safety Tips   **273**
      Safety Around the House • Safety and Falls
      Street Safety • Bicycle Safety • Automobile Safety
      Swimming Safety • Boating Safety • Personal Safety

Fact Book

TEXT

Consultant on Sports
Richard Rote, Director of Physical Education, Pleasantville, N.Y., High School

ILLUSTRATIONS

Lloyd Birmingham pp. 193–200, 228–234
Marcus Hamilton pp. 274–286
John Rice/The Ivy League of Artists pp. 236–249
David Rickman/Publishers' Graphics, Inc. pp. 202–216
Joel Snyder/Publishers' Graphics, Inc. pp. 251–272
James Watling/Publishers' Graphics, Inc. pp. 219–226

The Earth and the Stars

The Earth and the Sky

HAVE YOU EVER LOOKED UP AT NIGHT into a clear sky full of twinkling stars? Did you wonder how many stars exist and how far away they are? Did you see the moon that night? Perhaps you wondered why the moon looks so much larger than the stars, and why each night it seems to change shape slightly—growing from a slim crescent to a brightly shining full moon, and then back again, until it seems to disappear completely.

As you looked up into the clear night sky, you probably thought of other questions, too. Why are some stars bright and easy to see and others dim and hard to see? What makes stars twinkle? Is a shooting star really a star? What is a star?

Did you know that even when you are sitting still in your favorite chair at home, you are actually traveling through space faster than any racing car can go?

THE EARTH AND THE SKY

Did you know that the sun and moon do not really rise and set at all?

Did you know that human beings have walked on the moon, and that when they returned to Earth they brought back samples of moon rocks? Scientists have studied these rocks to help them learn how the moon, Earth, and the other planets were formed.

Did you know that thousands of satellites have been launched into orbit around Earth? Or that the moon is a satellite, taking a little more than 27 days to go around Earth?

The moon is called a natural satellite because it was made by the forces of nature. The satellites we launch from Earth are called artificial or man-made satellites. Other planets also have natural satellites. Mars has two moons. They are made of rock, the same as our moon. But did you know that some planets have moons that are made up mostly of ice and frozen gases?

Did you know the sun is really a star? How is sunlight made? Why does sunlight feel hot in summer but only slightly warm in winter?

There are so many questions you might ask about the sky and Earth. Why does the sky look blue? Where does the wind come from? What are clouds? What causes lightning? Where does rainwater go? Why does seawater taste salty?

Why are some rocks soft and others hard? Why are rocks different colors? Are moon rocks the same as Earth rocks? Where does beach sand come from?

What causes volcanoes and earthquakes? How are mountains made?

People have always wondered about the world around them and have asked questions like these. Sometimes their beliefs were far from the truth. For example, long ago people believed that Earth is flat and that ships traveling too far in any direction would sail right off the edge of the world. It took brave adventurers like Christopher Columbus to show that Earth is shaped like a giant ball, or *sphere*.

THE EARTH AND THE SKY

To a person in space, Earth looks like a blue-green marble with swirls of white in it. The blue is the color of the great oceans. The green is the color of the continents, the vast stretches of land that rise out of the water. The white swirls are the clouds that float over land and sea.

Today we know the answers to many questions people have asked about Earth, our home. Yet it seems as though every answer produces at least one new question. There is no limit to the things we can learn about our planet.

Earth is a big place, but we have learned that it is tiny compared with the rest of the universe. The universe is so large that scientists are not certain how big it really is. For example, think of a sandy beach at the shore and of how many grains of sand there are on that beach. The universe has a great many more stars than the beach has grains of sand.

Learning about Earth and the stars is a great adventure that never ends but is different each day. Are you ready to begin that adventure?

Then let's go!

Earth—Our Home

OUR PLANET IS QUITE A BIG PLACE, but it is also a very small place. How can Earth be both large and small? It depends on your point of view.

Look at a map of the United States and imagine what it would be like to walk from the shore of the Pacific Ocean to the shore of the Atlantic Ocean. That is a distance of about 2500 miles. If you were to walk at a rate of 2½ miles per hour, you would finish the trip in 1000 hours. That means you would have to walk for more than 41 days without stopping. If you were to walk 5 miles per day, your coast-to-coast trip would take 500 days—almost a year and a half.

Now imagine you are in space, orbiting Earth in a satellite. Your spacecraft circles Earth once every 90 minutes. That means it takes about 9 minutes for your spacecraft to fly over the United States.

Seen from far away in space, Earth looks like a very small place indeed. Our little blue-green planet looks mostly blue because the blue water of the oceans covers almost three-fourths of Earth's surface. The seven large landmasses, called *continents,* and the many islands of the world make up only about one-fourth of Earth's surface.

From out in space, the great mountain ranges of Earth look like long, bumpy wrinkles on the land. But to people on Earth, these mountains—some of which are more than 5 miles high—look gigantic. Out in space, great rivers such as the Mississippi in North America, the Amazon in South America, and the Nile in Africa look like little wiggly lines. Anyone who has stood on the shore of any of these rivers will tell you that there is nothing little about them at all. They are large and powerful bodies of water.

Earth's surface is a combination of many different things—mountains, valleys, deserts, rivers, lakes, seas. Earth would be a boring place if its surface were the same everywhere. Scientists have learned that the rock beneath Earth's surface is not all the same either. In fact, Earth seems to be made up of different layers of material, something like the layers of an onion.

Scientists believe that Earth's center, or *inner core,* is solid material mostly made up of iron mixed with smaller amounts of two other metals, cobalt and nickel. This inner core is extremely hot—about 9000 degrees Fahrenheit, more than three times the temperature needed to melt steel. The inner core remains solid because of the tremendous weight pressing in on it from the material all around it. Most materials must be able to expand when they are heated and change from solid to liquid. Because Earth's inner core is under such high pressure, it cannot expand, so it cannot change to liquid.

Around this solid inner core is an *outer core.* This, too, is made up mostly of iron and is very hot. Scientists think the outer core is either in liquid or near-liquid form.

Around Earth's outer core is a layer of very hot rock called the *mantle.* Many scientists believe that the heat

EARTH—OUR HOME

and pressure deep inside Earth make mantle rock flexible and *plastic*—that is, not quite solid but not quite liquid. Because of this, mantle rock can move very slowly, perhaps a fraction of an inch per year. According to this theory, Earth's top layer, the *crust,* is actually floating on top of the mantle.

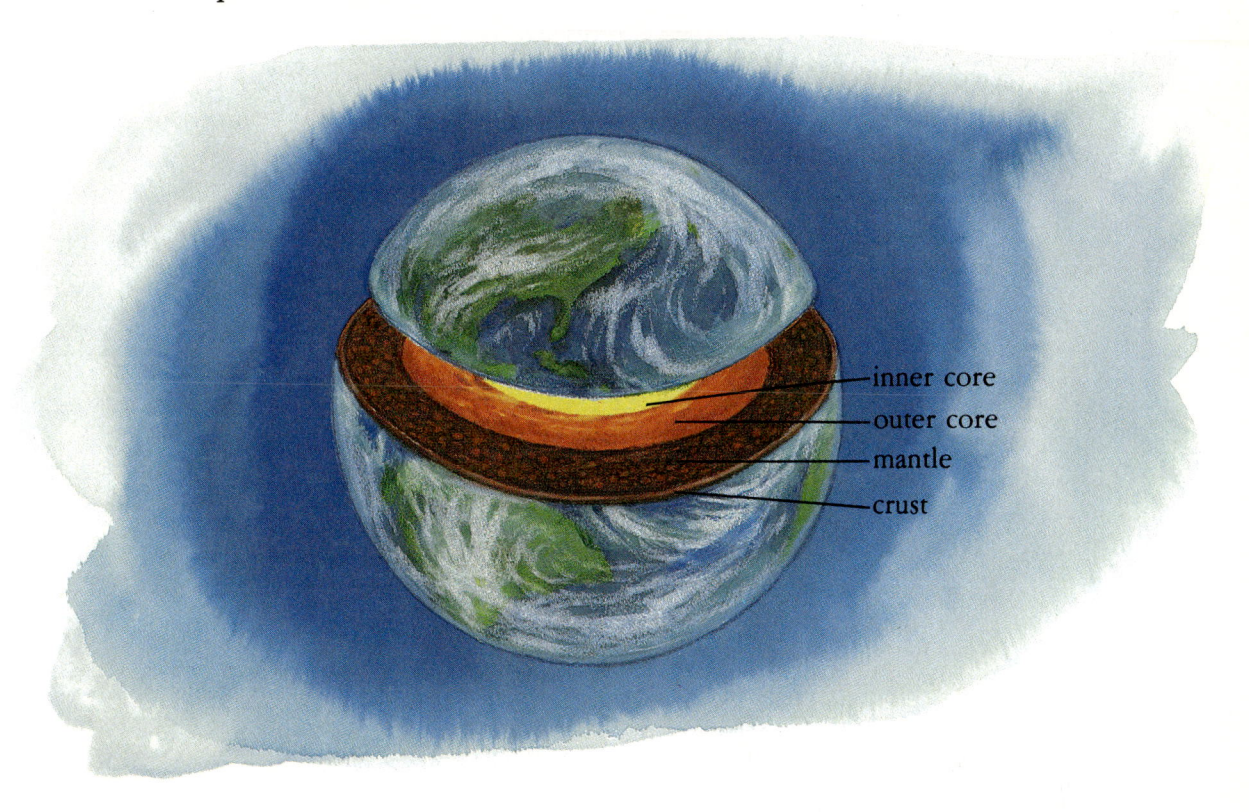

Earth's crust is made up of solid rock. The crust is thin compared with the mantle and core. On land the crust is about 20 to 40 miles thick. In some spots on the ocean floor, the crust is only about 3 to 5 miles thick. The mantle is about 1800 miles thick. The inner and outer cores combined are about 2100 miles thick.

The distance from the surface of Earth to the center of Earth's inner core is a little more than 3963 miles. Earth's *diameter*—the distance through Earth at its middle, or equator—is a bit more than 7926 miles.

Sometimes the mantle pushes up against Earth's crust and lifts it to form mountains. Sometimes the mantle forms mountains by pushing the crust together at one point, forcing it to buckle and fold upward.

9

EARTH—OUR HOME

Sometimes different currents moving in the mantle cause part of the crust to stretch and bend in one direction and part to stretch and bend in another. When the crust can no longer stretch, it breaks, causing an earthquake that sends waves of energy through the ground for many miles in all directions.

Most earthquakes are so weak that people do not even notice them. Some earthquakes are very powerful and can cause great damage.

Sometimes liquid, or *molten,* rock from deep within Earth works its way up through the mantle and crust to form a volcano. Volcanoes do not always occur on land. Sometimes they send their molten rock, or *lava,* up through the ocean floor. If enough lava is released, the volcano forms a new island in the ocean.

The world's great oceans play an important part in making and controlling the weather. The *atmosphere,* the layer of air covering Earth's surface, also plays a part. The atmosphere gathers up moisture from the oceans and carries it over the land, where it is released as rain. The rain makes it possible for plants to live on the land. Plants are an important source of food for animals. They are very important for another reason. They renew the oxygen in the air. Most animals—including people—need to breathe oxygen in order to live.

Earth's atmosphere does another important job. It helps protect us from harmful *ultraviolet radiation* from the sun. Ultraviolet light is the invisible part of sunlight that gives you a suntan—or a sunburn. Too much ultraviolet light causes skin damage and possibly eye damage. The atmosphere filters out most but not all of the sun's ultraviolet light.

As you can see, the different parts of Earth—the land, the oceans and seas, and the atmosphere—all work together to make our planet a good place in which to live.

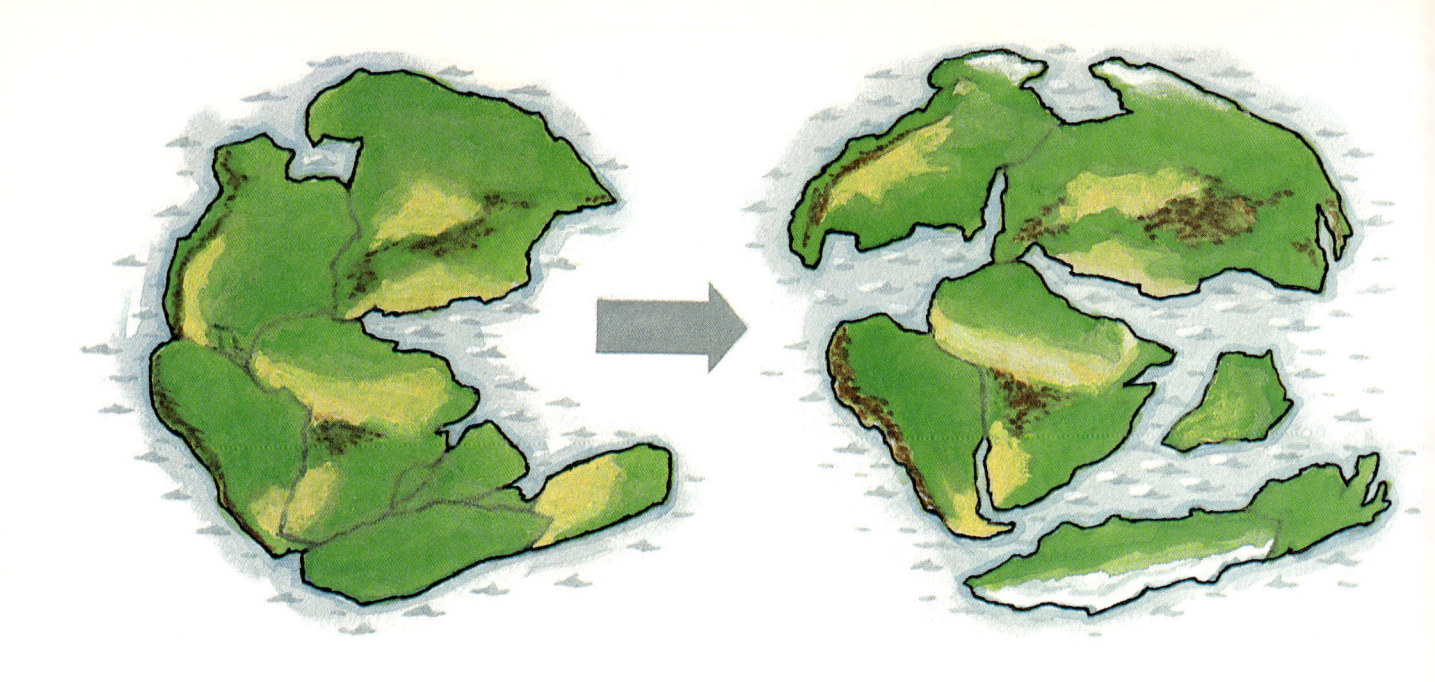

The Continents

SEVEN GREAT LANDMASSES, called *continents,* take up most of Earth's land. The countries of the United States, Canada, and Mexico are located on the continent of North America. To the south is the continent of South America. To the east of these two continents, across the Atlantic Ocean, are the continents of Europe and Africa. To the west, across the Pacific Ocean, is the continent of Asia. To the southwest is the continent of Australia. And to the south of South America, at the southernmost end of Earth, is the frozen continent of Antarctica.

Long ago, scientists thought that Earth's seven continents always had been located where they are today and always had looked the way they look now. In 1915 a scientist named Alfred Wegener suggested a different idea. He said that long ago, all the land was connected in one great continent, which he called Pangaea. Wegener proposed that forces deep within Earth caused this

12

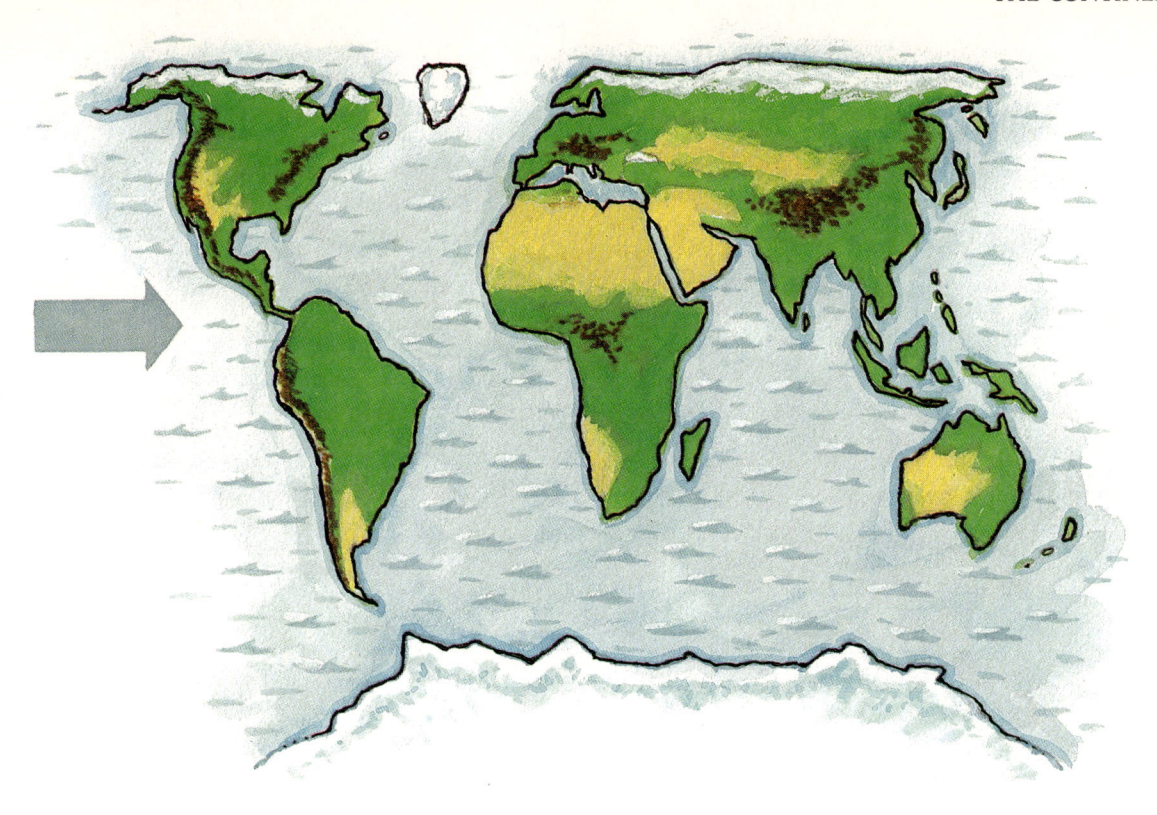

continent to break up into several big pieces, which very slowly drifted away from each other to become the continents we know today.

The way the continents are shaped made Wegener believe that they once had been one large landmass. The continents of North and South America look as though they could be fitted against Europe and Africa. Greenland looks as though it could be moved down to fit between North America and Europe. Australia and Antarctica look as though they broke away from the southern parts of South America and Africa. The island of Madagascar, off the eastern coast of Africa, looks as if it had once been part of that continent.

Wegener believed that as the continents of North and South America drifted west, the crust on their western coasts folded up to form the great chain of mountains that stretches from Alaska to the tip of South America.

THE CONTINENTS

He said that his theory also explains how certain animals came to live in different places that are separated by large stretches of water. For example, hippopotamuses lived on the island of Madagascar as well as in Africa. How could hippos possibly have crossed 250 miles of ocean to get to Madagascar, he wondered. His answer was that Madagascar must have been part of Africa long ago.

Wegener also noted that fossils of a certain type of extinct fern had been found in coal deposits not only in warm countries like India, South Africa, and Australia, but also in the cold and barren mountains of Antarctica. How did these tropical ferns ever spread to all those places, especially to the icy region near the South Pole? Wegener suggested that Antarctica once had been located far closer to the warm equator, at the bottom of the supercontinent Pangaea.

When Alfred Wegener first presented his theory of *continental drift,* most scientists scoffed at it. They were used to thinking of Earth as a ball of solid rock. It was hard for them to consider seriously the idea of drifting continents.

The scientists complained that Wegener had not explained how the continents could drift. Later Wegener suggested that the rock deep within Earth was so hot that it could move very slowly, in much the way a piece of glowing hot steel can be bent and shaped. Such rock could move in currents, just as water heated in a pan rises to the top, cools, and then sinks to the bottom of the pan to be heated again.

Miners had known for centuries that the farther down into Earth they dug mine shafts, the hotter the mines became. Some scientists thought it was possible that rock deep within Earth was in liquid or near-liquid form, but nobody could drill or dig into Earth far enough to prove this.

Over the years, however, many important facts have been discovered that support the theory of continental drift. One clue was the way different rock layers, or *strata,* are arranged.

THE CONTINENTS

If you have ever seen a picture of the Grand Canyon, you probably know that the rainbowlike layers of rock forming the canyon walls are made up of different kinds of rock, placed one on top of the other, like the layers of a cake.

Scientists studying rock strata in different places of the world discovered an important fact that supported the idea of continental drift. They found that a group of rock strata in eastern Brazil matched exactly groups of rock strata in South Africa and India. All three were exactly the same. How could this be, they argued, unless the three were once joined together?

Now the theory of continental drift is accepted by most scientists. But many questions remain to be answered, and much is still to be learned about Earth and how it is constructed.

No matter how the seven great continents of Earth were formed, they are quite different from each other in many ways. Each continent has its own interesting story to tell, through its land, its people, and its history.

Asia—
The Largest Continent

ASIA IS THE BIGGEST continent on Earth. It stretches from Europe in the west to the Pacific Ocean in the east and from the Arctic Ocean in the north to the Indian Ocean in the south. Also, Asia has more people than any other continent. It has 3 billion people, or three-fifths of all the people on Earth.

The westernmost part of Asia is Turkey, which is located between the Black and the Mediterranean seas. A small part of Turkey is on the other side of the Dardanelles and Bosporus straits, which connect the Black and Mediterranean seas. This small part of Turkey is actually in Europe.

The easternmost part of Asia is located at the Bering Strait, which connects the Arctic Ocean and the Bering Sea. About 55 miles across the Bering Strait is Alaska and the continent of North America.

ASIA—THE LARGEST CONTINENT

The distance between the westernmost and easternmost parts of Asia is about 5300 miles. The distance between its northernmost and southernmost parts is more than 5000 miles. The islands of Indonesia, the Philippines, and Japan are also considered part of Asia, even though they are not attached to the Asian mainland.

There are many countries in Asia. Most of Russia, one of the biggest countries in the world, is in Asia. The Ural Mountains mark the boundary between the European and Asian parts of Russia. Most of the people of Russia live in the European part, west of the Urals. But most of the land area of Russia is located east of the Urals.

When you hear people talking about Asia, probably the first country you think of is China. China has more people than any other country in the world—more than 1 billion.

China is often pictured as a land of flat, watery paddies, where rich crops of rice are grown. This is true of only a small part of China. Most of China is too dry or hilly to grow crops. Most of the farmland in China is in the south and east, near the ocean. Much of this part of China is steep and hilly, but over thousands of years the Chinese have leveled off, or *terraced,* the hillsides in order to have more farmland.

China is rich in coal, iron, and many other natural resources, but its most important resource is probably its people and their civilization. The Chinese had built up a great civilization long before the Roman Empire began in Europe.

Mongolia, located between China and Russia, is another interesting land. In the 13th and 14th centuries, the Mongols conquered most of Asia and established a powerful empire.

ASIA—THE LARGEST CONTINENT

Korea, which was divided into the countries of North and South Korea at the end of World War II, also has an ancient history. These countries are located on the eastern coast of Asia, next to China and Russia.

The island nation of Japan is another important Asian country. It has little land and few resources, so its people must work hard and make wise use of the land. Japanese factories produce all sorts of products, and Japan has become a strong and wealthy nation.

India, located in the southern part of Asia, has more than 860 million people. The neighboring countries of Pakistan and Bangladesh were part of India before they became independent. They also have large populations. The landmass that makes up these three countries is called the Indian subcontinent. The population of the Indian subcontinent is growing so rapidly that by the year 2000 there may be more people living there than in China.

Scientists think that long ago, when all the land on Earth was part of one large supercontinent, India was attached to what now is Africa. When the ancient continent started to break up, India broke off from Africa. Slowly it drifted to the northeast and pushed up against the southern coast of Asia. The pressure caused by India moving against Asia pushed the land up to form the mighty Himalaya Mountains, the tallest mountain range in the world.

The various parts of Asia look quite different from one another. Southeast Asia receives a large amount of rainfall and has tropical rain forests. Central Asia gets little rainfall, and several great deserts are located there. In northern Asia is Siberia, which has vast woodlands known as *taiga.* Here much of the ground is frozen year round, except for a thin layer of soil that thaws during the short, hot summer. North of the taiga, near the Arctic Circle, is the dry, flat, cold *tundra,* which has some small plants, mostly mosses and lichens, but no trees.

Lake Baykal, in southern Siberia, is the deepest lake in the world. It is a mile deep in spots and 420 miles long.

Asia also has the highest and lowest points of any continent. The highest point is the top of Mt. Everest, in the Himalaya Mountains, between Nepal and Tibet. Its peak is 29,028 feet above sea level. The lowest point is the shore of the Dead Sea, between Israel and Jordan. This point is 1296 feet below sea level.

The area in which Israel and Jordan are located is part of southwestern Asia and is known as the Middle East. The Middle East is where Asia, Africa, and Europe meet. As we have learned, Turkey is partly in Europe and partly in Asia. Egypt is thought of as a Middle Eastern nation, but most of Egypt is in Africa. Only part of Egypt —the Sinai Desert region—is located east of the Suez Canal and the Red Sea, which make up the dividing line between Africa and Asia.

Most of southwestern Asia gets little or no rainfall. Saudi Arabia is hot and dry and most of its land is desert. Iran and Afghanistan are rocky and dry. For these countries, raising rich food crops is very hard. But there is great wealth under the poor soil of these lands. Saudi Arabia is a rich country because of the vast deposits of oil under its sandy desert. Iran also has oil. The mountain regions of Iran and Afghanistan are rich in minerals and ores, but the land is so rugged that it is difficult to get to the minerals and mine them.

These are just a few of the many interesting things there are to learn about Asia.

Antarctica— The Frozen Continent

HAVE YOU EVER WONDERED what much of North America was like during the last Ice Age? You can get a pretty good idea by visiting Antarctica, the continent at the bottom of the world.

Antarctica is a vast, frozen continent. It is almost completely buried under an enormous layer of snow and ice. More than two-thirds of Earth's fresh water is frozen in this ice layer, which is more than a mile thick in places. The ice is always moving. Frozen rivers of ice called *glaciers* move slowly from the center of Antarctica out toward the ocean. At the water's edge the ice breaks into giant *icebergs,* which float north and eventually melt.

The ice layer stretches out past the land's edge and forms a shelf over the water. In the short warm season, the edges of this ice shelf break off and form ice *floes,* floating sheets of ice up to several miles across.

Antarctica is a land of bitter cold and high winds. The coldest temperature ever measured on Earth was recorded at Vostok Station in Antarctica. There, on July 21, 1983, scientists recorded a temperature of −128.6 degrees Farenheit.

Antarctica's winds begin in the mountainous area at the center of the continent and blow out toward its edges. Winds of 200 miles per hour have been measured in Antarctica.

Although Antarctica has so much water, it is actually a desert continent. It is a desert because its bitterly cold air carries little moisture. Only a small amount of snow falls in the center of the continent each year. Antarctica's outer edges, near the warmer oceans, receive more snow.

Even though there is so little snowfall, Antarctica has fierce snowstorms. The strong winds pick up the snow that has already fallen and blow it from place to place. This constantly changes the landscape—or snowscape—of Antarctica.

Antarctica is the fifth largest continent. It is larger than Europe or Australia. It is shaped something like a disk that has two large dents on one side. These dents are two large seas, the Ross and the Weddell. Stretching across the continent is a great mountain range called the Transantarctic Mountains. Sticking out between the Ross and Weddell seas and stretching north toward the tip of South America is a narrow neck, or *peninsula,* of land called the Antarctic peninsula.

Near the shore of Ross Sea is Mt. Erebus, an active volcano that rises 12,448 feet above sea level. It is one of several volcanoes in Antarctica. The tip of the Antarctic peninsula has seen a number of eruptions in recent years. In this area there is a break, or *rift,* in Earth's crust. Sometimes molten rock pushes up from deep inside Earth and through the rift. If it rises on land, the molten rock cools and hardens. But if it rises under the sea, it turns the water instantly to steam and there is a great explosion.

Scientists have found evidence of such explosions in the shapes of the peninsula's islands and bays. The area also has hot springs—pools of water that are heated by volcanic rock deep underground.

Because Antarctica is so cold, it is home to very few living things. Most are simple plants called mosses and algae. Such animals as penguins and seals visit Antarctica to raise their young, but their real home is the icy Antarctic Ocean. The waters of this ocean are filled with tiny plants and animals called *plankton,* as well as small, shrimplike animals called *krill.* Plankton and krill are food for many larger animals, including fish, penguins, and whales. The fish are food for other animals, including squid and seabirds.

Large deposits of coal have been found in Antarctica. The coal was formed from the remains of ancient plants that were trapped in the ground. Over a long period of time, the force of the rock pressing on the dead plants turned them into coal.

ANTARCTICA—THE FROZEN CONTINENT

If Antarctica is so cold, how could all those ancient plants have lived there? Long ago Antarctica and all the other continents were part of the supercontinent Pangaea. This supercontinent was then located much closer to the equator and most of it was probably covered with tropical forests.

When Pangaea broke into several smaller continents, Antarctica began to drift slowly to the south, where Earth receives less of the sun's warmth. Eventually all the tropical plants died off and the remains of the great forests were covered over by rock, and then by snow and ice.

There are no countries in Antarctica, but many nations have built scientific bases there. Seven countries claim territory in Antartica, but they have agreed not to colonize their claims and instead to use the continent for peaceful scientific study. So who owns Antarctica? The answer is that nobody owns Antarctica, because everybody owns it.

Europe—
Land of the Explorers

EUROPE IS ONE OF THE SMALLEST continents. Only the island continent of Australia is smaller. Europe has less than one-tenth of the world's land, but that land has an interesting shape. Europe has a number of peninsulas.

We call Europe a continent, but it is not really a separate piece of land. Europe is attached to Asia, and together they make up a single landmass called *Eurasia.* In a way, Europe is simply a large, odd-shaped peninsula at the western end of Asia.

Europe's eastern border runs right through Russia. It goes north and south along the Ural Mountains, through the Caspian Sea, and along the Caucasus Mountains northeastward to the Black Sea. All of Russia west of the Urals is in Europe, and all of Russia east of the Urals is in Asia.

EUROPE—LAND OF THE EXPLORERS

Europe's southern border goes through the Black Sea and along the northern shore of the Mediterranean Sea.

At the western end of the Mediterranean Sea, Europe and Africa come very close to touching one another. The small passage that connects the Mediterranean with the Atlantic Ocean is the Strait of Gibraltar. On the northern side is the European country of Spain and on the southern side is the African country of Morocco.

At its narrowest point, the Strait of Gibraltar is only 9 miles wide. At the entrance to the strait are two enormous rocks that stand like giant stone soldiers guarding the gate to the Atlantic Ocean. The European rock is called the Rock of Gibraltar, and the African rock is called Jebel Musa. Together they are known as the Pillars of Hercules.

The Pillars of Hercules were named by the ancient Greeks after one of the important characters in their stories, or *myths*. One ancient Greek story says that mighty Hercules moved the rocks there so he would have a place to tie some oxen he had captured. Another story says that once there was a single mountain there, but Hercules split it in two with a single blow.

Scientists think that Europe and Africa were once joined at the Strait of Gibraltar but that natural forces caused the land bridge between the two continents to break apart.

EUROPE—LAND OF THE EXPLORERS

The western border of Europe is the Atlantic Ocean. The islands of Great Britain, Ireland, and Iceland are also part of Europe. Europe's northern border is formed by the Norwegian and Barents seas, which are part of the icy Arctic Ocean.

At the top of Europe is the Scandinavian peninsula. It is attached to Europe through the mountainous lands of Finland and the northwestern part of Russia. The countries of Norway and Sweden, located on the Scandinavian peninsula, and Denmark, just to the south, together are known as the Scandinavian countries.

Scandinavia was the land of the Vikings, a warlike, adventurous, seafaring people. Norway's rugged coastline contains many *fjords,* deep inlets with steep sides where the sea travels many miles inland. The fjords are deep valleys that were carved into the land by glaciers long ago. After Earth's climate warmed, the glaciers melted and the sea level rose, filling the valleys with water. The fjords made excellent harbors for Viking ships.

In southern Europe, the land that forms the country of Greece is also a peninsula. The ancient Greeks lived in many small, independent *city-states.* Although they never formed a single nation, the Greeks did many important things. They added to our knowledge of science, mathematics, philosophy, and the arts. Most important, the Greeks invented the idea of *democracy.* The word democracy comes from Greek words meaning "the people to rule." Our form of government is based on the Greek idea of democracy.

The Greeks put their understanding of science and mathematics to good use. They used their knowledge to build many beautiful buildings, such as the Parthenon in Athens. People who design buildings today still study the works of the ancient Greek builders.

To the west of Greece is the boot-shaped peninsula of Italy, land of the ancient Romans. The Romans conquered Greece and used many of the Greek ideas, but they did not use the idea of democracy. Instead they

EUROPE—LAND OF THE EXPLORERS

conquered an empire that stretched from northern Africa and western Asia through much of Europe.

Even the rugged and lofty mountains called the Alps, which stretch across the northern part of Italy, could not stop the advancing Roman armies. The Alps extend from France through Switzerland into Austria, a distance of about 750 miles. The Alps is the tallest mountain range in Europe.

The Roman Empire did not last, however, and when it ended Europe fell into a kind of sleep that we call the Dark Ages. Very little progress was made for centuries. Then, slowly, during a period called the Middle Ages, the countries of Spain, France, Portugal, England, Denmark, Sweden, Holland, and others started to emerge. After the Middle Ages came the Renaissance, a period when Europeans began to make great progress in trade, art, science, learning, and invention.

The number of people increased in Europe, and European rulers decided to look for new lands and more trade. So it was that explorers like Christopher Columbus set out on their voyages of discovery.

The physical shape of Europe has played an important part in making our modern world the way it is. All those peninsulas give Europe many thousands of miles of coastline. Because of this, Europe had many seaports and ships. Thus, the Europeans were just the right people to venture out on the seas and discover the New World.

Not all of the European countries were formed during the Middle Ages. Germany and Italy did not become countries until after the age of exploration. Some countries in eastern Europe, such as Czechoslovakia and Hungary, did not come into being until the 20th century. Russia was an empire for several hundred years. It was part of the Soviet Union, which came into being in the 20th century, for 70 years.

Some of Europe's countries are old and some are new, but the people of all these countries have rich histories that go back to before Roman times.

North America— Our Continent

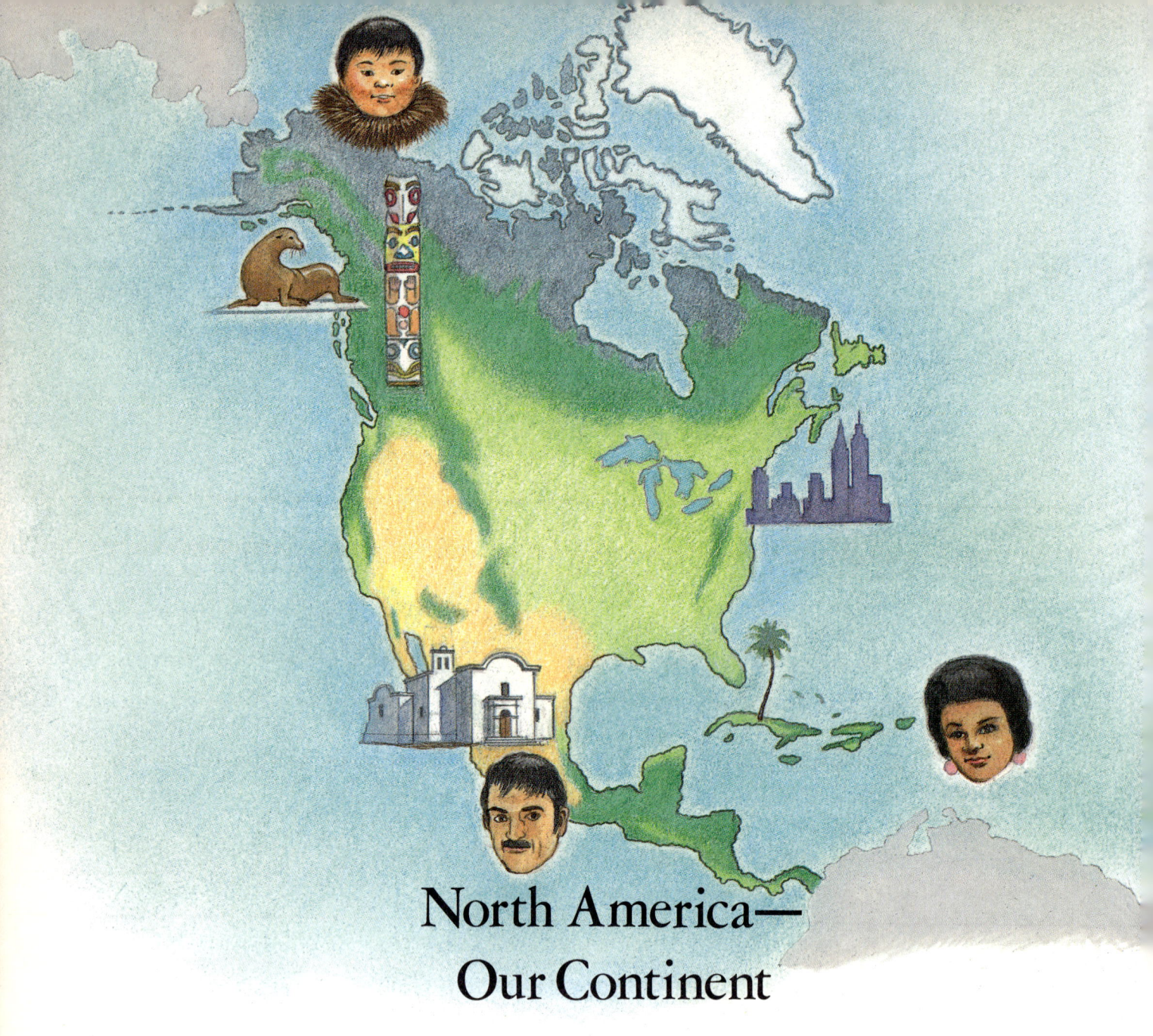

WHEN THE FIRST EUROPEAN EXPLORERS ventured into the Atlantic Ocean on their voyages of discovery, only the Norse, or Viking, explorers sailed west. The Portuguese, Spanish, and other explorers all sailed south, mapping the coast of Africa and looking for a way east to the rich lands of Asia. They found that this route to the Orient was long and difficult.

Christopher Columbus believed he could get to Asia by sailing west. In 1492 he set out to prove he was right. When he landed on the little island of San Salvador in the Caribbean Sea, he did not know he had discovered a new land. He thought he had arrived in the Asian land called the Indies. So Columbus gave the name Indians to the people he found living in this new land.

Later explorers showed that Columbus had found an unknown land that stretched from the Arctic Ocean in the north to the Antarctic Ocean in the south. They called this vast place the New World. This new world came to be named America after another explorer, Amerigo Vespucci.

America turned out to be two large bodies of land attached by a narrow strip of land. The northern part was called North America and the southern part was called South America. And, of course, the narrow central strip of land between the two was named Central America.

North America is usually said to include Central America, the islands of the Caribbean Sea and the western Atlantic Ocean, and the large island in the north known as Greenland.

Greenland was discovered by the Norwegian explorer Eric the Red. About a thousand years ago, in the Middle Ages, Norwegian settlers from Iceland came to live in Greenland and the northern coast of the North American mainland. Their settlements in North America did not last. Eventually people forgot that the settlements had ever existed. The rest of Europe did not learn about North America until Columbus found it again.

North America stretches from the cold tundra near the Arctic Ocean to the tropical border of Colombia in South America. The three main countries of North America are Canada, Mexico, and the United States.

The highest and lowest points in North America are both in the United States. The highest point is Mt. McKinley in Alaska, whose peak is 20,320 feet above sea level. The lowest point is in Death Valley in California —282 feet below sea level.

Canada, the northernmost country of North America, is the second largest country in the world. Only the Soviet Union is larger. Canada's northern frontier is still just that—a frontier. Many of Canada's Eskimos, or *Inuit,* live in the northern lands near the Arctic, but most Canadians live in the southern and eastern parts of the country. In those areas there are beautiful towns and cities and rich farms and orchards.

The middle part of Canada is a vast flatland. Here Canadian farmers grow large harvests of wheat and other crops. In the prairie to the west ranchers raise big herds of cattle. The western part of Canada, from the Rocky Mountains to the Pacific Ocean, has thick green forests and is rich in valuable ores and minerals.

Mexico is in the southern part of North America. Before Europeans got to the New World, Mexico was the home of several advanced civilizations. The first was the Mayan. The Maya built large cities on the southeastern tip of Mexico, called Yucatán. Their empire stretched south into Central America.

After the Maya came the Toltecs, who built their empire in the middle part of Mexico. After them came the Aztecs, whose great empire spread through central and southern Mexico. When the Spanish *conquistadors,* or conquering soldiers, learned of the great wealth of the Aztec Empire, they came and made war. The Aztecs had no horses or guns and were soon beaten and forced to work as slaves for the Spaniards. Mexico became part of Spain's New World empire, which included most of Central and South America and part of North America.

Mexico is a beautiful and varied land. The parts of Mexico near the oceans are hot and humid. In the Sierra Madre Mountains of western Mexico it is cool and dry. In the middle of Mexico it is usually hot and dry.

The official language of Mexico is Spanish. It is also the official language of six of the seven countries of Central

America. In Belize the official language is English. This is because Belize was a British colony for many years.

The United States is located between Canada and Mexico. Along its eastern coast is a long mountain chain called the Appalachians. The Appalachian Mountains are old and rounded by ages of weathering. In the west is a younger, taller, and steeper mountain range, the Rocky Mountains. In between the Rockies and the Appalachians is a great flat plain. There American farmers and ranchers produce vast amounts of food for the world.

In this middle part of the United States is one of the great rivers of the world, the Mississippi. The Mississippi River begins far to the north in Minnesota and travels more than 2300 miles south to New Orleans, Louisiana, where it empties into the Gulf of Mexico. Almost all of the rivers between the Rockies and the Appalachians, including the Ohio, Missouri, and Tennessee rivers, empty into the Mississippi.

Two states of the United States—Alaska and Hawaii—are not located between Canada and Mexico. Hawaii is a group of islands located in the middle of the Pacific Ocean. Hawaii is part of the United States but it is not part of North America. Alaska, located north and west of Canada, is part of North America. Alaska is a rugged, beautiful state. The largest of the states, it is rich in oil, minerals, forests, and other natural resources. It is known especially for its vast unspoiled wilderness areas.

The United States is rich in natural resources, but perhaps its greatest resource is its people. The United States probably has more different kinds of people than any other country. People have come to live in the United States from every other nation in the world.

South America— Our Neighbor Continent

SOUTH AMERICA, THE FOURTH LARGEST continent, is shaped like a triangle. It is a little smaller in area than North America. South America is about 4700 miles long, stretching from the warm Caribbean Sea in the north to the icy Antarctic Ocean in the south. It is about 3200 miles wide at its widest point, near the middle, where Brazil bulges out into the Atlantic Ocean. Most of South America is located south of the equator.

People often think of South America as being directly south of North America, but this is not so. It is actually located to the south and east of North America. In fact, the westernmost point of South America is almost directly south of Florida, which is on the eastern coast of North America.

Along South America's western coast are the steep, rugged Andes Mountains. The Andes curve like a long rocky spine down the back of South America. There are many very tall mountains in the Andes. The tallest is Mt. Aconcagua, in the southern part of South America on the border between Argentina and Chile. Its peak is 22,831 feet above sea level.

There are a number of active volcanoes in the Andes. Earthquakes often occur there, and some are quite strong. The earthquakes and volcanoes are signs that Earth's crust is changing its shape along the western coast of the continent.

In the southern part of South America, on the coast of Chile, glaciers have carved deep valleys and fjords from the mountains down to the sea. Sometimes we think of the steep-sided fjords as being found only in Norway, but they are also found in South America and other parts of the world.

The Andes Mountains are rich in ores and minerals. Bolivia has rich tin deposits; Chile and Peru have vast deposits of copper; and Ecuador has large amounts of oil deep within the ground. In the mountains of Colombia are great plantations where much of the world's coffee is grown. Colombia is the world's second biggest producer of coffee, after neighboring Brazil.

Next to Colombia and Brazil is the country of Venezuela. Venezuela is one of the world's leading suppliers of oil. Venezuela's oil industry has made it one of South America's richest countries.

Caracas, the capital of Venezuela, was the birthplace of Simón Bolívar. Known as the Liberator, Bolívar helped lead the people of South America in their fight to free themselves from Spanish rule in the 19th century.

East of Venezuela are the countries of Guyana and Suriname. East of Suriname is French Guiana, which is owned by France.

Peru was the hub of the Inca Empire, which became a great power in the 15th century. Its center was at Cuzco, in the southern part of Peru. The Inca extended their empire about 2000 miles from north to south along the Andes Mountains and from the Pacific coast hundreds of miles inland. The Inca built beautiful stone cities, fitting giant blocks of building stone together so well that the blocks did not need cement to hold them together.

The Inca were conquered by the Spaniards in the 16th century. Their civilization disappeared in a short time, but the ruins of such cities as Machu Picchu, near Cuzco, are reminders of their great empire.

East of the Andes, in the northern part of the continent, the land slopes down to one of the last great rain forests, the Amazon. This tropical rain forest covers much of northern South America. It receives a great deal of rainfall year round. Much of the rain runs off the mountains and hills and flows into streams and rivers. The streams and rivers empty into South America's largest river, the Amazon.

The Amazon River is the second largest river in the world. The Nile River in Africa is longer, but the Amazon carries much more water than any other river on Earth. Oceangoing ships can travel about 1000 miles up the Amazon. At its mouth—where the river empties into the sea—the Amazon is so wide it looks more like a sea than a river.

The Amazon rain forest has many animals and plants that are found nowhere else on Earth. Scientists have not even discovered them all yet. Some of the plants are used to make medicines.

For years South American farmers have been burning the rain forest to get farmland. The soil is not good for farming because most of the chemicals needed to grow good crops are not in the soil but in the trees. The farmers get only one or two good crops and then have to move on and burn more of the rain forest. After the farmers leave, the rain forest does not grow back. Instead, a thick covering of tough scrub plants grows in its place.

In the southern part of the continent the trees thin out and the land opens to a large prairie grassland called the *pampas.* Here the cowboys of Argentina, called *gauchos,* raise herds of cattle, much as the cowboys of the United States do. Argentina is one of the leading producers of beef cattle in the world. Argentina also raises sheep and grows wheat and corn. To the north and east of Argentina are the countries of Paraguay and Uruguay. The land in these countries is also good for farming and cattle ranching.

In the Atlantic Ocean off the southern coast of Argentina are the Falkland Islands, which are owned by Great Britain. These islands have been claimed for many years by Argentina, but the people of the Falkland Islands want to remain British citizens.

At one time all of South America was owned by European countries. Portugal owned most of eastern South America, including Brazil. This is why Brazilians speak Portuguese today. The western half of South America was owned by Spain. The history of South America's fight for independence during the 19th century is a fascinating story, every bit as exciting as the story of North America's struggle to become free.

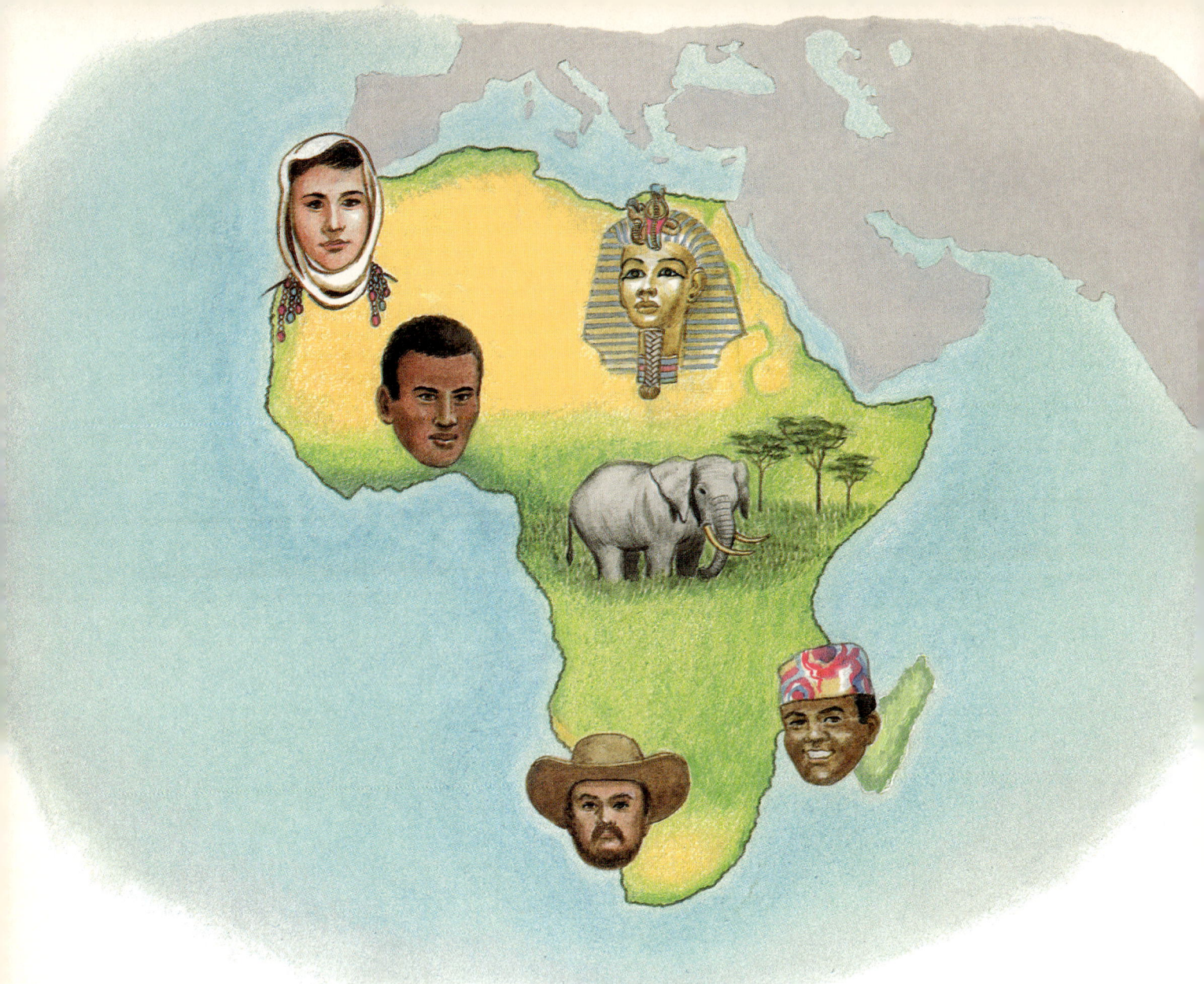

Africa—
A Large and Varied Land

AFRICA IS THE SECOND LARGEST continent on Earth. Only Asia is larger. Africa has more than one-fifth of all the land and more than one-tenth of all the people on Earth.

Africa is more than 5000 miles long, stretching from the shore of the Mediterranean Sea to the Cape of Good Hope, and from the South Atlantic to the Indian Ocean. It is about 4700 miles wide at its widest point, near the middle of the continent.

Africa has few mountains for such a large continent. The Atlas Mountains stretch across the northwestern corner of Africa between the coast and the Sahara Desert. The Sahara is the largest desert in the world. It stretches across almost all of northern Africa.

Another group of mountains is located in eastern Africa. In this mountain group stands the snowcapped volcano named Mt. Kilimanjaro, the tallest mountain in Africa. Its peak is 19,340 feet above sea level.

To the northwest of Mt. Kilimanjaro is Lake Victoria, the largest lake in Africa. The Nile River, the longest river in the world, starts nearby and flows into Lake Victoria on its long trip north to Egypt and the Mediterranean Sea.

A number of rivers empty into the Nile, and many have great dams to control their waters. Long ago, before the dams were built, the rivers would swell with spring rains and carry great amounts of rich, fine soil, or *silt,* northward. In Egypt the water would flood the riverbanks, spreading the silt out on the land.

The yearly gift of rich new soil from the river made it possible for Egyptian farmers to grow large crops along the plains of the Nile and on the great triangular *delta* that the river forms where it empties into the Mediterranean Sea. These large crops of food made it possible for the Egyptians to build a great and powerful empire. The Egyptian kings, or *pharaohs,* built many great cities, temples, and statues. They also built the Great Pyramids of Giza, near the modern city of Cairo. The pyramids were the tombs of the pharaohs. It took thousands of workers many years to build each one.

AFRICA—A LARGE AND VARIED LAND

Cairo, the capital of Egypt, is located on the Nile. It is the largest city in Africa and one of the largest cities in the world. Most of the people of Egypt live along the Nile. Much of the rest of Egypt is desert. The Egyptians owe much to the majestic Nile, which brings them life-giving water from the middle of Africa.

Large tropical rain forests stretch across the middle of Africa. The rain forests contain many colorful plants, buzzing insects, and interesting animals. Gorillas, monkeys, birds, snakes, and other animals make the rain forest their home. Crocodiles, hippopotamuses, and other animals live in the rivers.

South and north of the rain forests are flat grasslands called *savannas*. Among the animals that live in the savannas are lions, elephants, rhinoceroses, zebras, antelopes, giraffes, and many kinds of birds.

Ancient Egypt was only one of many kingdoms that rose and fell in Africa. Africa has a great number of different groups, or tribes, of people. Some of these tribes built powerful kingdoms that lasted for hundreds of years. There were kingdoms in Africa long before the first European kingdoms arose.

In the eighth century Arab explorers and traders began to travel through northern and eastern Africa. They converted many Africans to their religion, Islam. Northern Africa became part of the Arab Empire, which stretched from Spain into western Asia.

In the 15th century a Portuguese prince known as Henry the Navigator sent explorers to map the western coast of Africa and to look for an easterly route to Asia. One of the first things they learned was that the African coast is quite even and smooth, so there are few good harbors and bays. This meant that there were not many good places for the Europeans to start colonies and explore inland.

The explorers also learned that most of Africa's large rivers—the kind that explorers like to travel on—had large and dangerous waterfalls. This also made it difficult for them to travel into Africa. It took a good deal of time for the Europeans to learn about the inner part of Africa and its people.

At first the European countries traded with the African kingdoms. They found that some African tribes were willing to sell as slaves prisoners captured from other tribes. Sometimes the Europeans captured Africans and carried them into slavery. The slaves were sent to work in the European colonies in the New World.

Eventually the European nations stopped the slave trade, but they also decided at about the same time that Africa was a rich land worth conquering.

The European empires were stronger than the African kingdoms. In the 19th century almost all of Africa was conquered by France, Great Britain, Belgium, Germany, and other European nations. They divided Africa into colonies. Some Africans went to work growing crops on large plantations. Others went to work in mines, digging up Africa's wealth of diamonds, gold, metal ores, and valuable minerals. For a time Africa did not belong to the Africans.

In the 20th century the old European system of empires and colonies began to end. The two great world wars helped weaken Europe's hold on Africa. In 1945, after World War II ended, Africa began to awaken. Since then more than 45 new African nations have become independent.

Africa is a large and varied land. It is rich in natural resources, plant and animal life, history, and people. It is an old land but also a new land. In many ways, the story of Africa is only just beginning.

Australia—
The Island Continent

THE ISLAND CONTINENT of Australia is often called "the land down under." This is because the whole continent is south of the equator. The only other continent that is entirely south of the equator is Antarctica.

Australia is a little more than half the size of Antarctica and is the smallest of the world's continents. It is about 2500 miles from north to south and about 2300 miles from east to west. Australia includes a number of islands. The largest of these is Tasmania, which is located off Australia's southeastern corner.

Australia is a flat continent. Even its mountains are low and rounded. Australia's main mountain range, the Great Dividing Range, stretches along the eastern side of the continent. It divides the narrow, flat eastern coast of Australia and the flat grassland, or savanna, on the western side of the mountains.

The tallest mountain in Australia, Mt. Kosciusko, is located at the southern end of the Great Dividing Range. Its peak is only 7310 feet above sea level—less than half as high as Mt. Kilimanjaro in Africa.

Off Australia's northeastern coast is the Great Barrier Reef, the longest coral reef in the world. A large variety of colorful and interesting plants and animals live in and near the reef.

The northern and eastern parts of Australia are covered with lush green forests and woodlands. Farther inland, on the other side of the mountains, is the gently rolling savanna. Toward the middle of Australia the land becomes a great, flat *plateau* that is dry and hot and mostly desert. The desert goes almost all the way to Australia's western coast. The southwestern part of Australia gets a good deal more rainfall than the middle of the continent. It has forests and grassland like northern and eastern Australia.

Most of Australia's large lakes are saltwater lakes. They cannot be used to water crops because the salty minerals in the water would damage or kill the plants. Many of the rivers and streams get smaller or dry up completely during the warm summer season, so they cannot always be used to water crops either. Australia would not be a good place for farming except for one important thing. Deep within the ground in many places are vast pools of cool, clean water. Australian farmers and ranchers have drilled wells to get to the water. This underground water supply has helped Australia to become an important producer of beef, lamb, wool, wheat, sugar, and fruit.

Australia's land is rich in minerals and other natural resources such as timber. Its mines produce large amounts of such metals as nickel, gold, iron, aluminum, and copper. Australian factories use these metals and other raw materials to make everything from electrical wires to jet airplanes. Australia's forests provide a steady supply of wood to the country's lumber mills and paper factories.

The Dutch were the first Europeans to explore Australia, but the British were the first to settle there. In 1788 Great Britain started up a *penal colony,* a place to send people who had broken the law. They started this colony where the modern city of Sydney now stands. The people served out their prison sentences and then usually settled in Australia.

The British started up more colonies. Soon most of the settlers coming to Australia were people who were not in trouble with the law. Eventually Great Britain claimed all of Australia. In 1901 Australia became a self-governing nation.

When the first British settlers arrived, they found that the continent was already the home of a number of tribes of dark-skinned people. They called these people *aborigines,* which comes from Latin words meaning "from the beginning." Nobody knows for certain when the aborigines arrived in Australia or how they got there. They probably arrived by boat from the islands north and west of Australia. To the British settlers, the aborigines were the original Australians who had been there from the beginning.

The aborigines hunted and gathered their food and lived in small, simple shelters. They used stone tools and hunted with spears, which they threw with the help of a tool called a throwing stick. They also used a curved blade of wood called a *boomerang.* When the boomerang was thrown, it would fly on a curving path through the air and come back toward the thrower.

The settlers learned that the aborigines were an artistic people. They made beautiful paintings in caves, on rocks, and on pieces of tree bark.

When the British settlers came to Australia, they took the best land for themselves. This forced the aborigines to move to the hot, dry western lands. Today many aborigines live in lands set aside for them in the middle part of Australia. Others live and work in Sydney, Melbourne, Brisbane, and other cities.

Australia has many plants and animals that are found nowhere else in the world. Perhaps the best known of these animals are the kangaroo and the koala. The kangaroo is one of Australia's many *marsupials.* A marsupial is an animal that carries its babies in a pouch on its body when the babies are still very young.

Other interesting Australian animals include the kookaburra, a bird whose call sounds like wild laughter, and the platypus, a furry marsupial whose bill is wide and flat like the bill of a duck.

East of Australia are the two large islands of New Zealand, and to the north is the island of New Guinea. To the north and east are thousands of small islands, including the Hawaiian islands. Sometimes the area that includes Australia and all these South Pacific islands is called Oceania. This island world has many different kinds of people to learn about and things to see.

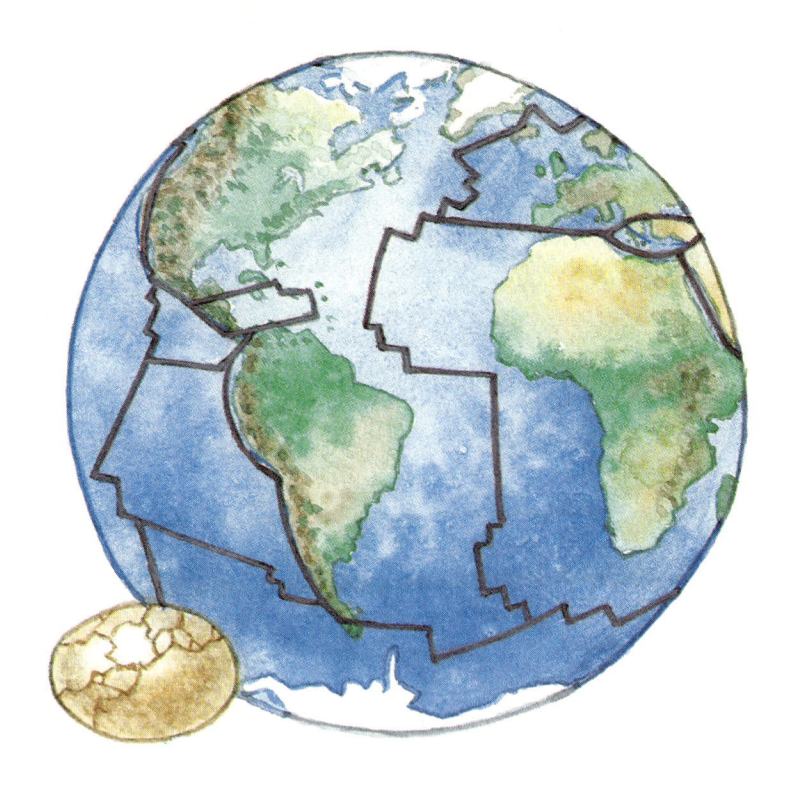

Natural Forces at Work

ALL AROUND US the land is changing. Every day Earth's surface is a little different. Most of the time the change is so slight we do not notice it and even scientists cannot always measure it.

There are powerful forces building up and tearing down Earth's thin outer layer, the crust. Some of these, such as wind, water, and ice, work to tear down the land. If they were the only forces, Earth eventually would be worn down to a smooth, ocean-covered ball. But there are forces just as strong as these at work building up the land.

Earth is made something like a hard-boiled egg with its shell cracked into a number of big pieces. The shell is like Earth's crust, which is also broken into big pieces, called *plates*. The white part of the egg is like Earth's mantle, and the yellow part of the egg like Earth's core.

The mantle is very hot and its rock moves very slowly. Earth's plates float on the surface of the mantle like rafts on a pond. They are made up of different layers, or strata, of rock.

Sometimes the mantle forces two plates against each other or squeezes the crust together in one place. When this happens, the crust may fold upward to form mountains. The Appalachian Mountains in the eastern United States and the Ural Mountains in the Soviet Union were formed this way. Europe's snowcapped Alps were also formed by Earth's crust folding upward.

The rock in Earth's crust is usually very hard and firm. It is difficult to imagine that anything could cause it to bend and fold. When rock is hit hard enough with a hammer it does not bend. It breaks. How is it, then, that the forces in the mantle rock can cause Earth's crust to bend?

The answer to this question has to do with time. When rock is hit with a hammer, energy goes instantly from the hammer head into a small spot on the rock. This sudden burst of energy causes the rock to break. But the forces within the mantle work on a large area over a great length of time. The particles of matter, or molecules, in the rock have time to adjust themselves to the force, and the rock very slowly bends.

Sometimes the moving mantle causes the crust to break apart along a line, or *fault.* This forms two blocks of rock, one on each side of the fault. The blocks push against each other but sometimes they cannot move because of friction. The motion of the mantle underneath builds up energy in the blocks. When enough energy is stored up to overcome the friction, the blocks suddenly slip and move, causing waves of energy to move through the ground. This is how the sudden motion of Earth's crust causes earthquakes.

These blocks of rock, called *fault blocks,* can move sideways or up and down. The San Andreas Fault in California is a sideways-moving fault. The land on the western side of the fault is sliding north, toward Alaska.

NATURAL FORCES AT WORK

When fault blocks move in an up-and-down direction, one block is pushed up higher than the other or sinks lower than the other. Sometimes one block rises and the other sinks.

The Sierra Nevada mountain range in California is a giant fault block about 400 miles long. One edge is tilted down beneath the Pacific Ocean. The other edge, in eastern California, has been pushed up many thousands of feet. The gently sloping western side of the Sierra Nevada is actually the flat top of this giant block. The steep walls of rock that make up the eastern side of the mountain range are the upturned edge of the fault block. Mountains that are built this way are called *fault block mountains.*

Another way the land is built up is through *volcanic action.* Volcanoes are formed when molten rock, or *magma,* deep within Earth pushes its way up through a crack in the crust and forces its way to the surface. When it reaches the surface it is called *lava;* the mountain it builds is called a volcano. Sometimes the lava is thin and flows quickly in all directions, forming a low, wide volcano cone. Other times it is thick and moves only a short distance before cooling and hardening, forming a steeper

NATURAL FORCES AT WORK

cone. Sometimes the volcano spews lava and ash and hot gases high into the air. The lava cools in small chunks called cinders. The volcano's cone is called a cinder cone.

Sometimes the magma moves up through the crust but does not go to the surface. It builds up in an underground *dome* that pushes up the top layers of rock to form a mountain; then it cools and hardens.

Devil's Tower in Wyoming shows one way in which Earth's surface is changed by building-up forces and tearing-down forces working together. Devil's Tower is made of volcanic rock that pushed up through layers of softer rock and then cooled before it reached the surface. Over a long period of time the softer rock layers were worn away by wind and water, leaving only the tower of volcanic rock.

NATURAL FORCES AT WORK

Volcanic action happens under the oceans, too. In the middle of the Atlantic Ocean is a ridge of tall volcanic mountains. Here lava pushes its way up and is cooled by the ocean water. New seafloor is being built up at the ridge, and the old seafloor moves east and west of the ridge. Far away the opposite is happening. Some edges of the crust's plates are slowly sinking back into the mantle, where the rock will be remelted. After a long time it will rise up again somewhere in the world to become new seafloor or new land.

Volcanoes and earthquakes often happen at the edges of the great plates. The plates are slowly moving against each other, building up energy for earthquakes and forming cracks for magma to rise to the surface.

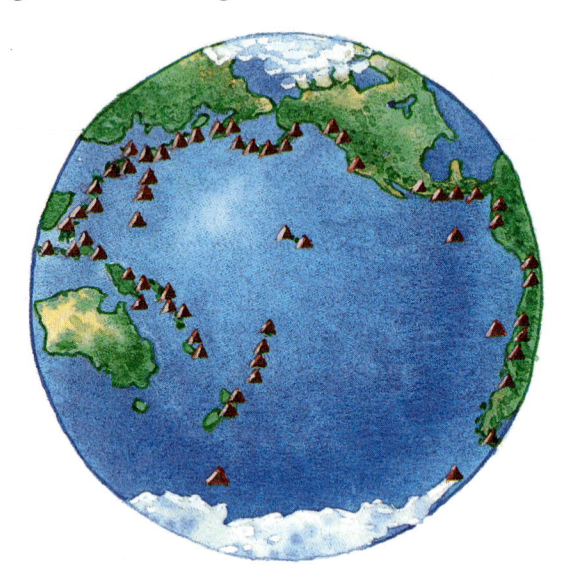

One of Earth's plates makes up the floor of the Pacific Ocean. All around its edges is a ring-shaped area known for earthquakes and volcanoes. This area, called the Pacific Rim, includes the mountain ranges of western South America and North America and the mountain ranges of eastern Asia. The Pacific Rim includes Japan, Indonesia, and the islands of the western Pacific. Because there are so many volcanoes in this area, it is often called the Ring of Fire.

Wind, Water, and Rocks

WE HAVE SEEN that powerful forces are at work building up the land. There are also forces just as powerful that are wearing down, or *weathering,* the land. Together, these two kinds of forces give our Earth its many interesting landforms—its mountains and valleys, rolling hills and flat plains, high plateaus, steep canyons, and sandy white beaches.

The Grand Canyon is an example of building-up forces working together with weathering forces to change Earth's surface. This beautiful canyon in Arizona runs through a high plateau area. For about a million years the Colorado River has been cutting its way through the soft plateau rock. Rain, wind, and frost also have been helping to break down the rock and widen the canyon. At the same time, forces within Earth have been lifting the layers of plateau rock upward. The result of these two forces working together is that the Grand Canyon is more than a mile deep.

WIND, WATER, AND ROCKS

Water does much to weather the surface of Earth. Rain falling in the mountains soaks into the soil and then runs off, carrying some of the soil into streams and rivers. The streams and rivers carry the mountain soil down off the mountains into the valleys and to the sea. The dissolved minerals carried by rainwater to the sea give seawater its salty taste.

Sometimes rainwater cuts deep grooves, or gullies, into mountains and hillsides. This usually happens in places where the slope of the land is steep and there are few plants to hold the soil with their roots. When the rain falls in such places, the soil, rocks, and plants are carried away quickly, leaving the land scarred and ugly.

Wind also carries away the soil. When the land is dry and there are few plants to hold the soil in place, the wind can pick up the dirt and dust and carry it great distances.

In the 1930's a long dry spell, or drought, struck the United States. In the farm area formed by parts of the states of Colorado, Kansas, Oklahoma, Texas, and New Mexico, the dry weather killed off the crops and left the land bare. Strong winds picked up the dry soil and carried it away. In some places the wind removed all of the soil. In other places farms were covered with tall dunes of soil. Some of the soil was carried more than a thousand miles by the wind. Thus, this farm region came to be called the *Dust Bowl.*

Whenever water and wind damage the land by carrying off the soil, the damage is called *erosion.* Farmers have learned much about how to protect the land from erosion by both water and wind. They have learned to plant rows of trees between fields as *windbreaks* to break the force of the wind and make it less able to blow away the soil. They have also learned to let some of their land rest so it will not dry out. Instead of planting crops in a field every year, they let grass grow there for a season or two before plowing it and planting a new crop. This helps return important chemicals to the soil and also helps the deeper soil build up a reserve of moisture.

Farmers have also learned not to plow their land straight down the sides of hills or slopes. By plowing along with the shape, or *contour,* of the land, the long rows of plowed soil, or furrows, act like little dams or steps down the side of the slope. When the rain comes, the furrows help keep the water from racing down the hillside and carrying the soil away.

A form of water, ice, also works to wear away the land. In the cool upper parts of mountains, snow sometimes collects faster than it melts. Over time it packs down into a frozen river of ice. Then the ice river, called a *glacier,* begins to move slowly, plowing up rocks and soil and carving deep gouges out of the mountainside. Glaciers move very slowly, perhaps only a few feet each year. Down in the valley, where the weather is warmer, glaciers melt, dropping all the rock and soil they have dug out of the mountain.

Long ago, when Earth's climate was cooler than it is now, most of North America was covered with a sheet of ice. Glaciers carried vast amounts of rock and soil from northern Canada into the eastern and midwestern United States. Europe, too, was almost covered with ice. The steep slopes of the Alps were carved by great glaciers. There are still some glaciers in the Alps, slowly scouring the sides of the mountains and moving the rocks and soil into the green valleys.

Ice wears down rock in another important way. Water gets into tiny cracks inside rock. When cold weather comes, the water freezes and expands, pushing like a wedge against the inside of the rock and weakening it. After many freezings and thawings, the rock breaks into smaller pieces.

The wind helps to wear down mountains. It picks up sand and dirt and blows it against the rock. This acts like sandpaper on the rock, chipping and grinding away at it to make new soil and sand.

Another force at work changing the land is the movement of the ocean. The ocean's waves are at work day and night, wearing down shore rocks and breaking them into smaller and smaller pieces.

Water, wind, waves, and ice all work to break rock down into smaller and smaller pieces—gravel, pebbles, sand, soil. These are called *sediments.* The sediments are carried away and laid down, or deposited, in new places. Sometimes they are deposited in low places on the land and sometimes in the sea. Over long periods of time many layers of sediment are built up, one on top of the other. The weight of the top layers presses down on the bottom layers. When the bottom layers have been pressed long and hard enough, they become a new kind of rock called *sedimentary rock.*

Most of the rock layers of the Grand Canyon are sedimentary rock formed ages ago. Scientists think that at one time, the whole area around the Grand Canyon was the floor of a great inland sea. This sea deposited layers of sediment that became rock. Then the sea dried up and the land lifted to form the plateau.

WIND, WATER, AND ROCKS

Sedimentary rock is one of three main classes of rock. The second class of rock is formed from the molten rock within Earth. It is called *igneous rock.* Sometimes igneous and sedimentary rocks are pushed deep into Earth's crust. There high temperatures and pressures can change them into the third class of rock, which is called *metamorphic rock.*

Granite is an example of igneous rock. Granite is very strong and hard and resists weathering. It is often used as a building material. Basalt, the hard rock that makes up most of the crust beneath the oceans, is also an igneous rock.

Sandstone is a sedimentary rock. So is shale, which was once very fine soil, or *silt.* Sometimes shale is changed by great heat and pressure into slate, which is a metamorphic rock.

Limestone is a sedimentary rock formed from the crushed remains of shellfish. The chalk that is used to write on blackboards is one kind of limestone. Marble is a metamorphic rock that was formed out of limestone. It is often used for statues, monuments, and the walls of buildings because its surface can be polished to a shiny smoothness.

Rocks differ in color, hardness, and appearance according to their consistency and makeup. There are a great many kinds of igneous, sedimentary, and metamorphic rocks, but every rock on Earth belongs to one of these three main types.

shale
sandstone   limestone
SEDIMENTARY

basalt
granite
IGNEOUS

marble
gneiss
METAMORPHIC

Weather

THE OCEAN WAVES at the seashore are continually wearing away rocks, building up or tearing down beaches, and helping to change the shoreline. But what causes these waves?

They are caused mostly by the invisible ocean of air that is all around us, which is called the atmosphere. The atmosphere is made up of several gases. Most of the atmosphere consists of a gas called nitrogen. About one-fifth of the atmosphere is oxygen, the gas that almost all animals and plants need to breathe in order to live.

The atmosphere is what gives the sky its blue color. Regular sunlight looks yellow-white in color, but it is really made up of light of all the colors of the rainbow. Tiny particles in the atmosphere cause the blue light to break away from the sunlight and scatter in the sky, so we see the sky as blue.

The atmosphere is moving all the time. When it moves quickly, we feel it as a breeze or as wind. It is the wind that makes the waves on the ocean. When the wind blows over the surface of the ocean, it pushes against the water, putting some of its energy into the water in the form of waves. The longer or harder the wind blows over the water's surface, the bigger and more powerful the waves will become.

Perhaps you have been at a lake or pond when the air was still and the water was as smooth as glass. Then a breeze started up, and small ripples soon appeared on the water. The breeze formed the ripples in the same way that the wind forms the waves in the ocean.

The atmosphere also contains moisture, which it gets from ponds, lakes, streams, rivers, oceans, and even little puddles left over from rainstorms. But most of the moisture comes from the oceans, which make up nearly three-quarters of Earth's surface. The atmosphere collects water from the oceans and carries it over the land. This water falls as rain or snow. Much of it flows into streams and rivers and is carried back to the oceans.

How does the water get into the air? The sun plays an important part in this process. Sunlight warms the water. Some of the water *evaporates*—changes from a liquid to a gas—and becomes water vapor. The water vapor rises into the atmosphere. High in the sky, where the air is cooler, the water vapor *condenses,* or changes back into a liquid. The water forms tiny droplets around specks of dust carried by the wind. If the air is cold enough, the water forms tiny ice crystals. Clouds are collections of these water droplets or ice crystals.

cirrus

cumulus

stratus

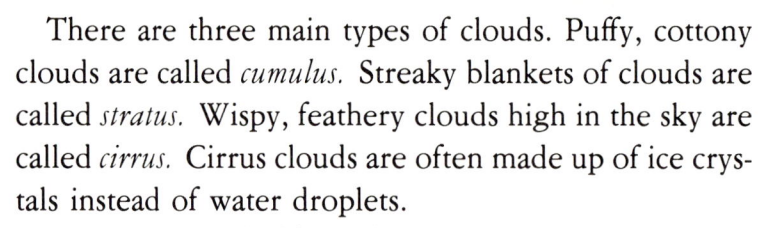

There are three main types of clouds. Puffy, cottony clouds are called *cumulus.* Streaky blankets of clouds are called *stratus.* Wispy, feathery clouds high in the sky are called *cirrus.* Cirrus clouds are often made up of ice crystals instead of water droplets.

Warm air can hold much more water than cold air. Sometimes the warm wet air blowing in from the oceans comes to a tall mountain range. It must rise to get over the mountains. That makes the air cooler and less able to hold water. The air must release some of its water as rain or snow. Mountain ranges near coasts—such as the Cascade range on the western coast of the United States and

Canada—often receive large amounts of rain on the ocean side and less rain on the inland side.

The atmosphere gathers almost all its moisture from large bodies of water. This is why in the middle parts of continents, away from oceans, seas, and large lakes, the land is often dry. The air that blows there has already dropped most of its moisture and has not gathered much while traveling over land.

Air temperature is the measure of the warmth or coolness of the air. The instrument used to measure temperature is a thermometer. There are two different thermometer scales. One scale often used in the United States is the *Fahrenheit scale.* With a Fahrenheit thermometer, the freezing point of water is marked at 32 degrees and the boiling point at 212 degrees. The second type of scale, the *Celsius* or *Centigrade scale,* is used in many other countries and also in most scientific laboratories. On the Celsius scale, water freezes at 0 degrees and boils at 100 degrees. The Fahrenheit and Celsius scales are just two different ways to measure the same thing.

Humidity is the measure of how much moisture is in the air. Air that contains much moisture is said to be humid. Relative humidity is the amount of moisture in the air compared with the greatest amount of moisture the air can hold. A relative humidity of 100 percent means the air is holding all the moisture it can. If the temperature drops, the air will not be able to hold as much moisture, and rain or snow will probably fall.

Air pressure is the measure of how closely the tiny particles, or molecules, of air are pressed together. For example, the higher the air is above sea level, the thinner it is. That means there is more space between air molecules and air pressure is low.

The winds move large bodies of air, or *air masses,* across the land. These air masses have different temperatures and pressures. Air pressure is measured with an instrument called a *barometer.* High pressure usually means fair weather. When the air pressure drops, rain or snow may be on the way.

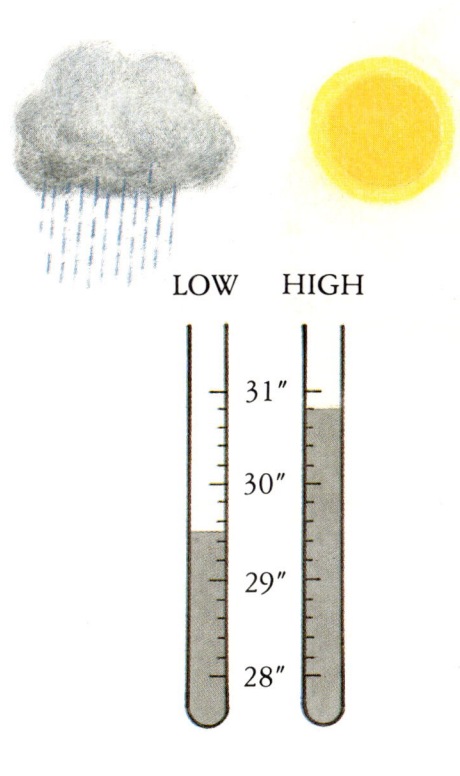

Storm fronts often form where air masses of different temperatures and pressures meet. By taking measurements at many different places, weather forecasters can make maps showing where storm fronts are located and how quickly they are moving.

A *thunderstorm* is a combination of rainstorm and electrical storm. *Lightning* is caused by the different electrical charges that build up between rain clouds, or between rain clouds and Earth. When the charges become strong enough, a sudden current of electricity will jump from one place to another as a flash or streak of lightning. The sudden lightning makes sound waves in the air that we hear as thunder.

Some storms have their own special names. Tropical storms that form over the warm ocean are called *hurricanes* when their winds reach 75 miles an hour. Hurricanes cause great damage with their high winds and heavy rains, especially near the coast. Hurricanes that form in the western Pacific Ocean are called *typhoons.*

Sometimes the wind starts to swirl so fast it forms a funnel-shaped cloud called a *tornado.* Tornadoes form mostly in flat, open country where there are few hills or trees to break the wind. Where the tip of its funnel touches ground, the tornado can cause great damage.

Scientists have learned that most of the world's winds are quite steady and follow clear patterns. Winds are usually named for the direction from which they come. In the northern hemisphere is a belt of winds that blow from west to east. They are called the *prevailing westerlies.* In the southern hemisphere is a belt of winds that blow from east to west. They are called *prevailing easterlies.*

Winds that blow around the North and South poles are called *polar winds.* On either side of the equator are belts of hot, dry winds called *trade winds.* These winds blow toward the equator. They were named trade winds during the age of sailing ships. The traders of those days knew they could rely on these steady winds to carry their ships from one land to another.

Earth and Space

LONG AGO, people knew very little about the world around and above them. They looked up into the night sky and wondered about the lights they saw there. They marveled at the fiery sun as it rose from one edge of the land in the morning and disappeared from the opposite edge at night. They stood on the tops of hills and gazed with curiosity at the distant horizon, where the edge of the sky seemed to touch the land.

Throughout the ages, people have asked questions about Earth and the sky. Does the sky touch the ground? What is the sky made of? What are the stars?

Perhaps the hunters and shepherds of ancient times, sitting around their camp fires at night, thought the flickering stars were the far distant camp fires of hunters who lived in the sky. If the flickering lights were camp fires, why did they never seem to go out? And why did they move slowly across the night sky?

In order to answer these and other questions, people in different parts of the world invented many colorful and interesting ideas. Some people in ancient India thought that Earth is flat and rests on the backs of three giant elephants. The elephants stand on the back of an enormous tortoise. The Shawnee Indians of North America believed something very close to this. They said Earth is balanced on the back of a giant turtle. If the turtle moves suddenly, it causes an earthquake.

The ancient Egyptians believed the sky is a river and that the god Ra sails his fiery barge—the sun—across the sky each day. Some Egyptians thought that the Milky Way—the belt of stars that stretches across the sky like a starry road—was formed by kernels of corn dropped by the goddess Isis.

Ancient people were very interested in the sun, moon, planets, and stars. They kept written records of the stars and planets, recording their brightness, location, and movement. They also kept records of the appearance of comets and meteors. This study of the stars and other heavenly bodies is called *astronomy.*

Ancient people thought that the stars and planets have power over things that happen on Earth. Many people thought that the appearance of a comet or meteor in the sky is a sign that something terrible is going to happen. The location of the planets in the sky was also important. In fact, the planets seemed to be so important that each was named after an ancient god.

The ancient astronomers thought that certain groups of stars made interesting pictures in the night sky. The astronomers named these groups of stars, or *constellations,* after things that the star groupings resembled—Ursa Major, the Great Bear; Ursa Minor, the Little Bear; Taurus, the Bull; Aries, the Ram; Leo, the Lion. Nobody is certain who named the first constellations, but we do know that early sailors soon found an important use for them. They learned that by noting where certain constellations were located in the night sky, they could figure out the right direction in which to point their ships.

EARTH AND SPACE

The ancient Phoenicians, who lived on the eastern coast of the Mediterranean Sea, were important early astronomers. Their understanding of the constellations helped them to become the greatest sailors of their day. The Egyptians also made important discoveries in astronomy and mathematics.

The ancient Greeks took all the knowledge gathered by the Phoenicians, Egyptians, and other peoples and added to it. During the Golden Age of ancient Greece, a new view of the world began to take shape.

The Greek philosophers often disagreed with one another about Earth and the heavens. Some thought Earth to be flat. Others believed it to be round, like a sphere. One philosopher, named Aristarchus, said that Earth and the planets travel around the sun. He was correct, but he was unable to convince others.

One of the most famous astronomers of the ancient world was Ptolemy, who was born in Greece but lived in Egypt. In his book, the *Almagest,* Ptolemy said that Earth is a sphere located at the center of the universe, and that the sun, the moon, the planets, and the stars all revolve around Earth. Ptolemy's ideas were accepted by almost everyone. For the next 1400 years people believed Earth to be the center of the universe.

Most people never read Ptolemy's book. They simply assumed that Ptolemy was correct. But in the 16th and 17th centuries, a few scientists began to wonder if the *Almagest* was correct. With newly invented telescopes and other instruments, astronomers began making observations that did not agree with Ptolemy's system. Two scientists—first Nicolaus Copernicus, and later Galileo Galilei—showed that Ptolemy was wrong, and that Earth and other planets revolve around the sun.

At first these great men received only scorn for their efforts. Eventually, however, other scientists showed that Copernicus and Galileo were right. This new knowledge made it possible for such astronomers as Tycho Brahe, Johannes Kepler, Isaac Newton, and Edmund Halley to add still more to our understanding of the universe.

Our Star—the Sun

BECAUSE OTHER STARS SEEM TO BE very different from the sun, it was a long time before people learned that the sun is really a star. Other stars are just tiny specks of flickering light in the night sky, but the sun fills the daytime with bright light. We see the stars at night but we see the sun only during the day.

The stars do not really flicker. They seem to twinkle because our atmosphere bends, or *refracts,* the starlight one way and then another. Sometimes the light gets to our eyes, and sometimes it misses them. This makes the stars seem to flicker and twinkle.

The sun looks much larger than the other stars. This is because it is much closer to Earth than other stars. The sun is about 93 million miles away from Earth, but the next nearest star is more than 268,000 times farther away. Light travels faster than anything else in the universe—about 186,000 miles per second. It takes the sun's light about eight minutes to get to Earth, but it takes the light from the next nearest star more than four years to reach Earth.

The sun is vastly larger than any of the nine planets. In fact, the sun contains about 740 times as much mass as all the planets combined. Mass is the amount of matter, or substance, an object contains. From space, Earth looks like a tiny speck compared with the sun.

Unlike Earth, which is made up of solid or liquid matter, the sun is made up mostly of the lightest of all gases, hydrogen. A little more than one-fourth of the sun is helium, the second lightest gas.

One difference between stars and planets is that stars produce their own light and planets do not. All the light from a planet is reflected light. It is also reflected light that comes from our moon, from the moons of other planets, and from some other heavenly bodies, such as comets. Their light is really reflected sunlight.

How does the sun make its own light? The sun contains so much hydrogen and helium that its gravity is very strong. The weight of all this gas pushing in on the sun's center, or *core,* squeezes the molecules of gas together and produces extremely high temperatures and pressure. The pressure of the gases at the sun's core is several billion times greater than the pressure of our atmosphere on Earth.

This enormous temperature and pressure squeezes the atoms of hydrogen together and forces them to combine,

summer

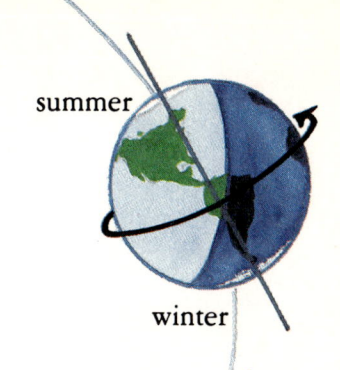

winter

or *fuse,* to form atoms of the heavier gas helium. This kind of nuclear reaction, called *fusion,* releases great amounts of heat and light.

On a hot summer day on Earth, the temperature might reach 100 degrees Fahrenheit. The temperature on the surface of the sun is about 10,000 degrees, and the temperature at the center of the sun is about 27,000,000 degrees.

The sun seems to be hotter and to warm Earth more in summer than in winter. This is because Earth is slightly tilted on its *axis*—an imaginary line through Earth's poles that helps us see how Earth spins, or *rotates.*

If Earth's axis were straight up and down, the equator would always be facing the sun, and the northern and southern hemispheres would each receive the same amount of sun all the time. But because the axis is tilted slightly, each hemisphere gets different amounts of sunlight at different times of the year. The tilt of Earth's axis is what causes the seasons.

During part of the year Earth's northern hemisphere is tilted toward the sun and its southern hemisphere is tilted away from the sun. Then it is summer in the northern hemisphere and winter in the southern hemisphere. When the axis is tilted away from the sun, the southern hemisphere is tilted toward the sun and the northern hemisphere is tilted away from the sun. Then it is summer in the southern hemisphere and winter in the northern hemisphere.

OUR STAR—THE SUN

The sun produces a tremendous amount of energy. Earth receives only about two-billionths of all the energy produced by the sun, yet that tiny amount is still enormous. The sun warms the oceans and causes the water to evaporate and form clouds in the air. Sunlight also warms the air and causes the winds to blow.

Some of the sun's energy is used by green plants, which are able to turn sunlight into food energy through a chemical reaction called *photosynthesis*. Plants are food for animals, so the sun makes it possible for both plant and animal life to exist on Earth. Also, the coal and oil within Earth were formed from dead plants. The energy in the gasoline for our cars, the coal for our electric power plants, and the heating oil for our homes originally came from the sun.

Around the sun is a cloud of superhot gas called the *corona*. The temperature of the corona is about 2000 times higher than the temperature at the sun's surface. The corona shoots out bright plumes and streamers of gas. It also forms bright lines that seem to stretch from the sun's north pole to its south pole. The corona is not nearly as bright as the sun's surface, so scientists take pictures of the corona when the moon comes between Earth and the sun and completely blocks out the light coming from the sun's surface.

Pictures of the corona show it only around the sun, but its gas particles spread far beyond, even past Earth. Far away from the sun, these gases are known as the *solar wind*. When comets travel toward the sun, the solar wind blows pieces of ice and dust off them, forming the part of the comet that we can see—its tail.

We cannot look directly at the sun because its light can damage our sensitive eyes. Scientists use special instruments to look at the sun's ever-changing surface. Sometimes great eruptions on the sun's surface shoot huge plumes of gas, called *solar flares*, into the corona. Solar flares send into space powerful radio waves, x-rays, and atomic particles which can cause problems with radio and television broadcasts on Earth.

OUR STAR—THE SUN

The sun often has spots on its surface that are cooler than the area around them. These are called *sunspots.* Sunspots have very strong magnetic fields that also affect radio and television broadcasts on Earth. The number of sunspots is always changing. Sometimes there are no sunspots to be seen, and other times there are dozens of large spots. About every eleven years the number of sunspots climbs from a low point to a high point and then drops back again to a low point. This is called the sunspot cycle.

Even though our sun is very large, it is only an average size star. Some stars are hundreds of times bigger than the sun. Other stars are small, burned out remains of once mighty stars. There are so many stars in the universe that it is impossible to count them. Yet, to us, the most important star is our sun.

The Moon

ON A JULY DAY IN 1969, two astronauts did something that had never been done before. They climbed out of their *Apollo 11* spacecraft and walked on the moon. It was the first time people had stood on the surface of another heavenly body.

As Neil Armstrong and Edwin Aldrin walked on the moon that day, a television camera aboard the spacecraft beamed the picture back to Earth, where millions of people around the world watched and marveled. Only a few years earlier, the idea of landing people on the moon and bringing them safely back to Earth had sounded like science fiction.

People have wondered about the moon for ages. The ancient Romans believed the moon is the shiny chariot of their goddess Diana. Many interesting ideas have been thought up about the moon. Some people thought the rough surface of the moon made it look like a person's face, which they called the Man in the Moon.

In the early 17th century, the Italian scientist Galileo Galilei began using a new invention, the telescope, to study the moon. The telescope *magnified* the moon and other heavenly bodies—made them look larger and closer. Because of the telescope's power to magnify, Galileo was able to see things that nobody had ever seen.

Galileo saw that much of the moon's surface is covered with mountains, valleys, and craters of all sizes. He also saw the low, dark areas that ancient astronomers thought were great seas. To this day they are called seas, although they have no water in them. The area that the *Apollo 11* astronauts landed in is called the Sea of Tranquility.

The moon revolves not around the sun, but around Earth. That means that the moon is not a planet like Earth, but a *satellite*. A satellite is any small object that revolves around a planet. Our moon is a natural satellite —meaning it was not made by humans. Spacecrafts launched into orbit are called artificial satellites.

The moon revolves around Earth once in about every 27 days. At the same time, Earth is revolving around the sun, and the sun is traveling through space. Because of these different motions, the distance from Earth to the moon is always changing. On average, the distance from Earth to the moon is about 239,000 miles.

Day and night on the moon are different from day and night on Earth. Earth rotates on its axis one complete turn every 24 hours, so each day and night on Earth lasts 24 hours. The moon rotates on its axis once about every 27 days—the same amount of time it takes to revolve around Earth. This means that the same side of the moon is always facing Earth.

Because the moon takes so long to turn on its axis, daytime on the moon lasts almost 14 Earth days and nighttime lasts just as long.

No one ever saw the far side of the moon—the side facing away from Earth—until space probes flew around the moon and sent back pictures. The pictures showed that the far side looked much the same as the near side.

It, too, had mountains, craters, and valleys and was covered with rocks and dust.

The moon would not be a good place to live. There is no water on its surface and it has practically no atmosphere. There are no clouds in the sky, no winds, no weather, no air to breathe. Astronauts visiting the moon must carry their own air supplies and wear leakproof space suits. The daytime temperature can reach about 261 degrees Fahrenheit. That is more than hot enough to boil water—if the moon had any water. At night the temperature can drop to 279 degrees below zero.

The moon is much smaller than Earth. Its diameter is only about one-quarter of Earth's diameter. Earth could hold about 50 moons inside it. The force of gravity at its surface is about one-sixth of Earth's gravity. That means a 180-pound man would weigh only about 30 pounds on the moon. This explains why the astronauts who visited the moon were able to jump so high and far.

The moon's gravity is strong enough, however, to cause ocean tides—the rise and fall of the ocean level. The moon's gravity pulls on the water, causing a bulge, or high tide, at the point on Earth nearest the moon, and another bulge at the point farthest away from the moon. Midway between these points, the ocean level drops, causing low tides.

The sun's gravity also makes tides, but the sun is so far away its tidal pull is less than half as strong as that of the moon.

When we look up at the moon in the night sky, sometimes we see a round full moon, sometimes a half-moon, and sometimes a thin crescent moon. Sometimes we cannot see the moon's light at all.

Half of the moon is always facing toward the sun and is lighted by it. The other half is turned away from the sun and is in darkness. We can see only the part of the moon that is lighted by the sun, but we do not always see all of the lighted part. How much we see depends on where the moon is in its orbit around Earth. When we see the whole lighted half, we see the full moon. When we see only half of the lighted half, we see a quarter-moon. There are two quarter-moons. When we can see none of the lighted half, we call that a new moon.

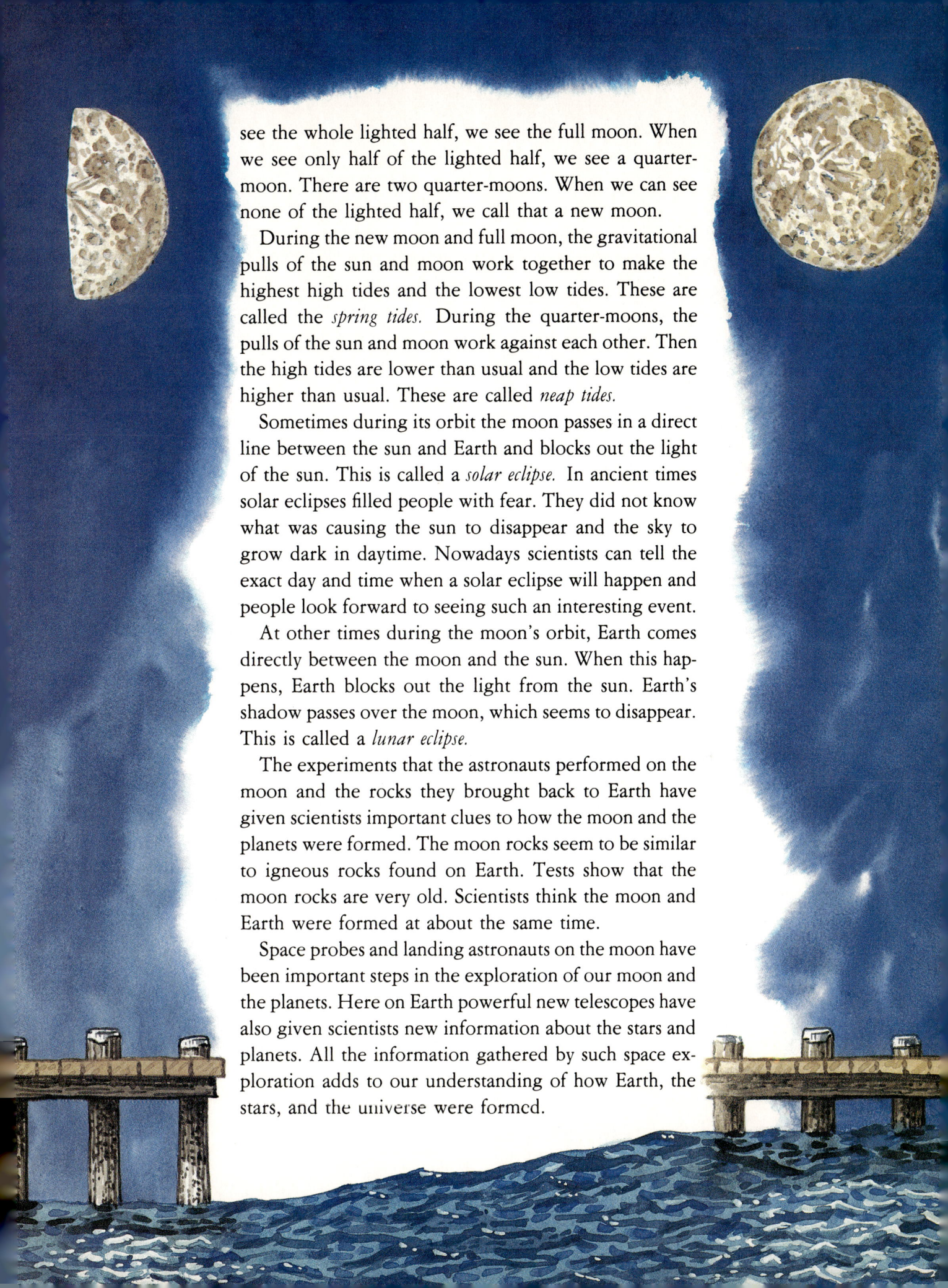

During the new moon and full moon, the gravitational pulls of the sun and moon work together to make the highest high tides and the lowest low tides. These are called the *spring tides.* During the quarter-moons, the pulls of the sun and moon work against each other. Then the high tides are lower than usual and the low tides are higher than usual. These are called *neap tides.*

Sometimes during its orbit the moon passes in a direct line between the sun and Earth and blocks out the light of the sun. This is called a *solar eclipse.* In ancient times solar eclipses filled people with fear. They did not know what was causing the sun to disappear and the sky to grow dark in daytime. Nowadays scientists can tell the exact day and time when a solar eclipse will happen and people look forward to seeing such an interesting event.

At other times during the moon's orbit, Earth comes directly between the moon and the sun. When this happens, Earth blocks out the light from the sun. Earth's shadow passes over the moon, which seems to disappear. This is called a *lunar eclipse.*

The experiments that the astronauts performed on the moon and the rocks they brought back to Earth have given scientists important clues to how the moon and the planets were formed. The moon rocks seem to be similar to igneous rocks found on Earth. Tests show that the moon rocks are very old. Scientists think the moon and Earth were formed at about the same time.

Space probes and landing astronauts on the moon have been important steps in the exploration of our moon and the planets. Here on Earth powerful new telescopes have also given scientists new information about the stars and planets. All the information gathered by such space exploration adds to our understanding of how Earth, the stars, and the universe were formed.

The Planets

IN THE 16TH CENTURY, scientists began to understand that Earth is not the center of the universe—that Earth and the other planets revolve around the sun.

In the days of Galileo Galilei, scientists knew of only five planets revolving around the sun. Today we know of nine planets. We call the sun and the planets that revolve around it the *solar system.*

One of the questions that puzzled early astronomers was why the planets stay in their orbits. Why do they not simply fly off into space? The explanation was found by the English astronomer Isaac Newton. He said that the planets are held in the solar system by an invisible force called *gravity,* which pulls objects toward one another.

Newton said that all objects produce gravity and that the more mass an object has and the closer it is to another object, the stronger is its gravitational pull on the other object. For example, Earth has a large mass and we are quite close to it, so Earth has a strong gravitational pull on us. When we jump into the air, gravity pulls us back down. Gravity even pulls the rain from the sky to the ground.

Newton said that because the sun has a very large mass, it has a strong gravitational force working to pull the planets into the sun. But the sun's gravity is balanced by *centrifugal force,* which is working to pull the planets away from the sun and send them off into space. The result is that the planets neither fall into the sun nor escape from it. The planets are trapped in their orbits.

If you tie a ball on a string and twirl it around in the air, you can feel that the ball is pulling against the string. Think of your hand holding the string as the sun and think of the ball as a planet. The string acts like the force of gravity. The pulling-away feeling of the ball is like the centrifugal force of a planet moving in its orbit around the sun.

The orbits of the planets are not perfect circles, however, and the planets are not always exactly the same distance from the sun. This is partly because the sun is in motion, too. As the planets travel along in their orbits, the sun is also moving through space. The planets move in a pattern called an *ellipse,* a circle that has been stretched out.

When scientists talk about the distance of a planet from the sun, they are really talking about the planet's average, or *mean,* distance from the sun.

In addition to revolving around the sun, each planet is also spinning on its own axis like a top.

Mercury, the planet closest to the sun, is the second smallest of the nine planets. Only Pluto, the planet farthest from the sun, is smaller. About 18 planets the size of Mercury would fit into one Earth. Mercury makes one complete revolution around the sun every 88 Earth days and rotates on its axis once every 58.7 days. This means that Mercury's year is a little less than 3 Earth months long, and one day and one night a little less than 2 months long.

Venus
sun
Earth
Mercury
Mars
asteroids
Jupiter

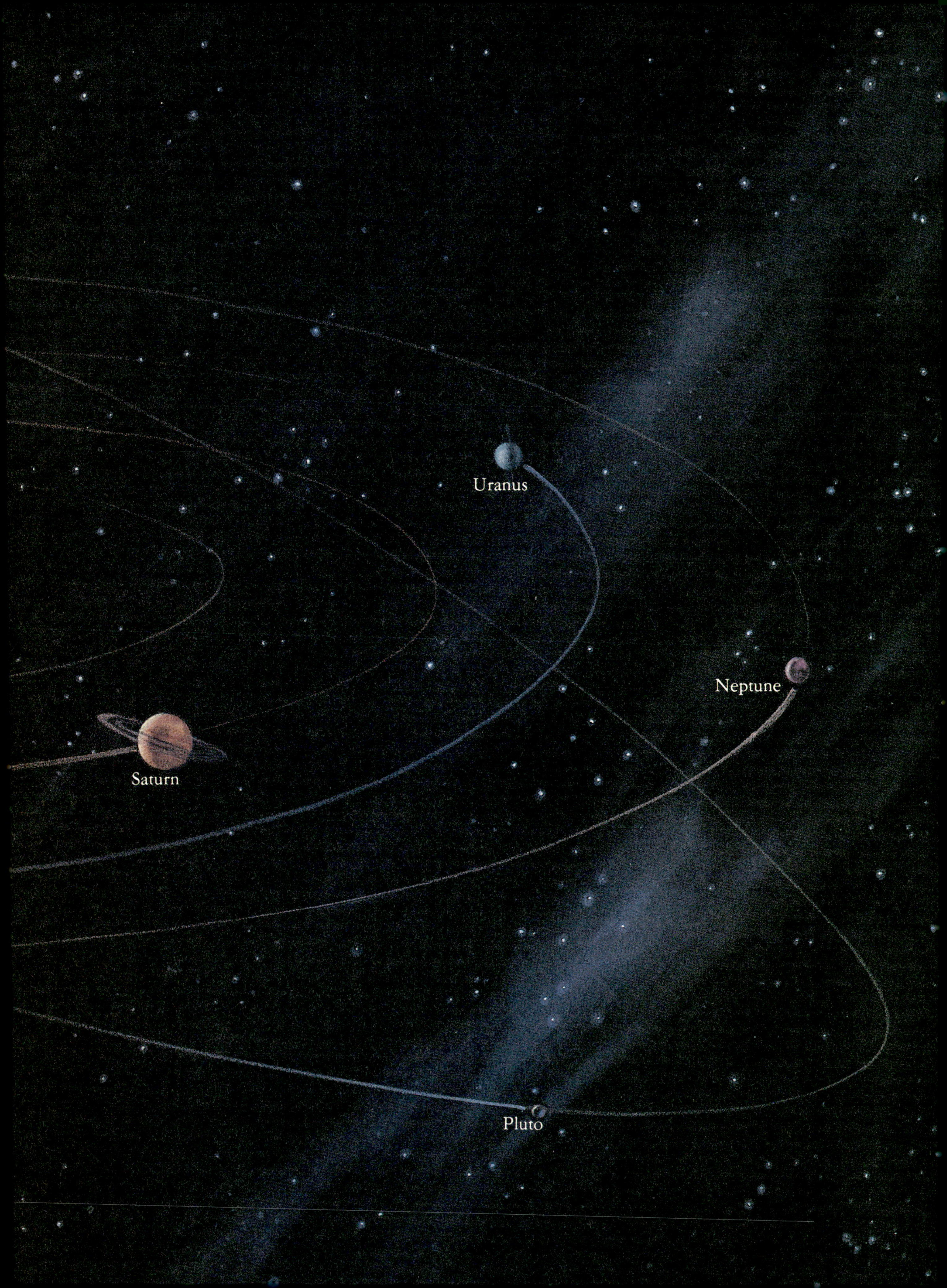
Uranus
Neptune
Saturn
Pluto

THE PLANETS

Mercury has little or no atmosphere. Temperatures on the side facing the sun can reach more than 800 degrees Fahrenheit. On the side away from the sun, temperatures can dive to 290 degrees below zero.

Venus, the next planet away from the sun, comes closer to Earth than any other planet. At its closest, Venus is only 25 million miles from Earth. It takes Venus 225 days to revolve around the sun and 243 days to rotate on its axis. Unlike most of the other planets, Venus rotates clockwise—from east to west. Because of this rotation, the time from one sunrise to the next on Venus is much shorter than 243 days. In fact, a day and night on Venus is only about 117 Earth days long.

Venus has a thick atmosphere of carbon dioxide gas. The temperature at its surface is more than 850 degrees.

Earth, the third planet from the sun, is our home. It takes 365¼ days for Earth to go around the sun. Our calendar has only 365 days, so every fourth year we adjust it by putting the extra quarter-days together and adding an extra day to the month of February. A year with an extra day in it is called a *leap year.*

Earth rotates on its axis from west to east about once every 24 hours. This west-to-east rotation is what makes the sun, moon, and other heavenly bodies appear to rise in the east and set in the west. Actually, they do not rise and set at all. The part of Earth we are on is really spinning toward—or away from—them. Day and night are caused by this rotation.

The closer you are to Earth's equator, the faster you are traveling compared to Earth's axis. Earth's surface at the equator is spinning around at about 1000 miles per hour. You do not notice it because everything—trees, ground, buildings, even the air—is traveling with you at the same speed.

Mars, the fourth planet from the sun, is called the Red Planet because the rocks and dust on its surface look reddish-orange in color through a telescope. It takes Mars 687 days to go around the sun. The Martian day and night is 24 hours and 37 minutes long, slightly lon-

Mars

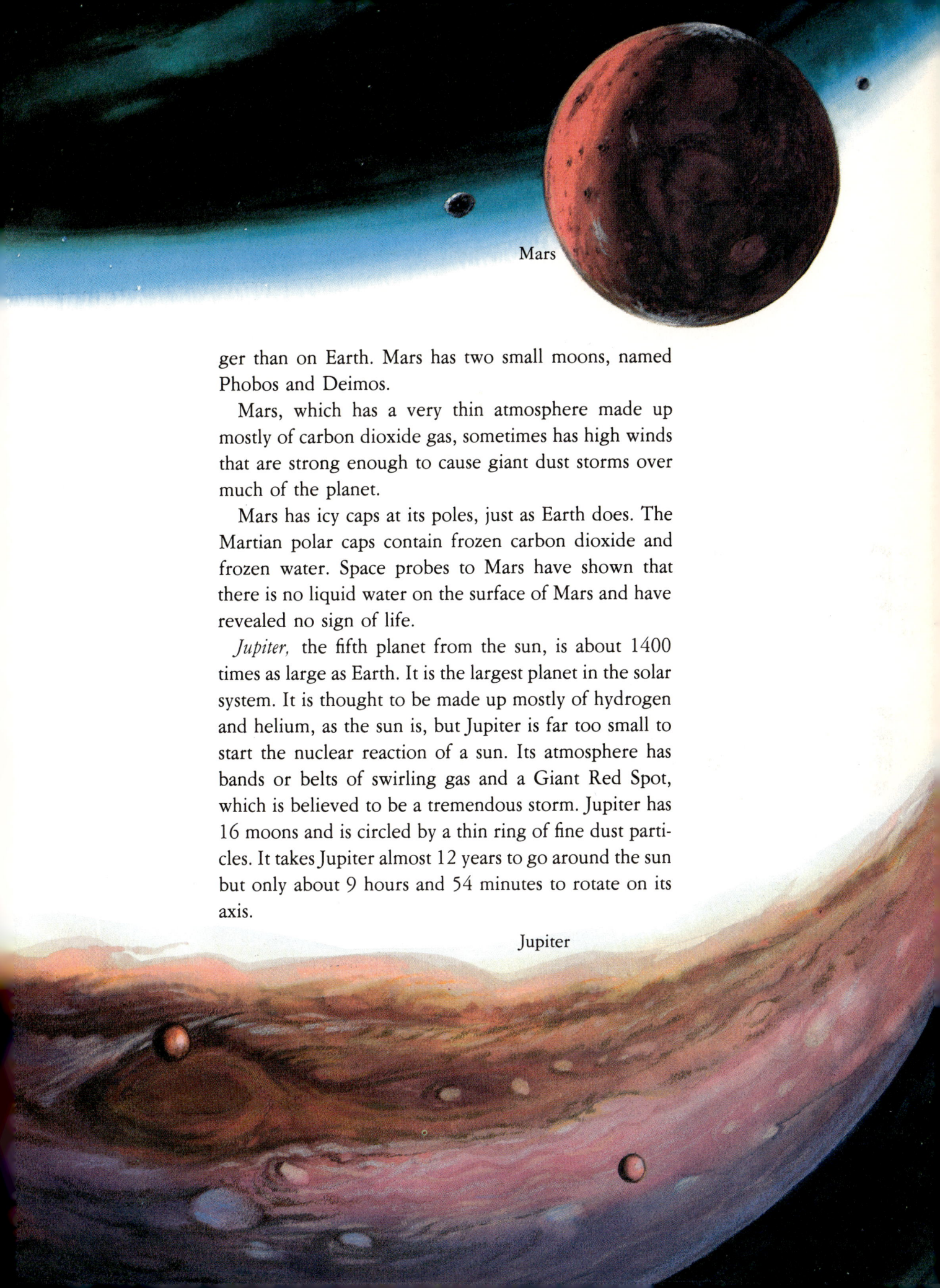

ger than on Earth. Mars has two small moons, named Phobos and Deimos.

Mars, which has a very thin atmosphere made up mostly of carbon dioxide gas, sometimes has high winds that are strong enough to cause giant dust storms over much of the planet.

Mars has icy caps at its poles, just as Earth does. The Martian polar caps contain frozen carbon dioxide and frozen water. Space probes to Mars have shown that there is no liquid water on the surface of Mars and have revealed no sign of life.

Jupiter, the fifth planet from the sun, is about 1400 times as large as Earth. It is the largest planet in the solar system. It is thought to be made up mostly of hydrogen and helium, as the sun is, but Jupiter is far too small to start the nuclear reaction of a sun. Its atmosphere has bands or belts of swirling gas and a Giant Red Spot, which is believed to be a tremendous storm. Jupiter has 16 moons and is circled by a thin ring of fine dust particles. It takes Jupiter almost 12 years to go around the sun but only about 9 hours and 54 minutes to rotate on its axis.

Jupiter

Saturn, the sixth planet from the sun, is about 755 times as big as Earth and is known for its broad belt of colorful rings. Saturn has seven rings, and each ring is made up of many small ringlets. Like Jupiter, Saturn is composed mostly of hydrogen and helium. It has 18 known moons. The largest moon, Titan, is larger than Mercury. It takes Saturn almost 30 years to go around the sun but only about 10 hours and 40 minutes to rotate on its axis.

Uranus, the seventh planet, is about 67 times the size of Earth, but because it is so far away, we can see it only with a telescope. Uranus is circled by a belt of rings and has at least 15 moons. It takes Uranus 84 years to orbit the sun and about 17 hours and 12 minutes to rotate on its axis.

Neptune, the eighth planet from the sun, is about the same size as Uranus. Its atmosphere is made up mostly of hydrogen, helium, and methane gases. The methane gives Neptune its bluish-green color. A great dark spot on Neptune is believed to be a giant storm. Neptune has winds of up to 1500 miles per hour. The planet has a belt of rings and at least six moons. It takes Neptune a little more than 164 years to revolve around the sun and about 16 hours to rotate on its axis.

Pluto, the ninth and smallest planet, was discovered only in 1930. It is about one-fifth as wide as Earth. Pluto is mostly rock. On top of the rock is a layer of ice, and on top of that is a layer of frozen methane. Pluto has a very thin atmosphere of methane. Its single moon, Charon, is a bit more than half as wide as Pluto. It takes Pluto about 248 years to go around the sun and almost six and a half Earth days to rotate on its axis.

In addition to the nine planets, our solar system has thousands of small, odd-shaped *asteroids* in orbit around the sun. Most of these are in orbit between Mars and Jupiter, and most are about a mile or less across. Asteroids are made of rock or metal or both.

Comets have long, narrow orbits that bring them very close to the sun and then take them far away, often completely out of the solar system. Halley's comet comes close to the sun about every 75 years and was seen last in 1986. It is made up of ice and frozen gases mixed with dust particles—like a dirty snowball.

As a comet nears the sun, it may form a brightly glowing tail. The tail is made up of particles of gas and dust blown off the comet by the solar wind, the steady stream of hot gas particles given off by the sun.

Sometimes a chunk of rock or metal called a *meteor* comes close enough to Earth to enter our atmosphere. A meteor travels so fast that the friction of the air usually causes it to glow white-hot and burn up. Sometimes we call meteors shooting stars or falling stars, but they really are not stars at all.

Most meteors are so small that they burn up completely before they can strike Earth, but some are big enough to get through the atmosphere and hit the ground. A meteor that has fallen to Earth is called a meteorite. Meteorites are parts of our solar system that we can study without having to leave Earth.

The Stars

WHEN YOU LOOK UP into the sky on a clear night, you can see thousands of stars. The sky seems to be filled with stars, especially in the long thin band we call the Milky Way. Actually, almost all the stars you can see without a telescope are part of a vast group of stars, or *galaxy*, we call the Milky Way galaxy.

How many stars can you see on a clear night? Sometimes it seems as though you can see a million, but there are only about 6000 stars that can be seen from Earth without the help of a telescope. Of these 6000 stars, you can see only about half that number at one time. This is because the sky is shaped like a great dome, or hemisphere. The sky you see ends at the *horizon,* the distant point where the sky seems to meet the edge of Earth. Actually, the sky goes all the way around Earth, but you can see only half of it because the horizon—Earth itself—blocks our view.

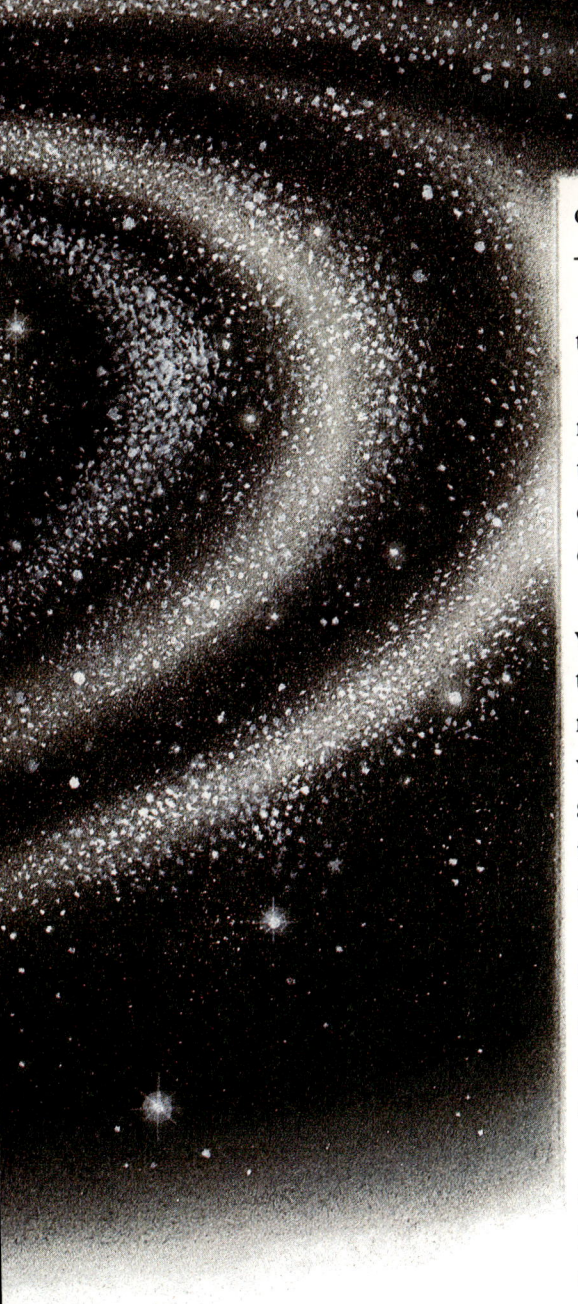

The 3000 stars you can see are a very small fraction of the stars in the Milky Way galaxy. There are really about 100 billion stars in the Milky Way, a figure so large that no one can really imagine it. Our sun is just one star in the Milky Way. A galaxy can be thought of as an island of stars in the vast sea of space. The Milky Way is just one of hundreds of millions of galaxies in the universe.

Even though there are so many galaxies in the universe, they are very large because the distances between the stars in them is great. Scientists have a special way of measuring these distances. The fastest thing in the universe is light, which travels about 186,000 miles per second. Yet even at this rate of speed, it takes light from the sun eight minutes to reach Earth. Light reflected from the planet Pluto takes about five hours to reach Earth.

Scientists measure distances between stars in terms of how far light travels not in a minute or an hour or even a day, but in a year. This distance is 5 trillion 880 billion miles. Scientists call the distance light travels in a year a *light-year*.

The nearest star to us, Alpha Centauri, is more than four light-years away. That means its light takes four years to get to us. If Alpha Centauri were to suddenly disappear, we would not know it for about four years.

The Milky Way galaxy is shaped like a disk with a bulging center. Spreading out from the center are two spiral arms full of stars. These spiral arms make the Milky Way look like a giant pinwheel. The distance across the Milky Way is about 100,000 light-years. Our sun is located in one of the spiral arms and is about 35,000 light-years from the center of the galaxy. The light we receive today from the center of the Milky Way began its journey long before the first great civilizations arose on Earth.

There are different kinds of galaxies. Some are spiral galaxies like the Milky Way. Others are called barred spirals, because their spiral arms seem to stretch out from a bar-shaped cluster of stars in the middle of the galaxy. Elliptical galaxies look like balls or spheres that have been stretched out. Irregular galaxies do not seem to have any special shape. They are just bundles of stars bunched together.

Galaxies seem to exist in groups, or *galactic clusters.* There are about 20 galaxies in the cluster that includes our Milky Way. Other clusters have hundreds or thousands of galaxies.

Most of the matter in a galaxy is in its stars. A small portion of a galaxy's matter is contained in clouds of gases and dust called *nebulae.*

There are different kinds of nebulae. An *emission nebula* is a cloud of gas and dust that is lighted by a star or stars within it, but only the glowing gas cloud can be seen. A *dark nebula* is a cloud of gas or dust that is too far away from any stars to be lighted by them. A dark nebula blocks our view of the stars beyond it, so it looks like a dark spot in the sky. A *planetary nebula* looks like one of the distant planets, but it is a cloud of material thrown off by a star toward the end of its life.

There are many different kinds of stars. Some are relatively young—about 10 million years old. Others are several billion years old. Some are large and are called giants. Others are many times larger than the sun and are called supergiants. Still others are much smaller and are called dwarfs.

Some stars are much hotter than others. The colors of stars depend on their temperatures. The hottest stars are the blue or blue-white stars, with surface temperatures of up to 45,000 degrees Fahrenheit. Then come the cooler white stars, and then the yellow, yellow-red, orange-red, and red stars, the coolest stars of all. Red stars have a surface temperature of up to about 5000 degrees. Our sun is a yellow dwarf.

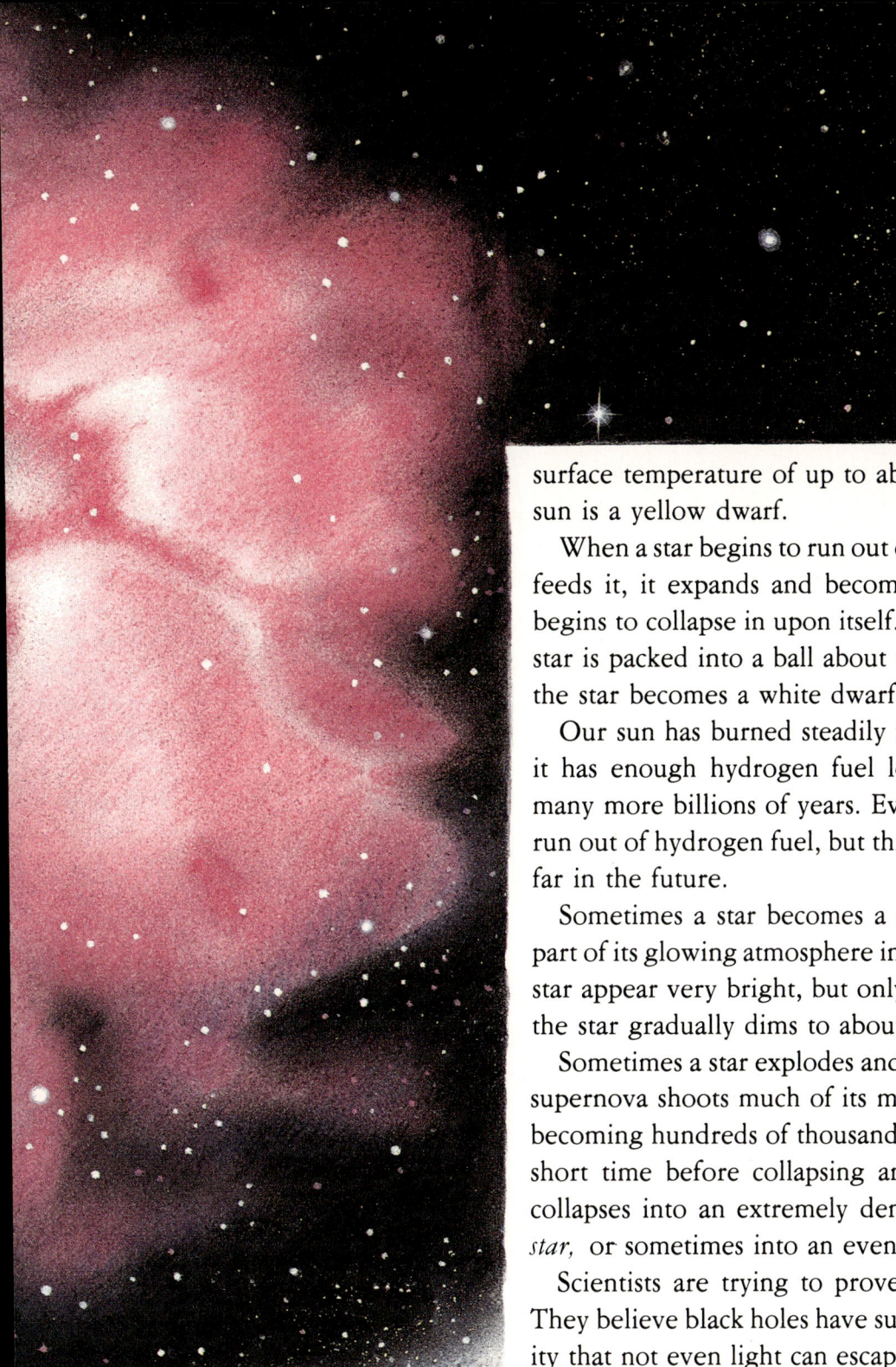

When a star begins to run out of the hydrogen fuel that feeds it, it expands and becomes a red giant. Then it begins to collapse in upon itself. All of the matter in the star is packed into a ball about the size of a planet, and the star becomes a white dwarf.

Our sun has burned steadily for billions of years, yet it has enough hydrogen fuel left to burn steadily for many more billions of years. Eventually it will begin to run out of hydrogen fuel, but this will happen very, very far in the future.

Sometimes a star becomes a *nova* and shoots a large part of its glowing atmosphere into space. This makes the star appear very bright, but only for a short time. Then the star gradually dims to about its original brightness.

Sometimes a star explodes and becomes a *supernova*. A supernova shoots much of its matter far out into space, becoming hundreds of thousands of times brighter for a short time before collapsing and dying. Sometimes it collapses into an extremely dense ball called a *neutron star,* or sometimes into an even denser *black hole.*

Scientists are trying to prove that black holes exist. They believe black holes have such strong forces of gravity that not even light can escape from them. Because a black hole does not give off any light of its own, and because no light is reflected from it, scientists cannot see it. But its strong gravity should have an effect on the motion of nearby stars. Scientists are hoping the movements of such stars will prove black holes exist.

Rockets and Space Travel

IN 1957 a powerful Russian rocket carried the first artificial satellite, *Sputnik 1,* into orbit around Earth, and the Space Age began. In 1969, only twelve years later, American astronauts walked on the moon. Today scientists are planning great space stations and a possible expedition to Mars. All these things were made possible by an important invention—the rocket.

The giant rockets that carry satellites and astronauts into space are relatively new inventions, but people have known how to build simple rockets for centuries. The Chinese built rockets in the 12th century. In the 13th century they used rockets in battle. The rockets were made of hollow tubes filled with gunpowder and attached to arrows. These rockets, which they called "arrows of fire," roared and filled the sky with smoke and sparks.

Arab traders learned about the Chinese rockets and carried the idea to Europe. Europeans used rockets in battle and also for colorful fireworks.

It was hard to hit a target with these early rockets. Cannons and muskets proved to be much better weapons, so people eventually lost interest in rockets for warfare. Then, in the 19th century, an Englishman named William Congreve made an improved rocket that the British army used against the armies of Napoleon. During the War of 1812 the British bombarded Fort McHenry in Maryland with Congreve's rockets. Francis Scott Key saw the bombardment and wrote of "the rockets' red glare" in the poem that became the national anthem of the United States.

Over the years rockets steadily became bigger and better. Today's giant rockets seem to be far different from the early Chinese "arrows of fire," but in fact, modern rocket engines work the same way as the early Chinese rockets.

Both types of rockets burn fuel and turn it into hot gases inside the rocket in the *combustion chamber*. The gases expand, pressing in all directions against the inside of the chamber. At the back of the combustion chamber is an opening, or nozzle, through which the gases can escape at high speed. The force of the gases blasting out through the nozzle creates an equal but opposite force that pushes against the front of the combustion chamber and moves the rocket forward. This opposite force is called *thrust.*

Rockets that burn fuel—that cause fuel to combine with oxygen and release energy—are known as chemical rockets. There are several kinds of chemical rockets. The main type, the *solid fuel rocket,* contains its fuel and its oxygen source—or *oxidizer*—in a solid mixture. Once the solid fuel is ignited, it burns steadily until it is used up.

Another main type of chemical rocket is the *liquid fuel rocket,* which contains liquid fuel in one tank and liquid oxidizer in another. The fuel and oxidizer are fed into the combustion chamber, where they mix and burn. In liquid fuel rockets, the amount of fuel and oxidizer that goes to the combustion chamber can be controlled. This means

launch

first stage separates

second stage separates

third stage and payload

that the amount of thrust, and the amount of time the rocket engine is running, also can be controlled.

Rockets often have two or more *stages.* Each stage is like a separate rocket. It has its own fuel and oxidizer supplies. The stages are stacked one on top of the other. The first stage, often called the *booster stage,* usually has several rockets working together. The booster stage gets the rocket off the ground and starts it on its way into the sky. After it has used up almost all of its fuel, the booster stage separates from the rocket, and the second stage starts up. Because the rocket has gotten rid of the extra weight of the first stage, it can now climb higher and go faster than if there were only one stage.

Many large rockets have three stages, and some have four. Each stage increases the rocket's speed, or *velocity.* These extra stages are needed so that the rocket's *payload* — such as a satellite or spacecraft — can reach the speed needed to break free of Earth's gravity and go into orbit.

Solid fuel rockets have been used to launch satellites into orbit around Earth. Solid fuel booster rockets are also used as the first stage of the space shuttle spacecraft. All of the rockets used to carry astronauts into orbit and send space probes away from Earth have been liquid fuel rockets.

Powerful chemical rockets have changed the world. They have lifted thousands of satellites into orbit and have sent many space probes to the moon and the planets. New kinds of rockets may someday carry people to other planets and space probes to the stars.

Scientists have been working on many new ideas for designing rockets of the future. One idea is to make a rocket powered by a nuclear reactor. Just as nuclear reactors are used to produce electricity here on Earth, they may be able to produce thrust for rockets in space. Another idea is to make rockets powered by electric or magnetic fields to produce thrust.

This is an exciting time for rocket scientists because the age of rockets and space travel has just begun.

Life on Other Planets

WE HAVE SENT SPACE PROBES to study the planets of our solar system and have learned many new things about them. But so far it seems that Earth is the only place in our solar system that has living things.

Are there any other places in the universe where living things can exist?

Scientists are unable to answer this question yet, but some scientists think that the answer may be yes.

Our sun is a star, one of perhaps 100 billion stars in the Milky Way galaxy. Let us suppose that of these 100 billion stars, only one in a thousand is like our sun. That would mean there are 100 million stars like our sun in the Milky Way. Now let us suppose that of these stars, only one in a thousand has planets orbiting it. That would mean there are 100,000 solar systems in our galaxy. Finally, let us suppose that only one solar system in a thousand has a planet something like Earth. That would

LIFE ON OTHER PLANETS

mean there are 100 planets in our galaxy where living things like those on Earth could exist.

The Milky Way is only one galaxy. There are hundreds of millions of galaxies in the universe. This means there may be billions of planets on which life could exist.

But scientists are not yet certain that other stars even have planets. Some astronomers believe they have gathered information showing planets circling certain stars, but what looks like a far-distant planet could be just the remains of a burned-out star. More work must be done before we will know for certain whether other stars have planets.

What if life does exist on other planets? What would these living things be like? Almost all life on Earth needs oxygen and water and sunlight to survive. Life on other planets might need a very different combination of things to stay alive. Scientists do not expect to find another planet exactly like Earth, so they do not expect to find living things on other planets that are exactly like Earth's plants and animals.

How can we ever know about life in outer space? Someday we may be able to travel in space ships to other planets. The rockets we now have do not produce enough energy for such long trips. We would have to invent a new kind of rocket for travel to the stars.

We might be able to communicate with creatures on other planets using radio waves, which travel at the speed of light. Scientists have built great radio transmitters that send powerful signals into space—special signals that cannot be made by a star or any other natural object. Perhaps somewhere intelligent creatures are listening for such signals. Scientists have also built giant radio receivers to listen for any faint signals coming to us from outer space. So far all they have received are radio waves given off naturally by the stars.

What sort of creatures would be able to communicate with us by radio? First of all, they would have to be able to think and to move around. They would have to have something like hands in order to build the complicated machines needed to send radio signals across space. And, of course, they would have to *want* to build machines to communicate with us.

Such creatures might have three eyes, or long antennae sticking out of their heads, or six legs. There is no reason why they would have to look like humans. They would, however, need to have an advanced civilization, a technological civilization, though not necessarily like ours today.

Radios first came into use less than 100 years ago. If a radio signal from some other planet reached Earth 150 years ago, we would have missed it because we did not yet have any radios to hear the signal with. Perhaps there are civilizations out in space that have not yet discovered radio. If so, they would not know about the signals we are sending into space and could not send a signal to us.

Perhaps someday, on some planet light-years away, an intelligent being will hear very faint radio signals that have traveled many light-years from Earth. Perhaps that being will answer by sending us a radio signal. That signal will take years to reach us. We might miss it if we are not listening in the right direction at the right time. But if we do receive such a signal, then we will know that we are not alone in the universe.

The Final Frontier

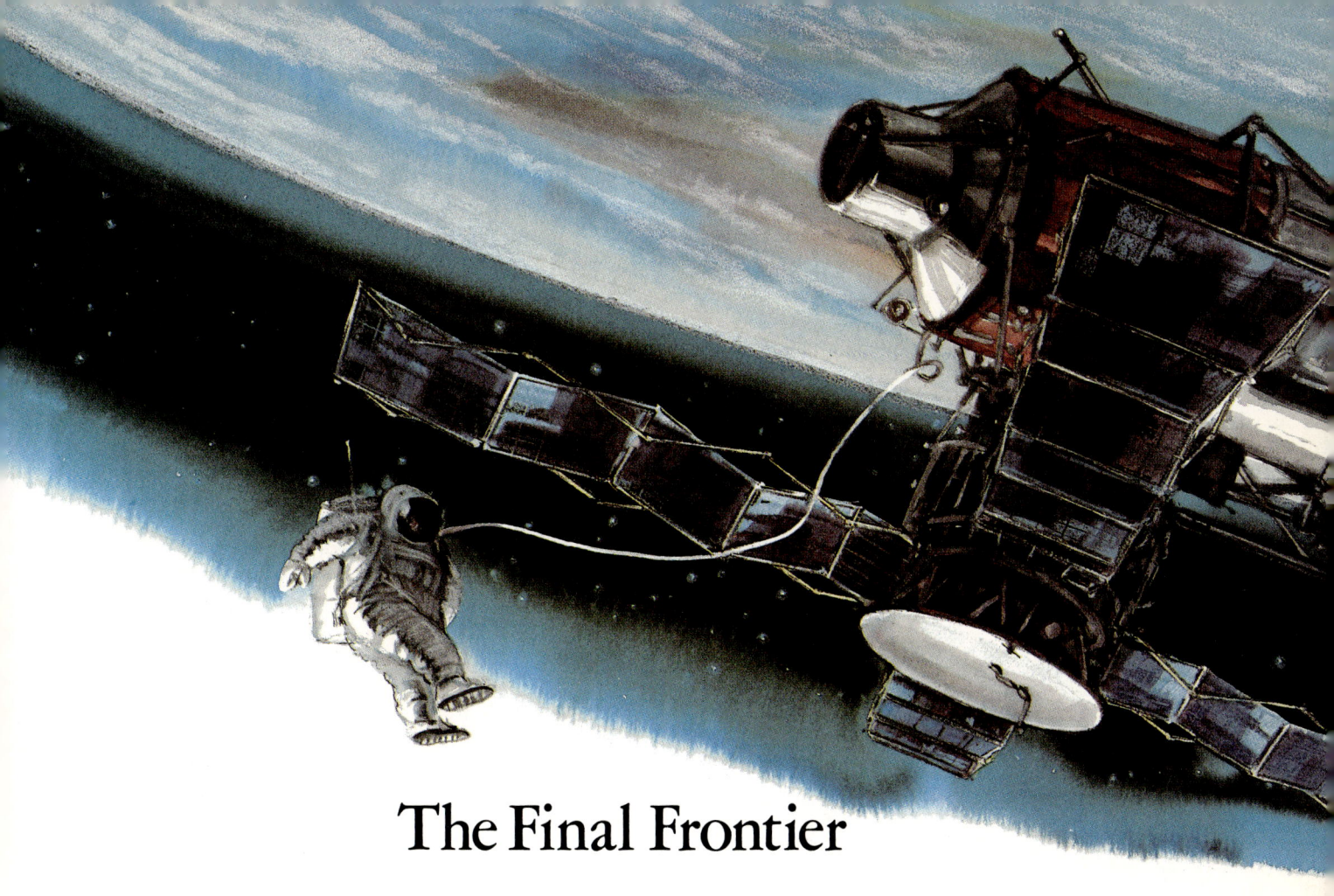

WHEN THE RUSSIAN COSMONAUT Yuri Gagarin became the first person to orbit Earth in 1961, the world took a big step forward in the exploration of space. In 1969 the world took another great step when astronauts Neil Armstrong and Edwin Aldrin walked on the moon. The early astronauts and cosmonauts—an *astronaut* is a person who travels in a spacecraft and a *cosmonaut* is a Russian astronaut—were the first explorers of the last and greatest of all frontiers—space.

Scientists learned a great deal from these and other early space missions. The moon rocks brought back by the Apollo astronauts helped scientists to understand the nature of the moon and how it is related to Earth. The missions also helped scientists to build better spacecraft to explore Mars, Venus, and the other planets.

In 1973 the United States launched Skylab, an orbiting laboratory the size of a bus. Astronauts stayed in Skylab for weeks and even months at a time to complete important experiments. They took long space walks outside

Skylab and learned a great deal about how staying in space for long periods affects human beings.

The astronauts learned that the absence of gravity in space makes a big difference in the way things can be done. For example, all food and drink have to be eaten from tubes or other containers. Otherwise the lack of gravity would cause them to float and drift around. Turning a bolt with a wrench was a great challenge for the astronauts. In the absence of gravity, an astronaut is just as likely to turn as the wrench is, unless the astronaut holds firmly onto something sturdy.

Another important lesson the astronauts learned was that in space, there is no real day and night. If an astronaut's spacecraft is circling Earth about once every 90 minutes, the astronaut's day is about 90 minutes long. Since astronauts are not ready for sleep every 90 minutes, they have to be told when it is time to go to sleep and when to wake up.

In 1986 Russia launched a new space station into orbit around Earth. It was named *Mir,* which is Russian for "peace." Since it was launched, *Mir* has had crews on board it almost all the time. In December of 1988 two Russian cosmonauts set a new space record by staying in the space station for a year.

The United States and other countries are planning a much larger space station. When it is completed, people will live and work in it year round. There will always be somebody living in space.

Such a space station might become a good place from which to launch missions to the moon and beyond. Scientists are discussing a number of possible new projects for these missions. One idea is to build a base on the moon. Workers could use the materials found on the moon to make the things needed to build more space stations. Because of the moon's weak gravity, it would be much easier to launch spacecraft from there than from Earth.

Scientists are also hoping to send a mission to Mars soon. Because Mars is so much farther away from Earth than the moon, an expedition to Mars would be an important step in our future exploration of space.

Travelers to Mars would have to carry enough food, water, and air to last them for several years. Their spacecraft would have to carry enough fuel for the long journey to Mars and back again. They would also have to carry supplies and spare parts to make repairs if anything should break down. Out in space there are no repair shops.

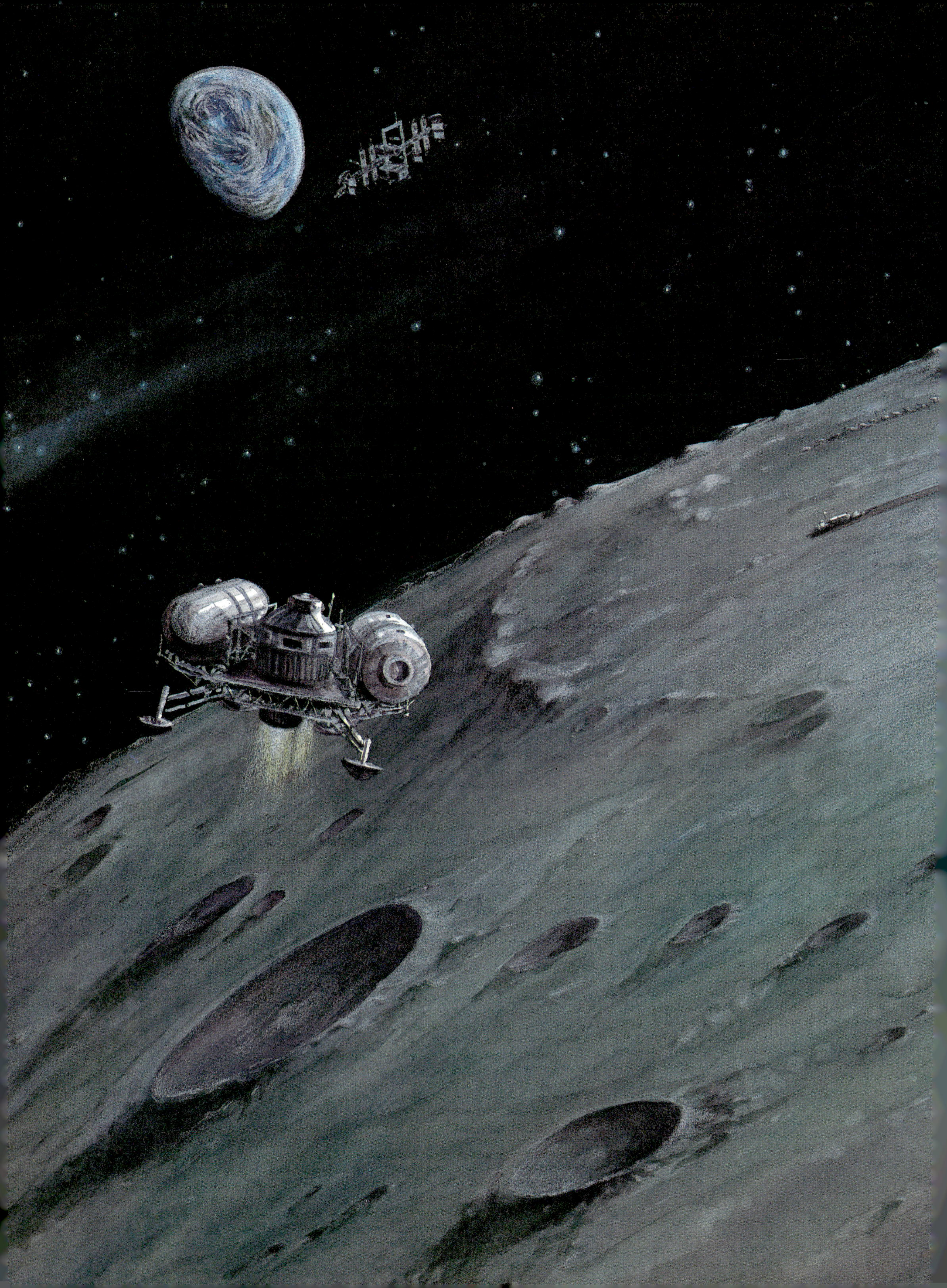

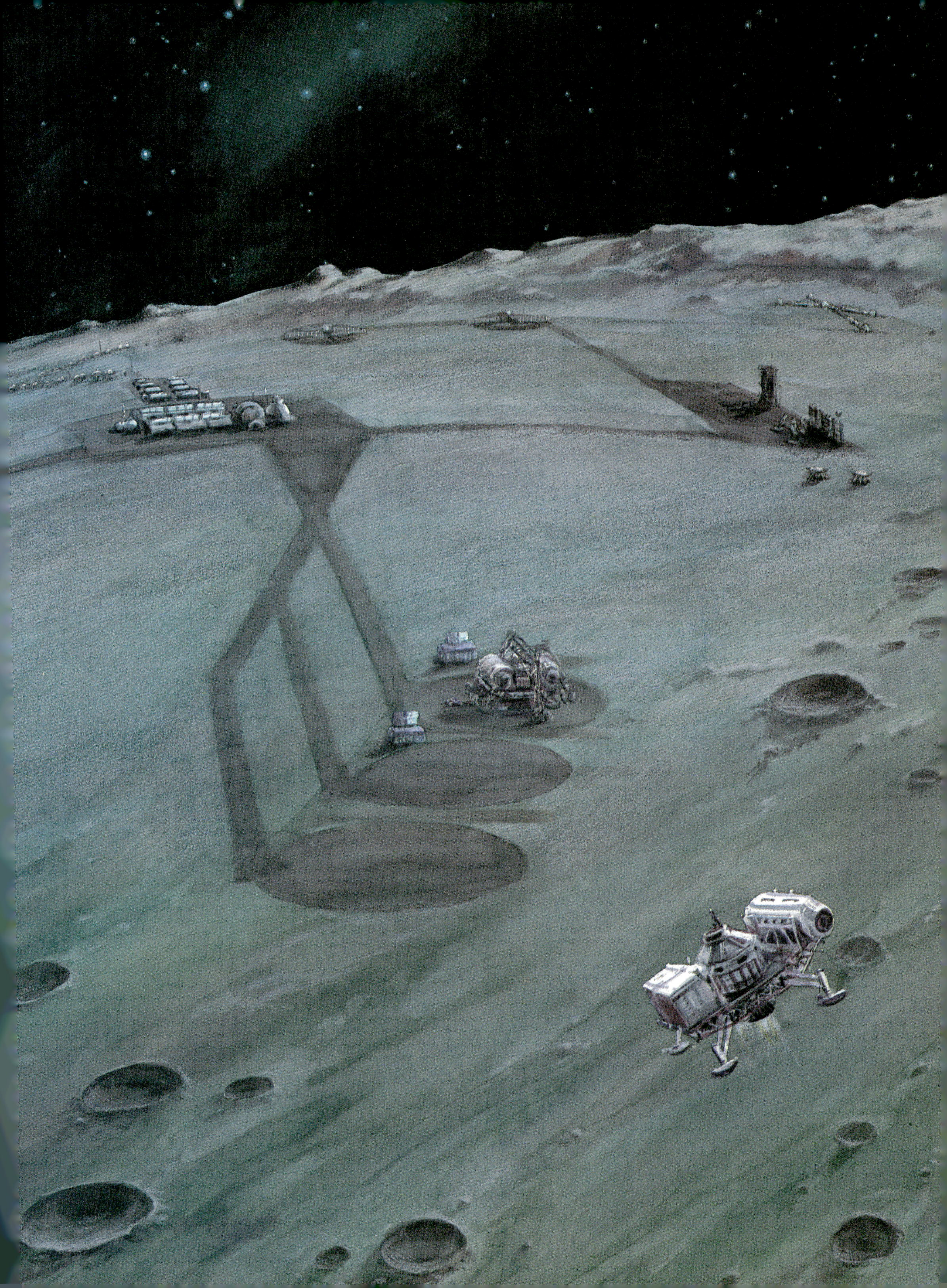

Imagine what space travel might be like in a hundred years. Your shuttle craft lifts you from Earth to a large and comfortable space station. You stay there a day, and then take another shuttle to the moon. There are several moon bases now, all the size of small cities. From the moon you travel to another space station and get aboard the speedy new Mars Express for the long journey to the Red Planet.

Three months later you are standing on Mars in one of the domed cities built by settlers from Earth. The domes protect the settlers from the harmful rays of the sun and from the Martian dust storms. Life is still hard in the domes, but every year it gets a little better.

The scientists who live in the domes are working on ways to change the whole climate of Mars. They want to warm up the frozen planet and give it a thicker atmosphere. Such an atmosphere will keep the warmth from escaping into space and also filter out the sun's dangerous rays. The scientists hope to melt the polar ice caps and create rivers and lakes where there is still only cold, dry Martian dust.

Right now such an idea is only science fiction, but today's science fiction has a way of becoming tomorrow's science fact. Who knows what great adventures still await us here on Earth and out among the stars?

Adventures in Science and Discovery

Early Ways of Counting

WHEN DID YOU LEARN HOW TO count to ten? You were probably very young, and now counting seems easy to you. Did you ever wonder where numbers came from, or when people first started counting?

Thousands of years ago people lived simple lives that were close to nature. They spent most of their time getting food and shelter. Perhaps their first use of counting was to keep track of their animals, to be sure none were lost. Early people may have tied knots on a vine or cut notches on a stick to keep count.

Perhaps people used pebbles to count their animals. One pebble would stand for one animal. Two pebbles would stand for two animals. A pile of pebbles would be needed to count a whole herd. But suppose a man wanted to tell a friend how many sheep he had. Using a big pile of pebbles to tell someone a number would have been clumsy. Perhaps he used a special sound or word to stand for the number of sheep he owned. Using words for different numbers would have been the start of a numbering system.

EARLY WAYS OF COUNTING

Early people probably counted with their fingers. One finger meant "one." Two fingers meant "two." Today some tribes in South America still count in groups of five for the five fingers on the hand. When they mean the number five, they say the word for "hand." When they mean ten, they say "two hands." When they mean twenty they say, "two hands and two feet."

Throughout history people have used different words and symbols for numbers. Some ancient people left a written record of their number systems. The earliest written records we have are clay tablets that were made about 5000 years ago by the people of ancient Mesopotamia, in what is today the country of Iraq. The Mesopotamians used a wedge-shaped stick called a *stylus* to make marks in tablets of soft clay; the tablets were then baked in the sun. When the clay hardened, the Mesopotamians had a permanent record of the marks.

In ancient Mesopotamia, people traded grains such as barley for other goods. The amount of grain a person had to trade was written down on a clay tablet. The stylus was used to make wedge marks. A mark up and down meant one bundle of barley. But on its side the same mark meant ten bundles. The Mesopotamians also had a special mark for the number 60, which they considered to be a very important number.

The ancient Egyptians also kept records using numbers. They wrote on paper made of papyrus reed, a kind of water plant. Their number system was based on the number ten, just as it is today. They used straight lines to show the numbers one through nine. When they reached ten, they drew a symbol that looked like a heel mark or an upside-down U. When they reached 100 they drew a picture of a coiled rope. For 1000 they drew a lotus flower. A bent finger meant 10,000.

The Egyptians used their system to keep track of the days and seasons so they would know when the Nile River was due to overflow its banks. They also used numbers when they surveyed their land and measured the building stones for the great pyramids.

EARLY WAYS OF COUNTING

Later, another number system was developed in Greece. The ancient Greeks used the letters of their alphabet to represent numbers. *Alpha,* their letter "A," was one, *beta,* their letter "B," was two, and so on for the first nine letters. The next nine letters were the names for "ten," "twenty," "thirty," and so on. This system was sometimes confusing because the same symbols were used for both letters and numbers.

The ancient Greeks were the first people to discuss different numbering systems and create a system of mathematics. The Greeks invented a kind of mathematics called *geometry.* Geometry is the study of shapes, such as squares, rectangles, and triangles. The Greeks' fascination with geometry led them to the idea that certain shapes are perfect—their lengths and widths are in perfect balance with each other. Many of the beautiful temples that the Greeks built were designed to be the perfect shape that the Greeks called the golden rectangle.

After the Romans conquered the Greeks, they adopted many Greek ideas, including their system of mathematics. But the Romans created a different system of number symbols, or *numerals.* These are the *Roman numerals* that you may have seen on the faces of clocks or cornerstones of buildings. In Roman numerals, the symbol I stands for one, V stands for five, and X stands for ten. The symbols are added on to make larger numbers. For example, XXXVII means "10 + 10 + 10 + 5 + 1 + 1," or 37. If a smaller number is placed before a larger one, it means the smaller number is to be subtracted from the larger one. For example, the Roman numeral IX means "one subtracted from ten," or nine.

Although there are Roman numerals for big numbers, such as L for 50, C for 100, D for 500, and M for 1000, large numbers can get very long. For instance, the date 1988 in Roman numerals is written MCMLXXXVIII. Roman numerals were very awkward for adding, subtracting, multiplying, and dividing.

The ancient Romans also used a simple calculating machine called an *abacus.* Other civilizations also used

EARLY WAYS OF COUNTING

abacuses. Perhaps the best known is the Chinese abacus, which uses rows of beads or disks strung on wires as counters. The beads are moved up and down on the wires to add or subtract numbers.

In ancient China, people drew beautiful pictures to represent numbers. Their numbering system was based on the number ten just as ours is. They also used the number zero, just as we do. To the Chinese, numbers were more than just tools to count things with. They believed that all the natural world is connected by numbers. The seasons, the planets, animals, and even musical notes can be given special numbers and these numbers will work together to achieve the harmony and beauty in nature.

The Chinese used their numbering system to measure very long distances. They placed these measurements onto a grid that helped them to draw accurate maps. Their measurements aided them in building the famous Great Wall of China.

Halfway around the world in the jungles of Central America, the Maya developed a very different numbering system. It was based on the number 20, not on the number 10 as ours is. They combined dots and bars to form their numbers. The dots stood for 1 and the bars meant 5. So the symbol ≝ represented the number 13. The Maya also discovered zero.

The Maya carved into stone the faces of animal gods that looked like jaguars, monkeys, and birds. They used these pictures to number their days and months. Keeping track of time was a very important part of the Mayan religion. The Mayan calendar was like a big circle—for the Maya, time had no beginning and no end. The Mayan calendar measured time in 52-year cycles. When one cycle of time ended, a new cycle began.

In Mayan ruins, scientists have found huge stone calendars and monuments with carved pictures on them. One carving shows a date almost 1500 years ago—February 11, 526 A.D. The Aztecs of Mexico also had a system of numbers that can be seen on stone calendars.

The Incas of Peru had a very different system. They did not have a way to write numbers. Instead, they counted by making knots in special ropes called *quipus*. A quipu had a main rope with many small strands tied to it. A single knot made on the strand farthest from the top of the main rope meant one. A knot on the strand next to it meant ten, a knot on the next strand meant one hundred, and so on. Quipus were used to keep track of everything from the amount of corn in a harvest to the number of arrows made in wartime. Different quipus were made of different colors. A yellow one might be used for counting corn, and a red one for counting weapons. The quipus were passed on from one generation to the next as a record of a family's wealth.

On the other side of the globe, in India, yet another numbering system came into use. Sometime in Indian history people began to use zero when they wrote their numbers. They wrote zero as we do: 0. The Hindus of India called zero *sunya*. The Hindu number system was based on the number ten, and they used *decimal places* to divide the number one into tenths, hundredths, and even smaller parts, as we do today.

Hundreds of years later, in the sixth century, the city of Baghdad became a great center of Arab learning, especially in medicine and mathematics. In the 800's, when the Arabs began to trade with India, they began to use the Indian number system. The Arabs changed some of the Indian number symbols to make their own system of *Arabic numbers.* It is from these Hindu-Arabic numbers that we get our system.

During the Middle Ages in Europe, Italians began to trade with people from all over the known world. Goods arrived by ship in the port cities of Italy. The traders had to keep track of all that was bought and sold. They added or subtracted by moving little beads along a metal wire on a square table, a device similar to an abacus. Then they wrote down the result in Roman numerals. It was a long, complicated job.

Then around the year 1200, Leonardo Fibonacci, the son of an Italian merchant, traveled to Africa. There he learned about the Arabic system of numbers. When he returned to Italy he wrote a book to explain how much better the Arabic system was. Many people did not like Fibonacci's idea because during this time of the Crusades, Europeans were fighting bloody battles with the Arabs. However, the new number system and the way in which it simplified arithmetic eventually became accepted. Over time the numbers were changed slightly, but the system is the one we use today.

The Arabic system uses only 10 symbols—0, 1, 2, 3, 4, 5, 6, 7, 8, and 9—to write any number. The order in which the numbers are written gives the numbers their meaning. That is why 12,345 is different from 54,321. Today this system is accepted around the world.

Even if you have help from a calculator or a computer, you still need to understand numbers to give your answers meaning. Whether you are counting your change at the store or measuring the distance to another galaxy, numbers help you to organize the world around you.

Pythagoras—
The Father of Mathematics

DO YOU LIKE TO LISTEN TO guitar music? Strumming guitar strings can produce notes that sound good together. That pleasing sound is called *harmony*. The idea of harmony is just one of the discoveries made by Pythagoras of ancient Greece about 2500 years ago.

Pythagoras is considered the father of mathematics. You may wonder how music and mathematics are related, but you can see for yourself that they are. If you pluck a string that is pulled tight, it will make a musical note. If you push down on the string exactly in the middle and pluck one of the halves, the note will sound very much like the original note, only higher in pitch. Pythagoras showed that by dividing the string in two and playing half of it, he could produce a musical note that harmonized with the original note. He also showed that other related notes could be produced by playing strings that were one-third, one-fourth, and one-fifth as long as the original string. In this way he showed that music and mathematics are related.

Pythagoras made many other important discoveries about mathematics. But the story of the Greek contribution to mathematics starts even before the time of Pythagoras. We must go back to his teacher's teacher, a man named Thales. Thales was considered one of the Seven Wise Men of Greece and its first great thinker. He lived in Miletus, the most important city of Greece at that time. Miletus, which was in Asia Minor, was close to the kingdoms of Mesopotamia and Egypt. Thales learned about astronomy from the Mesopotamians and mathematics from the Egyptians.

Thales learned from the Egyptians how to calculate the height of an object by measuring the length of its shadow and then comparing it with the shadow cast by a pole stuck in the ground. For example, if the pole were five feet tall and cast a shadow five feet long, then an object with a twenty-foot-long shadow would be twenty feet tall. This is how the Egyptians measured the pyramids.

Thales was the first person to show that a mathematical proposition is true by using a step-by-step method called a *proof*. For example, it is easy to see that a line drawn exactly through the middle of a circle divides the circle into two equal halves. But Thales said that we cannot really *know* this fact until we *prove* it to be true. Using mathematics, Thales proved that the line—called the *diameter*—does in fact divide the circle into two equal halves.

Thales was a teacher, too, and one of his students, in turn, became the teacher of Pythagoras. Pythagoras was from a Greek island called Samos, and it was there that he began to teach. When a harsh ruler took over the island, Pythagoras hid and taught his students in a small cave. Then he fled to the Greek city of Crotona, in southern Italy. There Pythagoras started a center of learning. He was most interested in philosophy and mathematics. Pythagoras had many students, and people came from far away to learn from him.

Pythagoras was looked up to by his students almost as a religious leader. He and his followers formed the

PYTHAGORAS—THE FATHER OF MATHEMATICS

Pythagorean Society, a secret society whose members pledged to keep their knowledge to themselves. The society allowed men and women to join. The members met secretly and used a special symbol to identify themselves to each other. Eventually they became a very powerful group.

Why did the Pythagoreans want to keep their knowledge secret? Some of their ideas about the world disagreed with the accepted ideas of the time. The Pythagoreans were thought to be rebels. At that time most Greeks believed that anything they could not explain easily was the mysterious work of the gods. But the Pythagoreans had a different way of looking at nature. They tried to show that nature is orderly and its rules can be understood by human beings. They said that the gods did not really have any power over natural events.

Pythagoras is remembered for saying, "All is number." By that he meant that everything in the world has to do with numbers. For example, you can count the number of petals of a flower, or the number of arms in a starfish, or the sides of a snowflake. In each of these natural wonders there is a beauty based on its shape and the number of its parts.

Pythagoras was the first to link different shapes with numbers. For example, think of a rectangle. Suppose the rectangle has a length of ten feet and a width of five feet. Since the length is twice the width, the sides have a two to one *ratio*. This ratio can also be called *proportion*. Pythagoras measured the proportions of such things as the spiral shape of a seashell and the shape of a many-sided crystal. In each he found a special kind of beauty—a beauty of proportions. Of all the shapes he studied, Pythagoras considered the sphere to be the most perfect.

The idea that there is beauty and harmony in shape led to changes in how the Greek people lived. The Greeks designed new buildings using special proportions of length, width, and height to make these structures more beautiful—and more stable. A shape known as the golden rectangle was considered the perfect shape for a building. Many of the Greek temples that are still standing today, thousands of years after Pythagoras, were designed in the form of the golden rectangle.

PYTHAGORAS—THE FATHER OF MATHEMATICS

Another mathematical observation that Pythagoras made was that the numbers one, two, three, and four add up to ten. Ten was considered the ideal number. But Pythagoras is probably best remembered for his idea about right triangles. Right triangles are triangles with a ninety degree angle—that is, they have one square corner. Even today we call his idea about right triangles the *Pythagorean theorem.* A theorem is a mathematical idea that can be proven.

The Pythagorean theorem states that in a right triangle, the *square* of the longest side is equal to the sum of the squares of the other two sides. A square is a number multiplied by itself. Suppose you have a triangle whose longest side—called the *hypotenuse*—is 5 feet and whose other two sides are 3 feet and 4 feet. The square of the hypotenuse is 5 times 5, or 25. The square of the other two sides are 3 times 3, or 9, and 4 times 4, or 16. Add 9 plus 16 and you get 25, which is the square of the hypotenuse. This rule works for any right triangle.

The Egyptians knew this fact about right triangles long before Pythagoras did and used it in planning and constructing their buildings. The Babylonians, Chinese, and Hindus knew it too, but Pythagoras was the first to prove this rule.

Pythagoras and his followers also observed the motions of the planets. They found that the planets moved in a regular, repetitive fashion. Each planet seemed to move at a different speed. Because the Pythagoreans related mathematics to music, they believed that each planet produced a different musical note. The Pythagoreans thought that Earth and the other planets traveled around a great fire at the center of the universe. This was the first idea of the universe that did not put Earth at the center.

The Pythagoreans considered geometry, astronomy, and music to be based on numbers and to be part of mathematics, the science of numbers. Eventually these four areas of knowledge came to be looked upon as the four most important subjects of all. This idea continued long after the time of Pythagoras, well into the Middle Ages. Today we study many other subjects, and they are all important. But the mathematical observations of Pythagoras are still as true and as fascinating as ever.

Archimedes' Bathtub

HAVE YOU EVER NOTICED what happens to the level of water in a bathtub when you get into the tub? The water level rises and may even overflow. If you have ever done this, you have repeated something observed by one of the great thinkers of ancient times. His name was Archimedes and he made one of his greatest discoveries while stepping into a bath. The rising water level gave him an idea that helped him solve a difficult problem.

Archimedes lived over 2200 years ago in ancient Syracuse, on what is now the Mediterranean island of Sicily. His cousin, king Hiero, had given a goldsmith some gold with which to make a crown. When Hiero received the crown he became suspicious. The crown was supposed to be all gold, but Hiero thought that the goldsmith might have kept some of the gold and added a less valuable metal, such as silver, in its place. Hiero asked Archimedes to figure out if the crown was really all gold. But he warned Archimedes not to melt down the crown to find out.

Archimedes was puzzled for a while about how to solve this problem. Then one day, as he stepped into a tub filled to the brim with water at the public baths, he got a great idea. Suddenly he realized that the amount of bathwater that overflowed took up the same amount of space as the part of his body that he placed into the tub. His body now took up the space where there had been water. The amount of space something takes up is called its *volume.* So his body had *displaced* or pushed away an amount of water equal in volume to his body. Excited that he had found a way to measure the amount of gold in the crown, Archimedes jumped out of the tub and ran home through the streets of Syracuse yelling, "Eureka!" which meant in Greek, "I have found it."

When he returned home, Archimedes weighed the crown. Then he took a lump of gold and a lump of silver that each weighed the same as the crown. The silver lump was larger, because silver is lighter than gold.

Archimedes filled two bowls to the brim with water and placed the lump of silver in one and the lump of gold in the other. The silver lump made more water overflow than the gold lump even though the two lumps weighed the same. This is because an object displaces an amount of water equal to its own volume, not its weight. So if the crown were pure gold, it would have to displace the same amount of water as the lump of pure gold. But the crown made *more* water overflow than the lump of gold did. That meant there was another metal in the crown besides gold—probably silver.

ARCHIMEDES' BATHTUB

Archimedes had also noticed that water is able to lift some things and cause them to float. This lifting power, called *buoyancy,* is what enables ships to stay afloat even when they are loaded with heavy cargo. Archimedes did many experiments and finally came up with a rule, or principle, about buoyancy. He concluded that anything that floats displaces its own weight of water. Anything that sinks displaces an amount of water equal to its own volume.

A submarine works on Archimedes' principle of buoyancy. Inside a submarine are large tanks called ballast tanks. To make the submarine go underwater, water is pumped into the ballast tanks. When the tanks are full, the submarine becomes heavier than the water it displaces, and it sinks. When water is forced from the tanks, the submarine becomes lighter than the water it displaces, and it rises.

Archimedes also made some important discoveries about simple machines, devices that make work easier. One machine he experimented with is called the *lever.* A lever is a flat, long object—such as a pole or bar—that rests against a support, called a *fulcrum.* Crowbars, seesaws, baseball bats, and boat oars are all examples of levers.

In the case of a seesaw, the fulcrum is in the middle of a long beam with seats on either end. A fulcrum can be moved to different positions on a lever. You probably know what it takes to balance a seesaw when two people are of different weights. The heavier person must sit closer to the middle of the seesaw, or the fulcrum.

To use a crowbar, the fulcrum is placed near the end that goes under the object to be moved. The person using this kind of lever pushes down on the other end of the crowbar. Pushing down on the crowbar applies a *force,* or energy, to the bar. The fulcrum changes the direction of the force from a downward to an upward one. Thus, a person can push down on a lever to lift up an object.

In the case of a baseball bat, the batter's hand closest to the middle of the bat acts as the fulcrum. The batter swings the bat handle toward himself. This causes the bat head to swing away from the batter and toward the ball.

Archimedes showed that the lever can change a weak force working over a large distance into a strong force working over a short distance. This makes it possible to use a small force to lift or move a large object. According to legend, Archimedes once said, "Give me a lever long enough and a place to stand, and I could move Earth itself." King Hiero challenged Archimedes to prove that he could accomplish such a feat, so Archimedes used some levers to pull a heavy ship safely into the harbor.

The pulley is another kind of simple machine that can be used to increase force or change its direction. A pulley has a wheel that can turn freely on an axle. Some pulleys are fixed, like the pulley at the top of a flagpole. A fixed pulley does not increase a force. It only changes the direction of a force. Some pulleys are movable, which means that a pulley wheel moves with the weight as a rope is pulled. A movable pulley nearly doubles the moving force. Several pulleys together, in a device called a *block and tackle,* can multiply the moving force several times.

If you have ever pushed anything up a ramp, you have used another kind of simple machine called an *inclined plane.* Suppose you want to move a heavy object up the steps leading to a house. If you use a board to make a ramp, the work is easier. The work is done by sliding the object over the length of the board. The longer the ramp, the less force is needed to move the object. Like the pulley, the inclined plane makes it possible for a weak force applied over a long distance to do the same work as a strong force over a short distance.

If you cut a long, thin, triangular strip of paper and wrap it around a pencil, you will observe a familiar shape—a screw. A screw is a simple machine that is basically an inclined plane wrapped around a cylinder. Like an inclined plane, a screw makes it possible for a small force to do a big job. Pushing a screw through a thick piece of wood would be difficult, but when you use a screwdriver to turn the screw, it moves slowly but easily through the thick piece of wood.

Archimedes invented a kind of water pump that used the principle of the screw. This simple machine, called the "screw of Archimedes," was first used to pump water from inside the hold of a ship. Today similar pumps are used in some waste water treatment plants.

Although Archimedes made many practical inventions, he did not think of them as his great contribution to the world. He considered himself a mathematician. Archimedes worked out many problems using mathematics, especially geometry. He studied circles, spheres, cylinders, and cones. He also devised a system of naming large numbers. Archimedes' system enabled mathematicians to name extremely large numbers, even the number of grains of sand in the world.

With his mind on counting sand grains and measuring perfect circles, Archimedes was probably rather forgetful and absentminded. This trait may have cost him his life. When the Romans invaded and conquered Syracuse, orders went out to capture Archimedes but not to hurt him. The Roman authorities knew of Archimedes' brilliance, and hoped he could be of use to them. Archimedes, calmly scratching a mathematical drawing in the sand, paid no attention to a soldier who ordered him to stand up. The soldier did not know Archimedes. When the order was not obeyed, the soldier drew his sword and killed Archimedes on the spot. Thus ended the life of one of the world's greatest mathematicians.

The Search for the Philosopher's Stone

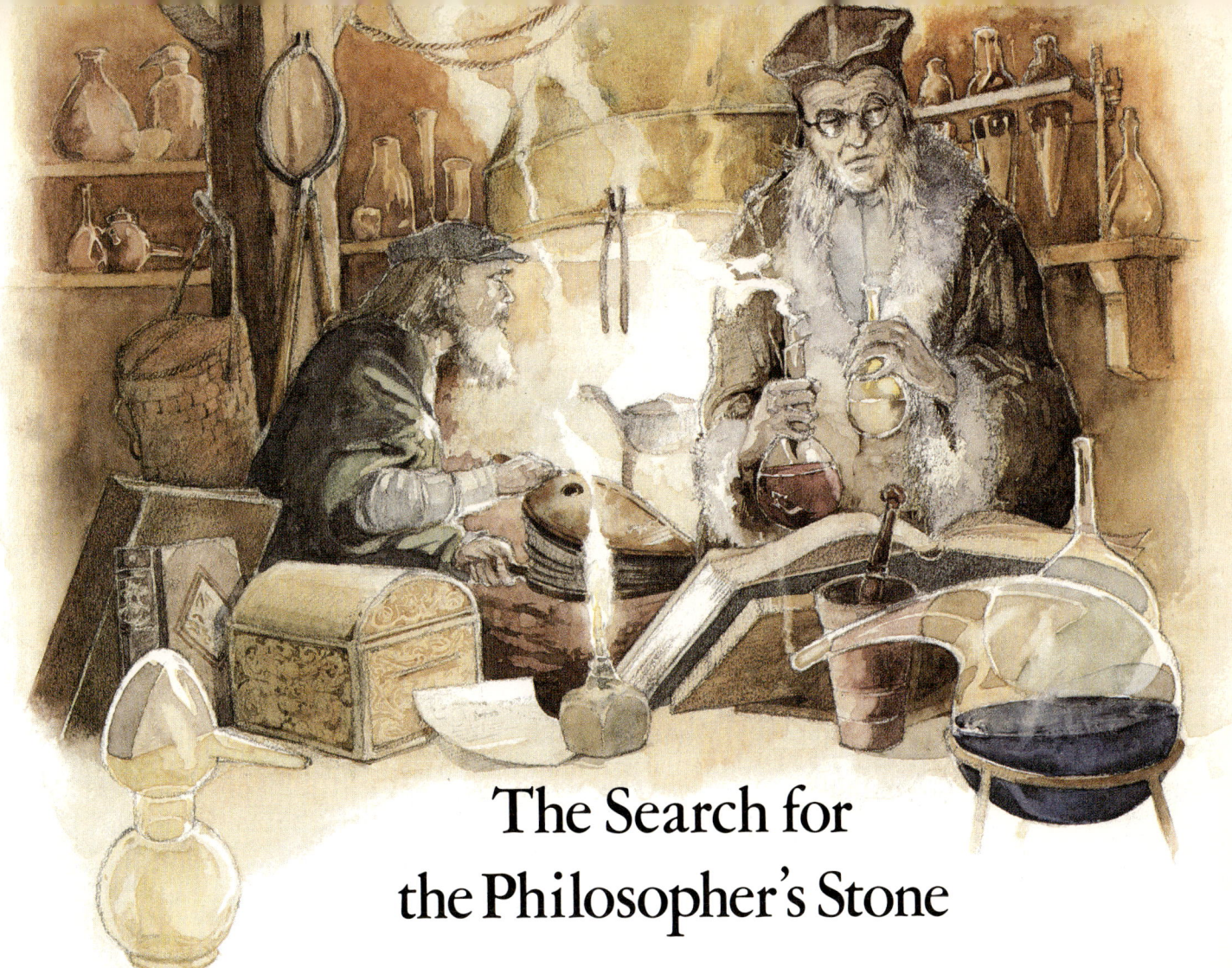

IT IS THE MIDDLE OF THE NIGHT. The only lights are a single candle and the deep red glow coming from a strange-looking oven. The room is cluttered with jars, bottles, skulls, and old books. An old man huddles over an egg-shaped glass bottle near the oven and adds a few drops of colored liquid to it. Suddenly, an explosion rocks the room. He is thrown back and glass and liquid are scattered everywhere.

This kind of event was not uncommon in the days of *alchemy,* a practice that started about 2000 years ago. Most alchemists were looking for a way to turn ordinary metals into gold. By adding materials together, they learned much about the nature of many substances. Although their methods were a blend of science and magic, alchemists made many observations and discoveries that gave birth to what we now call chemistry, the study of the substances and the way they behave.

THE SEARCH FOR THE PHILOSOPHER'S STONE

Alchemists tried to find a way to change, or *transmute,* other metals into gold. There were many incredible stories and claims about how this could be done. Some alchemists kept their experiments secret and used tricks to make others think they had been successful. They found they could make a decent living by this sort of fakery. Other, more honest alchemists had a much higher goal. They were searching for something called the Philosopher's Stone.

The Philosopher's Stone was not a rock for a thinker to sit on. Rather, it was a substance that alchemists believed could be created by mixing the right elements together under the proper conditions. Once made, just a tiny bit of the stone could change other metals into gold. Alchemists believed the stone could also be used to cure people of sickness. Some alchemists believed that it could give a person the ability to live forever, and so it was also called the Elixir of Life. The search for the stone was considered a religious and spiritual goal, and thus it was known as the Great Work.

As alchemists sought to learn how to make the Philosopher's Stone, they discovered many important chemical processes. For example, they heated liquids until they turned into gases, and then cooled the gases to turn them back into liquids again. This process, called *distillation,* is still used today. For example, crude oil that comes from the ground is distilled to make everything from gasoline to wax. Seawater is distilled to remove the dissolved minerals in it and make fresh drinking water.

The most important tool of the alchemist was the oven or furnace, something that could provide heat for experiments. The alchemists invented better furnaces to keep chemical mixtures at a steady temperature and created specially shaped bottles, flasks, and containers for every possible process. For example, they hoped to make the Philosopher's Stone in an egg-shaped glass they called the philosopher's egg. Many of the flasks and funnels that can be found today in a modern laboratory were developed from containers used by the alchemists.

Alchemists invented another important scientific tool called the *water bath.* With the water bath, different materials can be heated steadily at the same time and to the same temperature. The alchemists called a water bath a *bain-marie,* after a mysterious woman alchemist named Mary who lived almost 2000 years ago. The word "bain" is French for bath, and "Marie" is the French form of the name Mary.

The alchemists based their work on that of the ancient Egyptians and Greeks. The Greek philosopher Aristotle believed that everything is made up of four basic elements—earth, air, fire, and water. Each of the elements has special qualities—coldness, dryness, heat, and wetness. Everything in the world is made of different combinations of these elements. Aristotle and his fellow Greeks believed it was possible for elements to change into one another according to the qualities they had in common. For example, if earth became dry it could turn into the element fire, as when a field of dry grass in the summer catches fire from a spark or a bolt of lightning.

Another ancient Greek named Democritus had a slightly different idea. He believed that everything is made of tiny particles that cannot be divided into smaller particles. These particles he called atoms.

A thousand years later, the alchemists used the Greek ideas of elements and atoms. For example, one alchemist observed a metal that appeared to be made of earthy smoke. He thought the metal was made of atoms of earth that were becoming fire. This was the element we call sulfur. He also observed a watery vapor metal that appeared to be made of water on the way to becoming air. This was the element we call mercury.

Alchemists discovered many ways to make substances combine with each other to form a completely different substance in a *chemical reaction.* But their explanations of how the reactions worked were not very scientific. Although our ideas of elements and atoms are very different today, we owe a debt to the early alchemists for their descriptions of chemicals and chemical reactions.

Alchemists worked in secret, guarding their efforts against the prying eyes of the curious. The books that remain on alchemy are very strange, indeed. Many contain symbols instead of words. The alchemists wrote in a kind of shorthand, using symbols to stand for the materials and chemical processes they used. For example, a picture of a green lion eating the sun meant that a mixture of nitric and hydrochloric acid (the green lion) could dissolve gold (the sun). Gold usually contains a small amount of copper, which can turn the acid blue-green when combined with it. This is why the alchemists drew the lion with a green color.

Slowly, belief in the search for the Philosopher's Stone began to fade. One thing that helped change alchemy was the work of a man named Paracelsus. This colorful, arrogant character was born in Switzerland in 1493. He was a doctor who believed that alchemy should be used to find cures for diseases, not just to change metals into gold. He discovered some cures, but he also made many enemies. Paracelsus considered many scientists of his day to be ignorant fools—and told them so! He believed there were many kinds of elements, not just the four elements of the ancient Greeks. Paracelsus traveled from place to place spreading his knowledge about medicinal cures. He traveled so much mainly because he was often forced to move—and quickly. But some alchemists became interested in Paracelsus's ideas and started to investigate them.

After Paracelsus, it seemed that the days of alchemy were numbered. Many alchemists resorted to trickery. One such alchemist made a nail that was half gold and half iron and painted it all black. He would dip the nail into a solution that dissolved the paint, revealing the "gold" nail. But other alchemists did not get away with their tricks. One alchemist carried with him a chest containing a secret compartment. The compartment held pieces of gold that the alchemist could pull out at the necessary moment to convince others he had changed common metals to gold. He used his trick on a duke who was seeking to restore his fortune. The duke then gave the alchemist a huge piece of iron to change to gold, but the secret compartment did not contain enough treasure to do the job. So the duke had the iron made into a gallows painted with gold leaf, and promptly had the alchemist hanged.

In 1660 King Charles II of England founded the Royal Society of London. Its members made many careful experiments and observations that helped establish the science of chemistry. These early chemists wanted to learn about the structure and properties of substances. The scientists also shared information with one another. They did not work in secret as the alchemists did.

Alchemy was soon abandoned, as scientists learned more about elements, how they combine with each other to form chemical compounds, and the nature of chemical reactions. Yet the methods and observations made by the alchemists had an important influence on the new science of chemistry.

Copernicus, Galileo, and the Stars

HAVE YOU EVER SEEN a beautiful sunrise or sunset? You have probably noticed that the sun rises in the east and sets in the west. The ancient Greeks believed that the sun god Apollo rode his chariot of fire across the sky each day. In the Greek explanation of the universe, the sun and the planets travel around Earth. This idea was thought to be absolutely true for thousands of years. But in the 1500's the world started to change. Christopher Columbus and others had just discovered the New World. Ferdinand Magellan had sailed around the world. The time was right for new thoughts about Earth and its place in the universe.

One person who had such new thoughts was Nicolaus Copernicus. Copernicus was born in Poland in 1473. His uncle was a Roman Catholic bishop, and he helped young Nicolaus to travel to Italy to study law and medicine. Nicolaus soon began working for the church. One of his jobs was to help correct the calendar that people used. He had to figure out the length of the year and of each month. The calendar was supposed to agree with the motions of the sun, the planets, and the stars, but it seemed to be slightly incorrect, so Copernicus began studying the movement of the planets and the stars.

Copernicus was the very model of a good citizen and churchgoer. But his studies led him to some revolutionary new ideas that went against church teachings. The church held the belief that the sun and planets circle Earth, each held in place in an invisible layer of crystal; that the outermost crystal sphere holds all the stars; and that God lives outside these circles, turning them steadily for all eternity. As Copernicus made his observations, he realized that the motion of the sun, the planets, and the stars could be explained in a much better way. He decided that Earth and the other planets travel around the sun. If the sun were the center of things, the paths of the planets could be explained as circles around the sun.

Copernicus held this idea for many years, but did not say anything about it to others. He knew that his idea was completely revolutionary and went against church beliefs. So he waited until he was an old man to put his ideas in writing. In 1540 he gave his manuscript to a printer. He died three years later, the same year his book was printed. In his book, which was titled *On the Revolution of the Celestial Spheres,* Copernicus wrote, "The sun sits as upon a royal throne, ruling his children, the planets which circle around him."

Copernicus was a cautious man. He did not wish to anger the church. So he wrote at the beginning of his book that the reader could think of his system of the sun and planets as just a mathematical exercise and not a declaration of truth about the world. Yet some people saw the truth in Copernicus's ideas, and news about his book spread quickly.

One person who took the ideas of Copernicus very seriously was an eccentric Danish nobleman named Tycho Brahe. Brahe had begun studying astronomy after seeing an eclipse in 1560. He was something of a mathematician, and once he had even fought a duel with a classmate over who was the better mathematician. His classmate's sword had cut off part of his nose, and for the rest of his years Brahe wore a gold plate over the missing part. By the 1570's Brahe was considered a leading astronomer. He kept careful records of his observations — all made with his own eyes, for the telescope had not yet been invented.

Johannes Kepler, Brahe's young assistant, kept all of Brahe's records after the nobleman's death. From Brahe's records, Kepler made his own discoveries. He wrote that each planet travels around the sun not in a circle, but in an ellipse — an oval-shaped path. Kepler also wrote that the planets travel at different speeds, some fast and some slow. He thought of these speeds as different musical notes, some high and some low. Together, the planets' motions were in harmony with one another, making the "music of the spheres."

But no one as yet had really seen the planets clearly or measured their motions accurately. Without such observations, the planets remained just interesting lights in the night sky. Then, in the early 1600's, a man named Galileo Galilei finally showed that the Copernican theory was true.

Galileo was born in Italy in 1564. He studied mathematics and soon became interested in physics, the study of matter and energy. He invented many things, including the pendulum clock, which helped him to make accurate measurements. He cleverly designed many other kinds of scientific measuring instruments. Eventually he was hired by the rulers of the powerful Republic of Venice as a professor of mathematics.

In 1609 Galileo heard about an invention made by a Dutch lens maker. It was a spyglass that could be used to see ships out at sea. Galileo went about making his own instrument. He finally built a telescope with a magnification of about 32 — meaning an object 32 miles away would look as if it were 1 mile away. Turning the telescope to the sky, Galileo discovered what he thought were four new planets traveling around the planet Jupiter. They were actually the four largest moons of Jupiter.

COPERNICUS, GALILEO, AND THE STARS

He also studied the moon and drew pictures of its rough, cratered surface. The accepted belief was that all the heavenly bodies must be perfectly smooth spheres. The moon's rough surface disproved this idea.

With these new observations of the moon and planets, Galileo soon realized that Copernicus was right and that the planets travel around the sun, not around Earth. Galileo was somewhat arrogant. He thought that with his superior equipment and careful observations he could get others to see that the planetary system described by Copernicus was correct. Galileo published some of his drawings of the moon and planets in a book called *The Starry Messenger*. But people within the church were not willing to listen to his ideas about the motions of the planets. In 1616 the church ordered Galileo to stop writing about these revolutionary ideas.

Galileo kept up his observations. In 1632 he published another book in which the accepted idea of Earth as the center of the universe was made to sound foolish. The pope and other church officials were furious. They stopped the presses from printing the book and promptly placed it on the list of forbidden books. Worse still, Galileo was called to Rome to stand trial for *heresy*—for holding beliefs that disagreed with the teachings of the church. He was forced to sign a paper stating he did not believe in the Copernican idea, and he had to deny the truth of what he had written.

Why did Galileo deny what he knew to be true? By this time Galileo was an old man in his seventies and nearly blind. He knew he could not oppose the powerful Roman Catholic Church. But the seeds of change had already been planted. In time, Galileo knew, they would produce a rich harvest.

After this, the science of astronomy began to grow steadily in the northern parts of Europe, where scientists had a little more freedom to test and discuss their ideas. In 1642, the year that Galileo died, Isaac Newton, one of the great scientists of all time, was born in England. The age of scientific discovery had begun.

The Apple and Isaac Newton

ONE DAY IN 1665, a young man sat under an apple tree in an English garden. An apple fell and almost hit him in the head. That was not an unusual event. Many people before had seen apples fall from apple trees. But the man under the tree was thoughtful and observant. His name was Isaac Newton, and the falling apple suddenly raised an important new question in his mind. Why do objects—such as apples—fall down and not up? Nobody had ever explained this before, but Newton started thinking about it. He spent every waking moment thinking about it for the next couple of years. During that time he described the law of *gravitation*—the force that pulls all objects toward the center of Earth.

Isaac Newton, one of the most important scientists of all time, was born on Christmas Day in 1642. During his lifetime he developed original theories to explain light, color, motion, and gravity. He also developed a new kind of mathematics called *calculus.* In 1687 he published a book called *Principia* in which he described many of his

THE APPLE AND ISAAC NEWTON

theories. This book, one of the greatest scientific achievements, brought him great fame.

Yet the early days of Isaac's life had not gone very well. His father had died before Isaac was born. As a child, young Isaac was small and sickly. He could not join the other children in games. Instead, he read and made toys for himself. His family was poor and he was expected to work on the family farm when he was old enough. But Isaac was not cut out to be a farmer. He spent more time reading or working out mathematical problems than doing his farm chores. Luckily, his uncle realized this fact and sent him off to college in Cambridge, England. Soon he knew more about mathematics and science than his professors.

During the 1660's a great plague was raging throughout England. Newton's college was closed and he went home to his mother's farm. It was there in the garden that he saw the apple fall. Nobody is certain whether this story is true or not, but whatever got Newton thinking about the invisible force that acts on falling objects caused a turning point in scientific history.

Newton would sit for hours in his room and think about the force of gravity. He came to the conclusion that every object in the universe is attracted to every other object. The amount of attraction, or gravitational force, depends on how far apart the objects are and how much substance, or mass, they contain.

Newton studied the motion of the moon around Earth. He concluded that the moon has another force acting on it in addition to that of gravity. Because the moon revolves around Earth, it was a *centrifugal force* pulling it outward, away from Earth. This same kind of force can be seen when you spin a pail of water around in a circle. Centrifugal force keeps the water in the pail. Newton thought that the moon is balanced between its centrifugal force and the force of gravity. With these two forces balancing each other, the moon cannot be pulled closer to Earth, nor can it move farther away. Instead, the moon revolves around Earth.

To accurately describe his ideas about gravity, Newton invented a new kind of mathematics called calculus. Calculus is that part of mathematics that deals with numbers that are constantly changing. It is very useful for calculating such things as the motions of the moon and the planets, which travel in their orbits at speeds that are always changing. In using his calculus to explain the motion of the moon, Newton showed an important connection between mathematics and physics.

Newton was a modest, lonely man who never married. He was also somewhat absentminded. As one story goes, he was entertaining some friends one night and left the room to get a bottle of wine. After he had been gone for quite some time, his friends went to look for him. They found him working in his study, having completely forgotten about the wine and his guests.

Newton thought a great deal about the way things move. In his book he described what we now call Newton's laws of motion. The first law of motion is sometimes called the law of *inertia*. Inertia means that once something is moving, it will stay in motion until a force acts on it to stop it. It also means that if an object is not moving, it will remain at rest until a force acts on it to move it. You have probably seen this law in action. When you ride a bicycle or skateboard, it takes more effort to get started than it does to keep going once you are moving.

Newton's second law of motion shows the connection between force and the mass of an object. It states that the greater the mass of an object, the more force is needed to move it. That is why it is harder to throw a bowling ball than a Ping-Pong ball.

Did you ever let go of a balloon filled with air and watch it fly around the room as the air shot out of it? If you have, then you have seen Newton's third law in action. This law states that when one object acts with a force on another object, the second object exerts an equal force on the first one, but in the opposite direction. The force of the air escaping from the balloon produces an equal but opposite force that pushes the balloon forward. A rocket engine works the same way.

Newton was also fascinated with light. Once he bought some glass prisms at a county fair. He used them to show that white light is made of light of all the colors of the rainbow. He proved this by using one prism to break up a beam of light into many different-colored beams of light, and a second prism to make white light again from the different-colored beams. People had known for centuries that light passing through the edge of a lens seems to change color. They thought the light actually changed from white to red or green. By separating light and putting it back together again, Newton proved that white light could be physically separated into the different colors. He had formed an idea and had performed a real experiment to test it.

Newton's book, *Principia,* had a great effect on scientific thought of his time. His work was considered so brilliant that he was elected president of the Royal Society, voted into Parliament, and made a knight.

Newton did not let fame and honors go to his head. "If I have seen further than most men it is because I have stood on the shoulders of giants," he said. Those giants were the scientists and mathematicians who had come before him. Newton brought his own creativity to his work, using mathematics to explain natural events. He helped set the stage for the scientific revolution.

Leeuwenhoek's "Little Beasties"

ANTON VAN LEEUWENHOEK LIKED HIS JOB at the town hall in Delft, Holland, well enough. But he liked his hobby even more. He enjoyed looking at all sorts of things with a simple hand-held *microscope* that he had made by himself. Whenever he had the chance, Leeuwenhoek ground another *lens,* a carefully polished piece of glass. He placed the smoothly ground lens into a holder. Then he placed a small object, such as a thread of wool, a plant seed, or a drop of rainwater, onto a pinhead mounted on the holder. With the microscope held close to his eye, he looked at the object through the lens.

Through his microscope, Leeuwenhoek saw a whole new miniature world. The curve of the glass lens magnified objects so that they looked many times their real size. He could see that thread is made of many more tiny fibers than can possibly be seen with the eye alone. Using his lens, Leeuwenhoek saw the patterns on a fly's wing and the barbs on the sting of a bee. He looked at particles he scraped off his skin and teeth. Each new discovery made Leeuwenhoek even more curious about what other things looked like under his magnifying device.

One day he told his friend, Regnier de Graaf, about his microscopes. De Graaf was a scientist and a member of the Royal Society of London. He wrote a letter to the society urging them to ask Leeuwenhoek about his discoveries. In 1673 Leeuwenhoek sent his first letter to the Royal Society. The letter was entitled "A Specimen of Some Observations made by a Microscope contrived by Mr. Leeuwenhoek, concerning Mould Upon the skin, Flesh, etc; The Sting of a Bee, etc."

As the years passed, Leeuwenhoek wrote almost 400 long letters to the Royal Society describing his discoveries. His style of writing showed that he was not an educated man and had not been schooled as a scientist. Yet his ability to observe details and make new improvements on his microscope were a marvel.

In one letter, Leeuwenhoek told the society what he had seen when he had examined his own blood. He described the tiny particles that we now know as red blood cells, among the smallest cells in the body.

In another letter, Leeuwenhoek described the eggs of insects that he had found on spoiled meat and cheese. At that time people believed that insects were born out of nothing—that they arose spontaneously. This idea was called the theory of *spontaneous generation.* Looking at the microscopic eggs of the insects, Leeuwenhoek realized that, like other living things, insects do come from somewhere—they come from other insects.

Leeuwenhoek's greatest discovery occurred one day as he studied a droplet of rainwater. He saw tiny creatures that looked like miniature eels. "They swim and they play around," he told his daughter, Maria. "They are a thousand times smaller than any creature we can see with our eyes alone."

Leeuwenhoek quickly wrote a letter to the Royal Society. In it he described these "little beasties" swimming around in the water droplet. The Royal Society was not ready to believe him this time. They asked Robert Hooke, an English scientist familiar with microscopes, to look at rainwater, too. After his experiments, Hooke reported that Leeuwenhoek was right. There were such tiny living things in rainwater.

Leeuwenhoek became fascinated with this tiny world he had discovered. He caught a drop of rain and examined it. He found that it did not contain any swimming living things. But water that had collected in a dish for a few days did contain living things. Today we know that *bacteria,* tiny one-celled living things, can be carried by the wind to stagnant water, where they can quickly multiply. He looked at water from other sources, such as rain barrels, canals, and wells. He found not only bacteria, but also other tiny one-celled organisms of many different shapes and sizes. Leeuwenhoek observed that many had little tail-like structures that propelled them quickly through the water.

As a reward for all of his remarkable observations, the Royal Society made Leeuwenhoek an honorary member and sent him a diploma in a silver case. This was quite an honor for a man who had quit school at the age of 16. Leeuwenhoek continued his microscope studies. He even published a book, *The Mysteries of Nature,* in which he discussed his discovery of the "little beasties."

Through his long life, Leeuwenhoek built and used about 400 microscopes, all considered simple microscopes because they had a single lens. He used each microscope to look at something different. Leeuwenhoek did not tell anyone what he had learned about grinding lenses and making microscopes. He let only a few people look through his microscopes, and refused to sell any of them, although many people wished to buy them.

When Leeuwenhoek died in 1723 at the age of 91, he was known throughout Europe. Even the queen of England had traveled all the way to Holland to look through one of his microscopes. He left his most valuable microscopes to the Royal Society. For many years they remained the best microscopes in the world.

Leeuwenhoek's studies opened up a whole new field of science called *microbiology*—the study of living things that can be seen only with the aid of a microscope. Following Leeuwenhoek's lead, other scientists began to examine the various parts of living things using a microscope. Robert Hooke looked at the parts of a cork tree under a microscope and saw that they were composed of small, individual units of life. He called these units of life *cells.*

It took more than a hundred years for scientists to learn much more about Leeuwenhoek's "little beasties." More powerful *compound microscopes,* which use more than one lens, had to be developed. With these compound microscopes, scientists were able to carefully study and classify the tiny bacteria. Today we know of thousands of kinds of bacteria. Some, like the bacteria of decay that Leeuwenhoek may have seen in rainwater, are helpful. They break down dead plant and animal cells into chemical nutrients for other living things. Other bacteria cause diseases in animals and plants.

Today both helpful and harmful bacteria and other microscopic organisms can be observed under even more powerful microscopes called *electron microscopes.* These microscopes do not focus light through lenses to magnify objects. Instead, they use beams of atomic particles called electrons to produce a magnifying power hundreds of times greater than Leeuwenhoek's best microscope. With such microscopes, Leeuwenhoek's "little beasties" can now be magnified many thousands of times their real size.

Mr. Watt's Steam Engine

IN THE BRIGHT LIGHT OF A FULL MOON, an English factory owner named Matthew Boulton rode his horse to the monthly meeting of the Lunar Society. The Lunar Society met on bright nights so that its members could see their way by the light of the moon. In Birmingham, England, during the 1770's, there were no electric street lights and no automobiles to make travel at night easy and safe.

The Lunar Society was made up of a group of pioneering men who owned businesses and factories. These industrialists made and sold all kinds of things, from iron tools to kitchen dishes, buttons, and shoes.

Matthew Boulton came to the Lunar Society meeting with good news. James Watt, an inventor from Scotland, was coming to Birmingham to build steam engines. Watt still had not perfected his engine, but with the fine metal tools and machines at Boulton's factory, Watt was sure to get his engine running.

MR WATT'S STEAM ENGINE

James Watt had been working on steam engines ever since he had been given one to repair back home in Scotland. The idea of steam power had been around since the time of the ancient Greeks. In the early 1700's an English inventor, Thomas Newcomen, had invented a steam engine. This is how his engine worked. Water was boiled over a coal fire to make steam. When water changes to steam it expands and pushes out in all directions to take up more space. The steam entered a cylinder that contained a snugly fitting piston. The steam forced the piston to go up. When the steam cooled it changed back to water, taking up less space and allowing the piston to move back down. The piston was attached to a rod that moved back and forth and could be used to power a pump.

Newcomen's engine was not very efficient. Watt, a thrifty man who disliked waste, had been trying to think of a way to make Newcomen's steam engine less wasteful. At home in Scotland, Watt was taking a walk one Sunday afternoon when an idea hit him. He could make a separate chamber into which the used steam could go to be cooled after it had pushed the piston up. The separate chamber, called a *condenser,* made the engine much more efficient. Watt also made another change. The rod

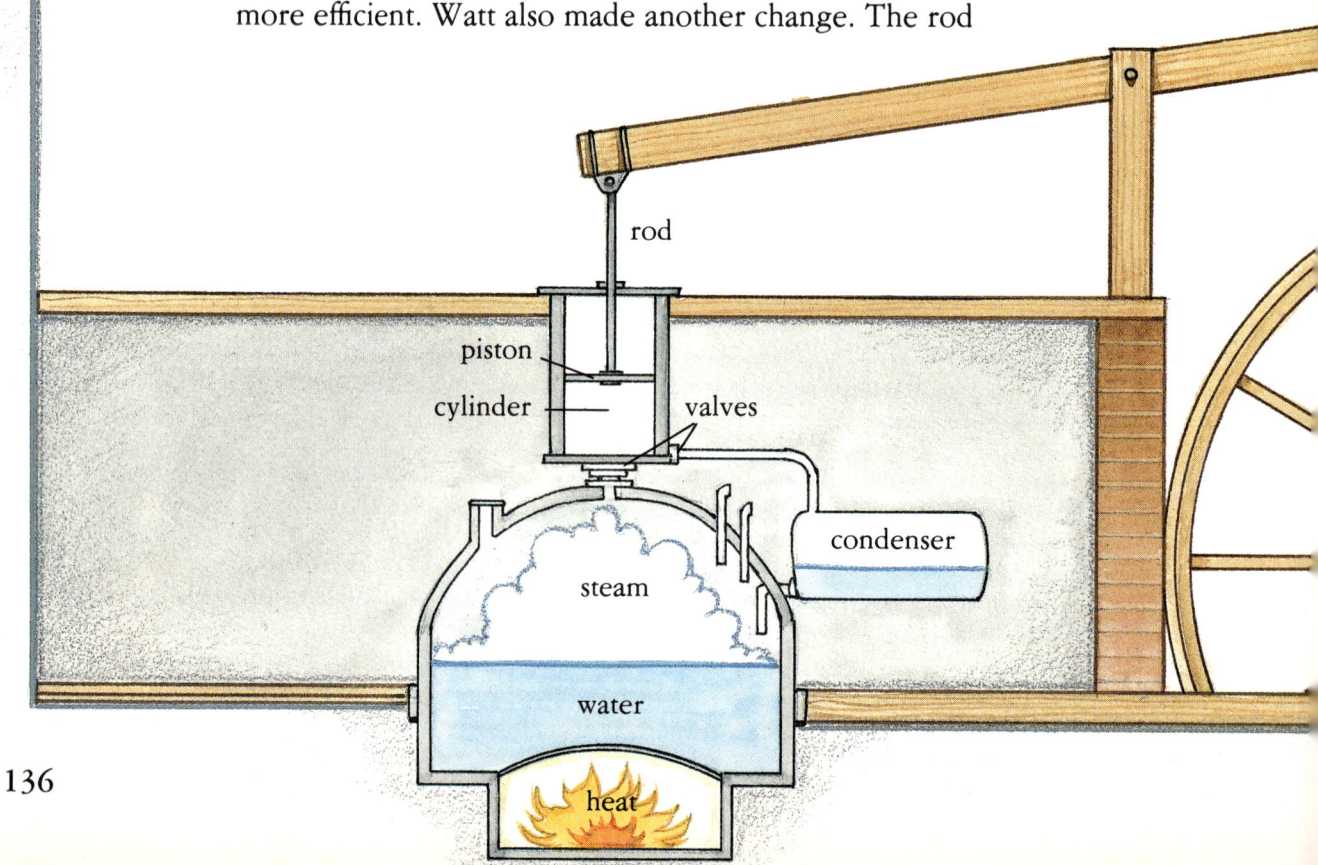

MR WATT'S STEAM ENGINE

that led from the piston was attached to a set of gears that turned a large wheel called a flywheel. The flywheel could be used to power a pump or run a machine.

James Watt soon built a smooth-running steam engine. Boulton used it to run his factory machines more efficiently and made more money. Because of their success, Boulton and Watt decided to form a partnership to sell steam power to other factories. Watt would not have done this on his own; he was a quiet and cautious man. But Boulton was excited about the idea and he was a good businessman. So together, Boulton and Watt set up engines in factories and mines all over England.

Boulton and Watt operated the engines for a fee. They charged one-third the difference between the cost of coal for the engines and the cost of hay for the horses that would have done the same amount of work. But just how much work could a horse do? No one was sure, so Watt decided to find out.

Watt put a strong horse to work lifting a heavy load with a rope and pulley. After making careful measurements, he announced that one *horsepower* was the amount of power required to lift 33,000 pounds a height of one foot in one minute. This was actually about one and a half times as much power as an average horse could produce. But it showed that a one-horsepower Watt engine could easily do the work of one average horse.

Once Watt's engine was available, everyone wanted one. Steam engines were soon operating in every factory town and mine in England. The use of steam engines spread throughout Europe and to the United States and helped bring about a new period in history—the Industrial Revolution, during which people harnessed the power of machines to make all sorts of goods.

The boom in industry produced by the steam engine brought with it the need for better transportation. How could manufactured goods be moved faster from factory to marketplace? One answer was by railroad. Around the year 1800, the first steam-powered locomotives were built to haul loads of coal in the coal mines. At first they

137

were used only to pull the coal cars from where the coal was being mined to the mine entrance, but soon the locomotives were hauling long trains of cars from the mines to nearby towns and cities.

During this time a British mining engineer named George Stephenson made many improvements to steam locomotives. He decided that locomotives and railroads could be used to haul passengers as well as coal. With his son Robert, Stephenson built an improved locomotive named the *Rocket,* and in 1829 the Stephensons opened up a railroad line from Liverpool to Manchester. The *Rocket* flew along the tracks at a speed of up to 29 miles per hour, and the railroad was a great success. Soon many others were building railroads in England, Europe, and the United States.

During the early 1800's, water was another important means of transportation. In England, many canals were being dug to connect rivers and other bodies of water. In some places it was cheaper and easier to send goods by barge along a canal than to send them by railway car.

In the United States an inventor named Robert Fulton was taking a great interest in water transportation. Fulton invented many things, including a submarine and torpedoes, but he is best remembered for his steamboat.

Although paddle wheel boats had been used for many years, the paddle wheelers always had been powered by people or animals. No one had been able to attach an engine to a boat equipped with paddles.

Several French and American inventors were also at work on steamboats. One, an American named John Stevens, had made a number of inventions for steam engines in the 1780's. By 1802 he had built a steam-powered boat that was driven by two propellers. It did not work very well because the steam engines were not powerful enough. So John Stevens went to work to design better engines for steamboats.

Stevens built and launched his improved steamboat, the *Phoenix,* in 1808. But by that time Robert Fulton had won the race to launch the first commercial steamboat.

Fulton had gone into partnership with Robert Livingston, a wealthy politician from New York. Livingston agreed to pay for the cost of building a steamboat of Fulton's design.

Fulton worked on several different steamboat designs in France and then returned to America with a good one. One momentous day in August of 1807, Fulton's steamboat *Clermont* made its way up the Hudson River from New York City to Albany. The rather clumsy, flat boat had its noisy, English-made steam engine in full view and paddle wheels on each side. The passengers were all decked out in their best ruffles and lace. The engine, fired with dry pinewood, gave off sparks and puffs of smoke and soon everyone was covered with soot. The boat was a great success, however, making the 150-mile trip in 32 hours, at a speed of almost 5 miles per hour.

Mr. Watt's steam engine had been given another use and the era of the steamboat had arrived. From the factories to the mines, from the rail yards to the shipyards, the steam engine ushered in a bustling new age of industry and transportation.

John Dalton, Atoms, and Molecules

JOHN DALTON WAS A MAN OF HABIT. Almost every day of his life he walked to the school in the town of Manchester, England, where he was schoolmaster. Each day for 57 years, rain or shine, he checked the temperature and wrote it down. It was this kind of routine observation and record keeping that led him to some important ideas that would change forever the way people thought about the nature of matter.

Every Thursday Dalton went to play a game of lawn bowling with his friends. One day, as he walked through the countryside in the rain, he thought about water. He wondered, how is it that water is made up of two gases—hydrogen and oxygen? Why do they always combine in the same amounts—two parts hydrogen to one part oxygen—to make water?

Dalton came to believe that an old idea handed down from the ancient Greeks was right. The idea stated that if a piece of a substance—gold, for example, or carbon—

were divided into two pieces, and then one of the pieces were divided again, and so on, eventually the substance would be divided into pieces that could not be divided any further. The Greeks called these smallest pieces of substance *atoms.*

John Dalton thought of atoms as little solid balls of substance, or matter. He said that the atoms of one kind of substance, or *element,* are all alike, but atoms of different elements are different from one another. One way they differ is that the atoms of each element have different weights.

Dalton had still other ideas, which he published in a book in 1805. He said that the atoms of one element cannot change into the atoms of another element. Instead, two kinds of atoms combine to make a third substance. Dalton noted that elements have combining powers that cause them to combine in definite ways. For example, when oxygen and hydrogen combine to make water, they always combine the same way—two hydrogen atoms with one oxygen atom. This combination forms one *molecule* of water. In another example, when one carbon atom and two oxygen atoms combine, they form one molecule of carbon dioxide.

Dalton had come to these conclusions as he worked in his own simple laboratory. He had also read about the work of two other scientists—an English chemist named Joseph Priestley and a French chemist named Antoine Lavoisier. Priestley had discovered that air is composed of several different gases, and that one of these gases makes burning, or *combustion,* possible. He also learned that animals need to breathe this gas in order to live. Lavoisier had named the gas oxygen and showed that it is an element.

Dalton concluded that each element is made of one particular kind of atom. He gave each element a symbol and showed that each type of atom has a definite weight, called its *atomic weight.*

But what are the properties of the elements that make them alike or different? Why does each element have a

JOHN DALTON, ATOMS, AND MOLECULES

different atomic weight? These questions were studied years later by a Russian scientist name Dmitri Mendeleev. Mendeleev was born about 30 years after Dalton published his theory of the elements. Mendeleev studied the elements and their atomic weights by inventing a card game he called Patience. On each card he wrote the name of an element and its atomic weight. He placed the cards in a column according to their atomic weights, starting with the element lithium. Mendeleev noticed that after he had put down seven cards, he came to the element sodium, which, like lithium, was a silvery white metal. So he started a new column, placing sodium next to lithium. When he had placed seven cards down in the second column he came to the card for potassium. This element was like lithium and sodium, so he placed it at the top of a third column. Mendeleev now saw that when he read the cards left to right, the elements in each row seemed to have a family resemblance. That is, they had similar appearance and chemical properties, even though their atomic weights were different.

Mendeleev continued his arrangement, placing calcium under potassium and next to magnesium. But the next card in his stack—the card for titanium—did not seem to belong in the next space. It did not resemble the other elements in that row across. So Mendeleev skipped that space and placed titanium next to the card for silicon. In leaving the space blank, Mendeleev predicted that an unknown element belonged there. Indeed he was right. During Mendeleev's time only 63 elements were known. Today we know there are 92 naturally occurring elements, and all the blanks he left have been filled.

Mendeleev used his cards to make a chart of the elements. The chart showed a definite order. Other scientists expressed interest in Mendeleev's chart, or *periodic table,* of atomic weights. Knowing the order of the elements gave them a way to start understanding atoms and how they are put together.

By the 20th century, scientists were beginning to realize that Dalton was wrong in thinking of atoms as solid balls of matter. The atom is not solid at all, but is made of still smaller particles, called *subatomic particles.* By the early 1900's experiments were begun to find the different parts of the atom. Scientists first discovered the *electron.* This tiny particle spins around the center of the atom, called the *nucleus.* Inside the nucleus of the atom are heavier particles called *protons* and *neutrons.* Each element on the atomic chart has a definite number of protons, neutrons, and electrons.

Understanding subatomic particles made it possible to unlock the energy within the atom that holds these tiny particles together. Scientists soon learned how to "split" atoms to release atomic energy.

Our modern age—the Atomic Age—has brought with it incredible new discoveries that John Dalton could never have imagined. Scientists are still at work uncovering many more secrets of the atom.

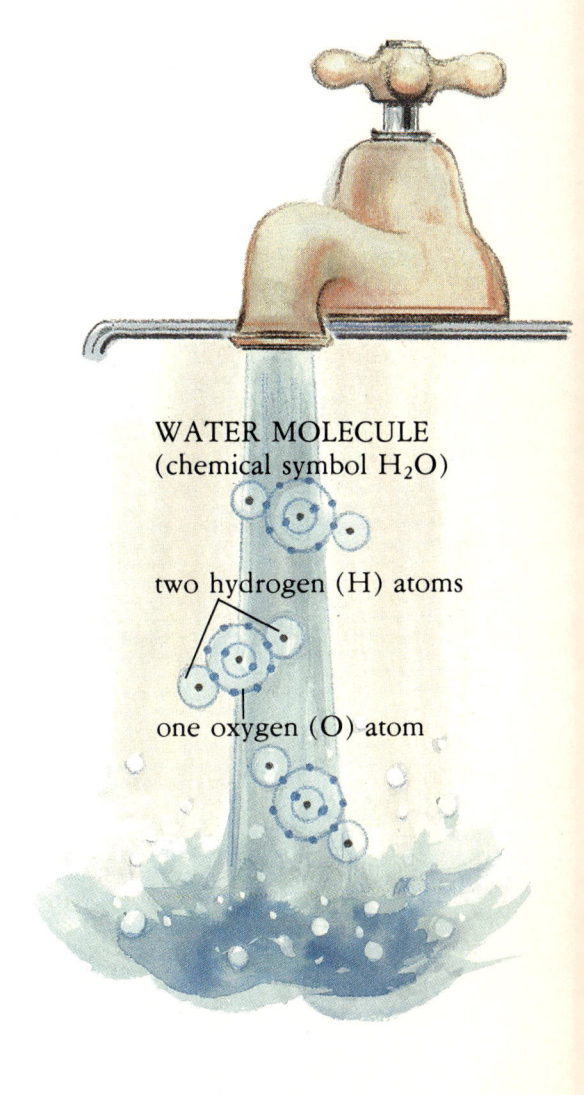

WATER MOLECULE
(chemical symbol H_2O)

two hydrogen (H) atoms

one oxygen (O) atom

Michael Faraday's Candle

IMAGINE THAT YOU ARE growing up in England in the 1800's. You are on your Christmas vacation and today you and your friends have come to a large hall to hear Michael Faraday, one of the most important scientists of your time.

A hush comes over the great hall as the aging Mr. Faraday enters. What exciting new experiment will he perform at the lecture today? Will he demonstrate how a magnet can be used to produce electricity? Will he use an electric current to break water down into oxygen and hydrogen gases? Not today. Today he is going to lecture on the remarkable properties of—a candle.

Michael Faraday's lectures at the Royal Institution of Great Britain were legendary. Faraday had attended many lectures there as a young man, and had decided that he would learn how to be a good speaker. To him, a good speech or lecture meant showing things—not just talking about them. He thought that by actually seeing scientific experiments, young people would become interested in learning.

One of Faraday's popular lectures to his audience of young people was on the "Chemical History of a Candle." A burning candle demonstrates many scientific principles, such as the way in which matter and energy are related. Matter is represented by the candle, the wick, and the air around the candle. Energy is represented by the light and the heat given off by the flame.

Matter is found in three forms, or states—solid, liquid, and gas. A burning candle shows all three. At room temperature, the candle wax is a solid. When the wick is lighted by a burning match, the wax at the top of the candle melts and becomes a liquid; it then rises up through the candle wick. The liquid wax changes to a gas, or vapor, at the top of the wick. There it combines with oxygen in the air in the process called combustion.

The light and heat energy released by the burning candle are easily observed. The molecules of gas that are produced by combustion release some of their energy. This energy causes the molecules to move very fast. The energized molecules rise up above the candle flame; the energy they release as heat can be felt.

The most energized molecules release energy in the form of light. If a lighted candle is placed near an object, such as a wall, the candlelight shines on it. When you put your hand between the candle and the wall, your hand forms a shadow. The rays of light coming from the candle are blocked by your hand, so they cannot reach the wall.

Why does the candle have a wick if the wax is the substance that is actually burning? The wick carries the liquid wax up to its tip where it is heated to a vapor. The vapor rises from the tip of the wick and actually burns just above it. Michael Faraday showed this is so in a clever way. He blew out the lighted candle, noting that the candle vapors were still rising from the wick. Then he struck a match and drew it slowly down toward the wick, being careful not to actually touch the match flame to the wick. When the match flame was still a little bit above the wick tip, the wax vapor burst into flame, and the candle was lighted once again.

The liquid wax rises up the wick—seeming almost to defy the force of gravity—through a process called *capillary action.* Capillary action is what causes liquids to flow up into a paper towel or a sponge.

By the time Faraday gave his candle lectures he had made many important scientific discoveries. He had begun his scientific career in an unusual way. A village blacksmith's son, born in London in 1791, he had had very little formal education. In 1804 he went to work as an errand boy for a bookseller and bookbinder. Soon he was put to work learning how to bind printed pages into sturdy books, using cloth, stitching thread, and glue. The skills he learned in this trade helped him in his experiments later on in life.

Young Michael Faraday read many of the books he bound. He read much of the *Encyclopaedia Britannica* and became very interested in science. In his spare time he did experiments. Walking in London one day he saw a poster for a scientific lecture at the City Philosophical Society. Faraday attended this and many other scientific lectures. These lectures on chemistry, electricity, astronomy, and other subjects were Faraday's real education, along with his almost constant reading.

One day he received tickets to hear Sir Humphry Davy lecture at the Royal Institution. Davy was considered one of the greatest chemists of the time. As always, Faraday was very attentive and took detailed notes. Later, he bound the notes in the form of a book and sent it to Davy. Along with the book he asked Davy for a job as a scientific assistant. The next year, Sir Humphry Davy hired young Faraday as an assistant at the Royal Society.

Though Faraday was only a laboratory assistant, Davy saw that the young man was very bright. Several months later, Davy asked Faraday to go with him on a grand tour of European countries to visit other scientists at work. This was a great opportunity for young Faraday, who had never been more than twelve miles from London. On this trip Faraday met some of the scientists who made important discoveries in the new field of chemistry.

Upon his return to England, Faraday decided to study chemistry further. He got three of the best chemistry books of the time, took them apart, and bound them together. He also bound extra blank pages into the new book. In this way he could read the text and fill in the blank pages with notes from his own observations and experiments.

Faraday experimented with gases and made a careful study of chlorine gas. He also discovered several new gases and learned how to cool some gases and change them into liquids. He experimented with adding different materials to steel to make it stronger, and produced new kinds of glass for improved telescope lenses.

Faraday became fascinated by another new scientific field—electricity. He had heard that a Danish scientist named Hans Christian Oersted had discovered that an electric current flowing through a wire could make a magnet move. At that time very little was known about electricity or magnetism. Faraday wondered how these two kinds of energy were related, and decided to make a few experiments. First he placed a bar magnet in the center of a cup of filled with mercury. Then he mounted a wire above the cup so that it could swing freely around the magnet. The tip of the wire ran through a cork, and the cork floated on the mercury. Faraday placed another wire into the mercury, and then connected both wires to a battery. Mercury conducts electricity, so when Faraday attached the battery, an electric current traveled through the wire. The current through the wire produced an invisible force that pushed against the magnet's magnetic field. The loosely hanging wire began to swing in a circle around the magnet. Faraday had made a simple electric motor. He had changed electricity (from the battery) into motion (the moving wire). All electric motors are based on this idea.

MICHAEL FARADAY'S CANDLE

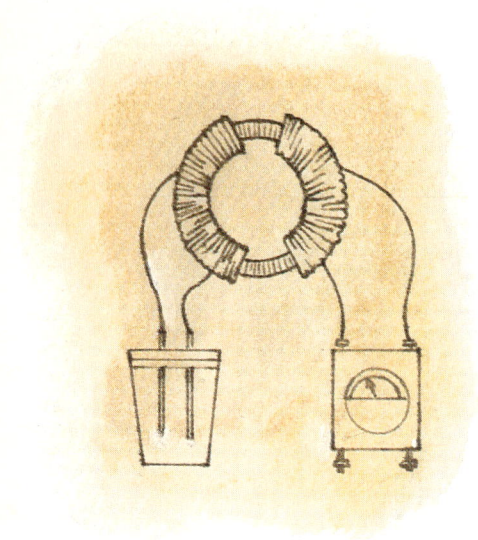

But Michael Faraday was more interested in finding out if electricity could come from magnetism. Faraday worked on this problem for many years. In 1831 he made something called an *induction ring.* It was a small ring made of soft iron. Around it Faraday wound two coils of wire. He connected one coil to a battery and the other coil to a *galvanometer,* an instrument used to measure electrical current. Faraday saw that when he connected or disconnected the battery, the galvanometer's needle would jump. He reasoned that the on-and-off flow of current connected to the battery in the wire produced a magnetic field around the coil. This magnetic field, he said, passed through the induction ring to the second coil. It caused, or *induced,* an electric current in the second coil that made the galvanometer needle jump.

Faraday had used electricity (the battery) to produce a magnetic field, and then had used the magnetic field to produce electricity (the current in the second coil). He had shown that electricity and magnetism are closely related. Faraday called his discovery magneto-electric induction. Today we call his discovery *electromagnetism.* Electric motors and electric generators work on the principle of electromagnetism. Even radio and television are based on electromagnetism.

The discoveries of Michael Faraday and many others helped make such modern inventions possible. During his lifetime Faraday was honored for his experiments on gases, electricity, and magnetism. His lectures on the science of a candle encouraged many young people to become scientists. Perhaps that was his greatest work of all.

The Germ Theory

HOW MANY TIMES HAVE YOU gotten a cold or the flu and thought you "caught" it at school? Do you remember getting vaccinations from the doctor to protect you from serious diseases?

Some diseases are *contagious*—they can travel from a person with the disease to a healthy person. Such diseases are caused by bacteria and viruses—germs so small they can be seen only with microscopes.

Only in the last 200 years did people realize that many diseases are caused and transmitted by germs. The story of this discovery began in 1796. Edward Jenner was a doctor in the English countryside. For years a disease called smallpox had spread throughout the land. It was the leading cause of death for English children. The disease caused high fever, pockmarks that scarred the face, and sometimes blindness or death.

One day Dr. Jenner treated a patient named Sarah Nelmes for cowpox, a disease that many farmers got from their cows. Cowpox was similar to smallpox, but

THE GERM THEORY

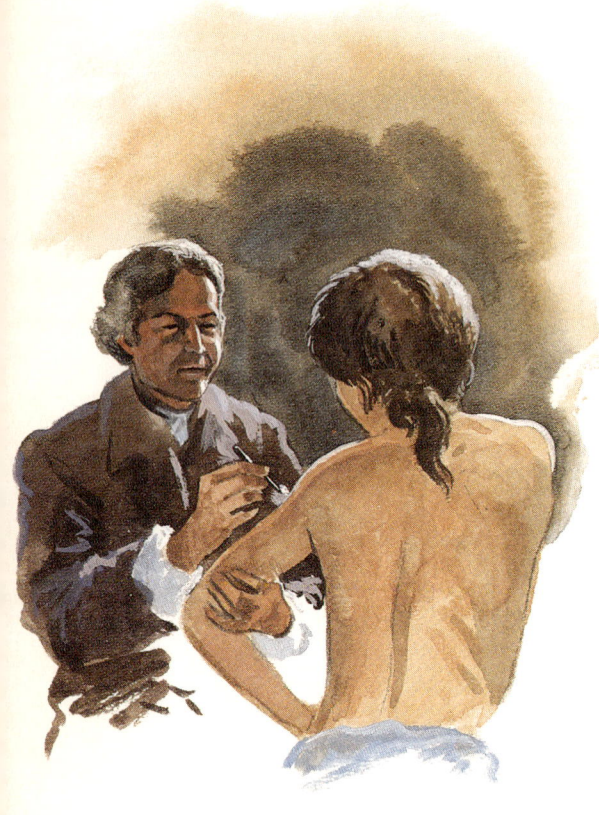

much milder. Jenner had heard that people who had had cowpox never seemed to get the dreaded smallpox. This gave Jenner an idea. When he treated Sarah, he took some of the fluid from her cowpox sores. Later, he rubbed the fluid into a cut on the arm of an eight-year-old boy named Jamie Phipps. A few days later Jamie came down with a mild case of cowpox, but soon got over it. Six weeks later, Jenner gave Jamie some fluid that was taken from a person who had smallpox. Young Jamie was not affected. The boy had become *immune* to smallpox—protected against the disease for the rest of his life. Jenner had made a *vaccine* that gave the boy immunity.

Jenner was not the first person to make a vaccine. Thousands of years earlier Chinese doctors had removed material from the sores of people who were suffering from smallpox and had rubbed it into scratches made on a healthy person's arm. The healthy person would often get a mild case of the disease and then become immune to smallpox. The problem was that sometimes the person would fall very ill with smallpox and die. But Jenner made his smallpox vaccine using fluid from the milder cowpox. His patients were not exposed to the deadly smallpox, yet they still became immune. Jenner's vaccine was much safer to use.

In the United States in 1801, President Thomas Jefferson wrote to Jenner congratulating him on his wonderful success. Jefferson insisted that members of his family be vaccinated against smallpox when Jenner's vaccine became available in the United States. Jefferson recognized that Jenner had done a great service to humanity. But not everyone back in England felt the same way. Many people mocked Jenner's method of using a cow's disease to prevent a human one. It was hard to change people's minds about preventing disease.

Early in the 19th century, improved microscopes made it possible for scientists to study bacteria carefully. Italian doctors gathered evidence showing that the deadly disease cholera is caused by bacteria. Later in the century scientists proved that many diseases are caused by germs, and that each disease is caused by a single type of germ. This idea is known as the germ theory. Two scientists who helped prove this theory were Louis Pasteur, a French chemist, and Robert Koch, a German doctor.

Louis Pasteur was a serious, hardworking scientist. Trained to be a chemist, he did important research on crystals. Then he became interested in *fermentation,* the process that turns the juice squeezed from grapes into wine. Fermentation is what puts the alcohol into wine and beer, but in Pasteur's day nobody understood what causes fermentation to take place. Pasteur showed that fermentation is caused by microscopic organisms called *yeasts.* As the yeasts grow and multiply in the wine or beer, they produce alcohol. Pasteur also showed that when bacteria get into the liquid and start to multiply, they can cause the wine or beer to turn sour and go bad. Pasteur showed that these bacteria fell from the air into the vats containing the liquids. Bacteria were responsible for turning fresh milk sour as well.

A few years later, Pasteur helped save the French silk industry. A mysterious disease was killing the silkworms, which spin the tiny silken threads from which silk cloth is made. Pasteur discovered that the disease was caused by bacteria. He showed that the disease was passed by infected silkworm moths through their eggs. By raising new silkworms from the eggs of healthy moths only, the farmers were able to control the disease and save the silk industry.

Then Pasteur became interested in cholera, a disease that had killed many people over the centuries. He began studying a type of cholera that was killing chickens by the thousands. Pasteur found a strain of bacteria that he was certain caused the disease. One day Pasteur injected healthy chickens with some of the deadly bacteria. Then he waited for the chickens to get sick. The chickens failed to get cholera, but they did become immune to the disease. Pasteur learned that the bacteria had become weakened and were no longer able to cause cholera, yet they were still able to make the chickens immune to the

THE GERM THEORY

disease. He had discovered that weakened bacteria make a good vaccine.

Pasteur then set out to conquer anthrax, a disease that killed many animals and infected humans as well. Robert Koch, a young German doctor, and others had identified the bacterium that causes anthrax. Pasteur grew cultures of the tiny killer and worked to develop a weakened form that could be used to produce a vaccine. Finally, in 1881, he developed a vaccine that could successfully prevent this deadly disease.

Then Pasteur began to work on rabies, a deadly disease that struck down animals and humans alike. People got this incurable disease from being bitten by an infected dog or other animal. Pasteur knew that rabies takes weeks or even months to develop after a person has been infected. Maybe if the victim could be given a vaccine soon after being bitten, it would prevent the disease from becoming active. Pasteur methodically developed a rabies vaccine using fluid from the spinal cords of infected rabbits. Now he needed a way to test it. Pasteur did not have to wait long. In 1885 a nine-year-old boy who had been bitten by a rabid dog was brought to Pasteur. Pasteur gave him a series of shots using the new rabies vaccine. Amazingly, the boy did not develop any of the deadly symptoms of rabies. People around the world cheered when they heard of Pasteur's success.

While Pasteur was working in France, young Robert Koch was studying anthrax and other diseases in Germany. Koch had heard of the early work done by Pasteur and was interested in the new germ theory of contagious disease. He set up his own laboratory in a small room next to his doctor's office. There he began experimenting with many types of disease-causing bacteria. Koch was also an amateur photographer and was the first person to take pictures of bacteria through a microscope.

In his laboratory in 1876, Koch proved beyond a doubt that one specific kind of bacteria causes anthrax. Koch took great care in his experiments so he could be absolutely sure that this is true. Koch later published a

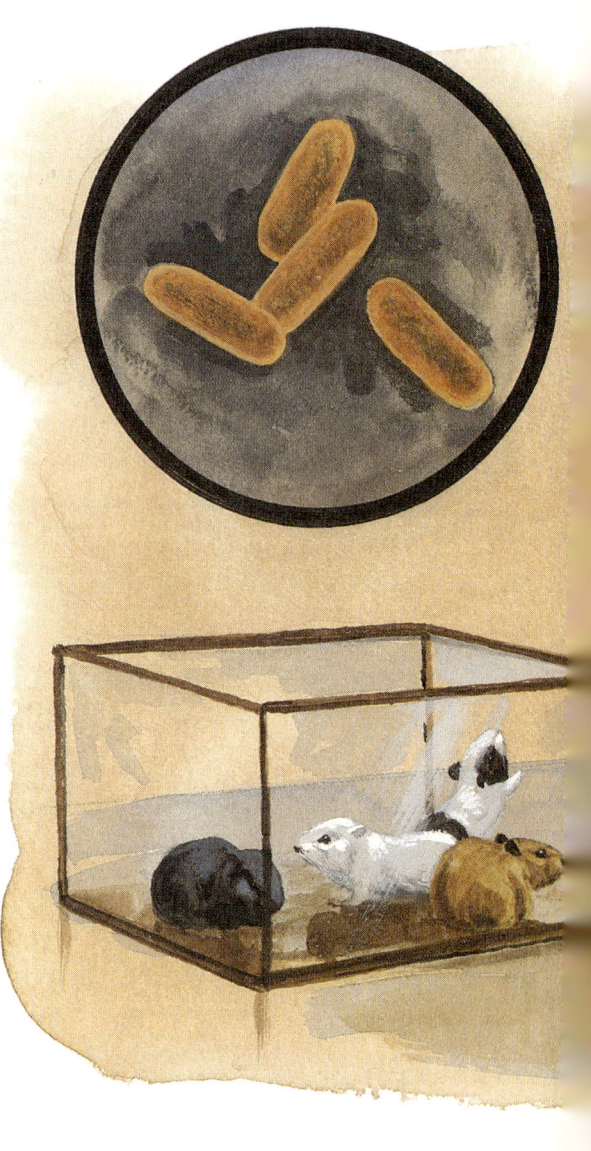

152

THE GERM THEORY

book showing that a number of specific diseases are each caused by a specific kind of bacterium.

In 1881 Koch was working with tissue taken from an ape that had died of a disease called tuberculosis, or TB. At that time this lung disease claimed many lives. After much hard work, Koch was able to isolate the rod-shaped bacteria that cause tuberculosis and grow pure cultures in his laboratory. Then he inoculated healthy guinea pigs with the bacteria. When the guinea pigs became sick, he found the tuberculosis bacteria growing in them. He removed some bacteria from the guinea pigs and grew another culture. Then he infected some healthy animals with this cultured bacteria. When those healthy animals contracted TB, he was certain that the rod-shaped bacteria, and they alone, are the cause of tuberculosis.

This long procedure invented by Koch became the standard way in which disease organisms are identified. Koch's work with tuberculosis helped point the way to new treatments and ways to control and prevent the disease.

As the 1800's drew to a close, other scientists and doctors worked toward isolating disease-causing bacteria. Most agreed that microscopic organisms cause many contagious diseases and they hoped to find a vaccine for each. The germ theory of disease finally had become scientific fact.

Edward Jenner, Louis Pasteur, Robert Koch, and many other scientists of the 18th and 19th centuries contributed much to our knowledge of disease and immunity. Thanks to these pioneers, many once-deadly diseases have been conquered.

George Eastman's Little Brownie

HAVE YOU EVER LAUGHED AT a picture of yourself that was taken when you were a baby? That photo recorded a special moment in your life that has since passed. To create a memory for your future, all you have to do is place a roll of film into a camera and take a picture. But taking photographs was not always so easy.

Like many useful technologies, photography owes its beginnings to the experiments of many people. One early experimenter was Louis Daguerre, a French painter of theater scenery who lived in the early 1800's. Sometimes Daguerre used a very old invention for making his large drawings for scenery. It was called a *camera obscura,* which means "dark chamber." A camera obscura is a small, lightproof chamber or room with one tiny, pinhole opening. Light coming in the hole projects an image of what is outside onto the inside wall opposite the hole. Daguerre would trace the scene that was projected on the wall. When the tracing was done, it could be painted and then used as stage scenery.

Daguerre's partner, Joseph Niepce, used a camera obscura to make the world's first photograph. But in the 1800's there was no such thing as photographic film. Instead, Niepce made his picture on a piece of paper coated with a chemical that would change color when light shone on it. Such a chemical is said to be *light sensitive.* He placed the paper on the wall of a camera obscura in his study and left it there all day. For eight hours the image of the trees outside his study window was projected on the paper. When Niepce discovered that a blurry picture of the trees had formed on the paper, he knew he was onto something interesting.

Niepce died in 1833 without ever making a clear photograph. For several years afterward, Daguerre experimented unsuccessfully with new materials to capture photographic images. Daguerre became so frustrated one day that he threw a glass plate that he had treated and exposed to sunlight into a cupboard of chemicals. Much to his amazement, the next day he found a perfect black-and-white photograph on the glass plate. He discovered that some mercury had spilled in the cupboard and had reacted with the chemical on the plate to produce the photographic image on the glass.

After much experimentation, Daguerre invented a system of photography that came to be called the *daguerreotype process.* This is how it worked. A metal plate was coated with a layer of silver. The silver side was polished into a shiny mirror. The plate was placed shiny side down into a box containing iodine crystals. A gas given off by the iodine reacted with the silver to form a light-sensitive compound called silver iodide. Then the plate was placed in a camera. The camera was really just a closed box with

2. taking the picture

1. preparing the plate

a small hole in it to let in light and a lens to focus the light on the plate. When light entered the camera, it reacted with the compound on the plate. The plate was exposed for many minutes. Then it was removed from the camera and placed in another box containing mercury vapors. Wherever there had been more light in the original scene, the mercury vapors formed a whitish deposit on the plate. Wherever there had been shadow in the original scene, there would be little deposit, so that part of the plate looked black. After the picture developed, the plate was washed with a strong chemical solution, then dried and mounted. The whole process took several hours of hard work using dangerous chemicals. Daguerre boldly announced to the world that with this process, the sun could draw his pictures.

The first photograph of a person was taken a couple of years later, in 1839. It took six minutes of exposure in full sunlight to produce a good image on the glass plate. That meant that the woman in the picture had to sit still all that time! Pictures of this type came to be known as sun pictures. The photograph showed every tiny detail, from the features of the woman's face to the fine lace of her dress.

3. neck brace to help person remain still

4. developing the photograph

GEORGE EASTMAN'S LITTLE BROWNIE

By 1840 photography studios began to open their doors for business. In a studio, people could sit for their formal portraits. A mania swept the United States and Europe. Everyone wanted to have their daguerreotype portrait made. A photo album or pictures arranged on a wall told a family's story and quickly became an important part of 19th-century life.

A big problem with the daguerreotype was that only one picture could be produced at a time. There was no way to make copies of the picture. Also, with time, the metal on the plate would tarnish and blacken, and there was no way to preserve the image.

In the 1850's a new kind of photographic process came into use. It was called *wet plate photography,* because the photographer had to soak a glass plate in a liquid chemical to make it light sensitive. While the plate was still wet, the photographer had to take the picture and then develop the exposed plate before it dried. This meant that the photographer had to travel with all of his equipment—camera, glass plates, chemicals, and a portable lightproof chamber, or *darkroom,* in which to prepare the plate, load and unload the camera, and develop the picture.

During the Civil War the famous photographer Mathew Brady sent teams of men to take pictures of the soldiers, their camps, and the scenes of battle. Each photographer traveled with his own wagon full of equipment. After the war, many of these photographs were destroyed, but the ones that remain tell us a great deal about the war and the men who fought it.

In 1871 came a big improvement over wet plate photography. A coating of a gelatinlike material was placed on the photographic plate. This material, called an *emulsion,* was sensitive to light even when dry. This change made developing much easier and safer. Now a photographer could buy ready-to-use plates and just load them into a camera.

But the biggest contribution to photography was made by George Eastman of Rochester, New York. A bank clerk by day and an experimental photographer by night, Eastman started making his own dry photographic plates. In 1885 he invented "American film." It was made of a strip of clear, flexible material that contained a light-sensitive gelatin emulsion. His new film had rows of holes on its edges, so it could be wound up in a roll on a spool. This made storage and developing much more convenient.

The developed film produced a *negative* image. Wherever the original scene had been light, the negative was dark, and wherever the original scene had been dark, the negative was light. The negative could be used to produce any number of photographs.

In 1888 Eastman introduced a camera that changed picture taking forever. Eastman called it the Number One Kodak camera. It had enough film already in it to take 100 pictures. When people had finished taking the pictures, they sent the whole camera back to Rochester. There the film would be removed and developed and the camera would be reloaded with fresh film. The customer would get the camera back complete with developed pictures and new film for a mere $10. In two years, Eastman sold 100,000 cameras.

Eastman continued to improve his cameras and his film. In 1900 he introduced his most famous camera, the Brownie. This small, simple camera was made especially for young people. It cost only $1, and a roll of film for it cost only 15 cents. Soon boys and girls everywhere were learning how to take photographs. No longer was the camera a bulky, troublesome thing. Eastman company advertisements proclaimed, "You push the button, we do the rest."

Eastman's flexible film brought on improvements in other areas. Thomas Edison used Eastman's film for the first workable movie camera. By the early 1900's a new industry was starting to grow—the movie industry. The first movies were only a few minutes long and had no sound. The picture on the movie screen flickered, too. People sometimes called the movies "flickers," or just "flicks." Even though early movies were not as good as today's films, millions of people went to see them.

Sometimes moving pictures were projected through different color filters to add color. However, an early kind of color film had already been invented in the early 1900's. This film had three layers and each was sensitive to a different color. In 1923 Eastman brought out the first home movie camera that used color film. The first movie made with color film to be shown in movie houses was a 1932 Walt Disney cartoon called *Flowers and Trees.*

Since the early days of Eastman's Brownie camera, many inventions have made picture taking easier. Today many cameras have built-in light meters and flashes so that there is always enough light. Cameras have gotten smaller and more streamlined. Instant developing was introduced with the Polaroid camera, which was invented by Edwin H. Land. In this type of camera, the photograph is developed as soon as the picture is taken. In a minute or so, the photograph is ready to be viewed.

There are disposable cameras, instant cameras, cameras powered by the sun, and even underwater cameras. But it was George Eastman's easy-to-use cameras that first brought people the fun of taking their own pictures.

The Age of Radio Begins

SOMEWHERE OFF THE Massachusetts coast, on a small fishing ship, a sailor had his turn sitting at the new wireless radio. His job was to listen for radio signals from shore or from other ships. The signals were sent in Morse code. The sailor listened for the dots and dashes of the code, which sounded like short and long scratchy buzzes. It was Christmas Eve of 1906, and the sailor had thoughts of home. Suddenly, he heard the sound of a human voice in his headphones. Then he heard an orchestra playing music, and then a violin playing a Christmas carol. Was he imagining things? Could voices and music actually be coming to him through the radio?

The sounds of voices and music really did come through the radio that night. And the violin was played by a brilliant Canadian inventor named Reginald A. Fessenden. That night in 1906 marked the first time that radio waves carried both the human voice and music.

The story of radio waves goes back to the 1880's, when a German physicist named Heinrich Hertz showed

THE AGE OF RADIO BEGINS

that electric energy can travel through space in the form of an electromagnetic wave. Think of a still pond into which a rock is dropped. The rock disturbs the still water, sending out rings of little waves, or ripples. Hertz discovered that both light and electricity travel in such wavelike patterns.

Waves can be measured two ways, by *frequency* and by *wavelength.* Think again of the ripples on the pond. If you pick a single point on the pond and count the number of ripples that pass through it in one second, you will know the frequency of the waves made by the falling rock. If you could measure the distance between the top of one ripple and the top of the next ripple, you would know the wavelength. Frequency and wavelength are related to each other in a very interesting way—the higher the frequency, the shorter the wavelength.

Energy wavelengths we can see make up visible light. Other wavelengths are longer, and our eyes are not sensitive to them. Hertz called these waves radio waves. He found that these longer waves could travel over long distances. They could even travel through walls, something that light waves cannot do.

Several years after reading about Hertz's waves, a young Italian inventor, Guglielmo Marconi, had an idea. At the time, the fastest forms of long-distance communication were by telegraph and telephone. But both of these inventions carried electric signals by wires, which were expensive to put up and keep in repair. Marconi decided to try using radio waves to send signals over long distances without wires.

162

THE AGE OF RADIO BEGINS

At first Marconi was able to send radio signals only a few feet, from one room of his house to another. Slowly and steadily he improved his wireless telegraph, as he called it. By 1895 he could send a wireless signal more than a mile. Two years later he started up the Marconi Wireless Telegraph Company in London, England. In 1899 he was able to send and receive wireless signals between England and France.

Marconi then showed that radio signals could be sent and received over distances of hundreds and even thousands of miles. In 1901 he sent a wireless telegraph signal across the Atlantic Ocean. Soon many ships were equipped with Marconi's wireless to receive and send radio signals. Ships in trouble could now radio other ships whenever they needed help.

While Marconi continued to improve his wireless telegraph, Reginald Fessenden was working for the United States Weather Bureau. Fessenden believed that voices and music could also be carried by radio waves. But the problem was that sound has a frequency of about 20 to 20,000 waves per second. Radio waves have much higher frequencies and we cannot hear them. How could radio waves carry the much lower sound frequencies?

Fessenden had a brilliant solution to this problem. He used a radio signal having a steady, high frequency and changed the height, or strength, of the waves according to the sound waves he wanted them to carry. For example, to send a sound signal with a frequency of 500 waves per second, the height, or *amplitude,* of the radio waves was changed 500 times per second. Fessenden added the sound and radio signals together in his transmitter. The radio receiver detected the combined signal and separated the sound information from it.

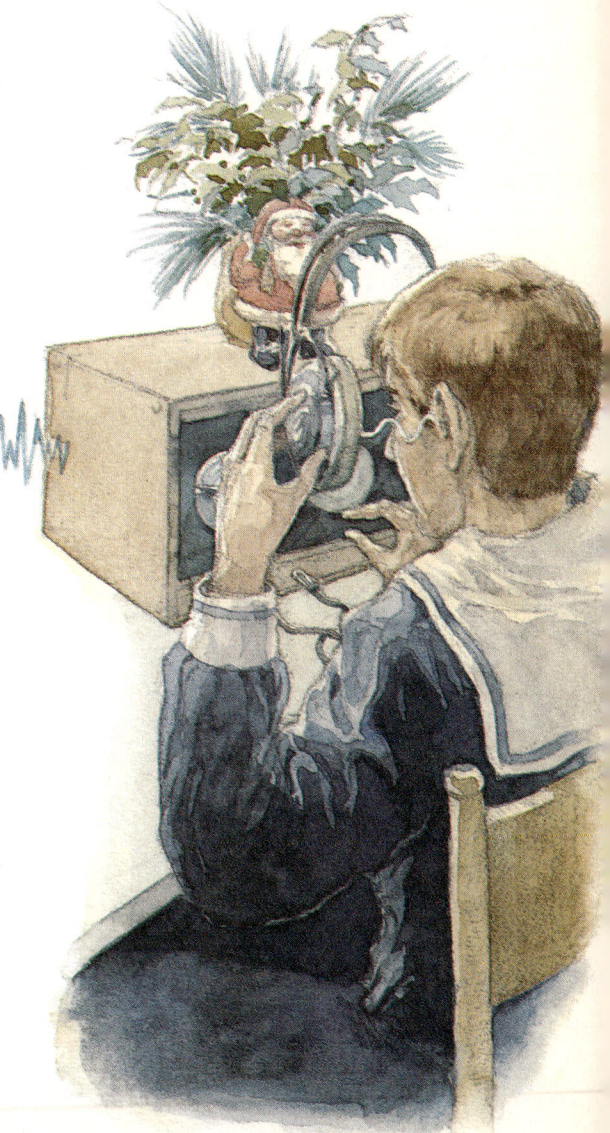

THE AGE OF RADIO BEGINS

After his successful broadcast on Christmas Eve of 1906, Fessenden worked to increase the range of his radio signals. Fessenden was a brilliant inventor but he was often difficult to get along with. He argued a great deal with his business partners, who gave him the money he needed to build and test his inventions. He had received many patents and spent much time in courts defending the rights to his inventions. Eventually he stopped working in radio and spent his later years on other projects.

Other inventors continued the work begun by Marconi and Fessenden. In 1904 Ambrose Fleming, a British scientist, invented an improved detector for radio receivers. He placed two metal conductors inside a glass bulb, pumped the air out of the bulb, and sealed it. The Fleming detector, or *diode* tube, detected the weak radio signals but could not *amplify* them—that is, make them stronger.

Fleming's diode detector was improved upon by an American inventor named Lee De Forest. He added a third conductor to the diode and invented the *triode* tube. By feeding an electrical signal into this third conductor, De Forest found he could control the amount of current that flowed between the other two. In this way he could use a weak electrical signal to make another signal—one that was exactly the same except that it was much stronger. The triode worked as an amplifier.

All the radio signals that were used during this time worked by changing, or *modulating,* the strength, or amplitude, of the radio signal. This system is called *amplitude modulation,* or AM for short.

AM waves are often interrupted by other stray signals that cause noise or static. In the 1930's Edwin H. Armstrong developed another kind of radio system. Instead of modulating the amplitude of a radio signal, he modulated its frequency. This system was called *frequency modulation,* or FM for short. An FM radio signal is not interfered with by noise and static. Also, FM can carry a bigger range of sound frequencies—higher high notes

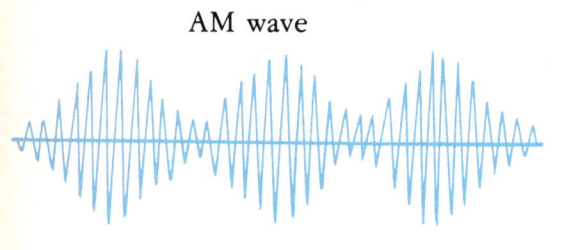

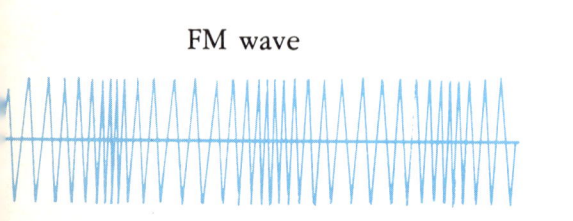

THE AGE OF RADIO BEGINS

and lower low notes—than the older AM radio system. This means that voices and music sound more real and natural on FM radio.

While Armstrong was working on FM radio, others were developing television, which uses radio waves to carry pictures as well as sound information.

Scientists are still inventing better ways to use radio waves to send and receive information. They are continuing the work begun by Hertz, Marconi, Fessenden, Armstrong, and other radio pioneers. So the next time you turn on the radio and sing along with your favorite song, think about all the people whose ideas have made radio possible.

Alexander Fleming Discovers Penicillin

THE YEAR WAS 1928. Alexander Fleming, a Scottish doctor, was at work in his crowded hospital laboratory. He was surrounded by stacks of laboratory dishes but was so busy that he had not looked at some of the dishes for a couple of weeks. Each covered dish contained varieties of bacteria that were known to cause diseases in people. Fleming carefully examined the bacteria that formed colorful patches inside the small, round dishes. One dish caught his attention. This dish, like the others, had bacteria in it, but something had happened to them. Some kind of greenish mold—a kind of plant—had gotten into the dish and grown there too. The bacteria closest to the mold seemed to have disappeared.

Fleming knew that something important was happening in this dish. The mold may have landed in the dish by accident, but it was no accident that Fleming set this dish aside. His trained eye had prepared him for a discovery. He carefully examined the mold that seemed to destroy the bacteria, and even photographed it. Fleming asked another scientist to identify the mold for him. The mold was called *Penicillium notatum.* Little did Fleming know at the time that this green mold would be the key to saving millions of lives.

What exactly had Fleming discovered? A mold had accidently gotten into a dish containing a pure colony, or *culture,* of bacteria. The mold had grown and produced a substance that killed the bacteria. Fleming, like other scientists, had often seen molds growing in laboratory culture dishes. Molds produce tiny spores that are carried through the air. They can easily land inside a dish when the protective cover is taken off. Many times such molds would ruin an experiment, and the scientist would have to obtain another pure culture of bacteria and start over. Fleming wanted to know what killed the bacteria in this culture dish.

At that time many people died of such diseases as pneumonia, which can be caused by bacteria. Many doctors and scientists were looking for substances that could kill these deadly bacteria. But the problem was that the substances that could kill bacteria were often harmful to people as well. Was the substance from the mold harmful too? Fleming experimented to find out.

Fleming used the greenish "fluff" on the dish to grow some more mold. Then he made up a mixture from the mold that his laboratory workers called mold juice. Fleming named the juice *penicillin.* When he gave the juice to

167

some laboratory mice that had been infected with a bacterial disease, he found that the penicillin killed the bacteria but did not harm the mice. This was an incredible discovery. What if this mold mixture could be made into a drug? Then, if someone with an infection took the drug, it would kill the bacteria that caused the infection but would not harm the person.

It sounded like a wonderful idea, but Fleming had several big problems. Whenever he grew some of the mold in a dish, it would kill bacteria for a time, but then it would stop working and the bacteria would return, as strong and deadly as before. He also found that he could not put the mold juice into a form that doctors could use. Although Fleming discovered penicillin and knew the value of it, he could not produce a drug that could be used by doctors. But Fleming used the mold in his laboratory to keep unwanted bacteria out of his culture dishes.

In 1929 Fleming wrote a report about his discovery. Other scientists read it, but the report did not cause much excitement at the time. Part of the problem was that scientists believed everything that is harmful to bacteria would also be harmful to humans. Even though Fleming showed that penicillin is safe, it was hard for him to convince other scientists to test it as a drug.

A couple of years after Fleming's discovery, one of Fleming's own students, Dr. C.G. Paine, used penicillin to cure several children of eye infections. Paine used a mixture similar to Fleming's mold juice. But very few people heard that Fleming's penicillin could cure disease, and Dr. Paine found it difficult to work with the mold juice.

It took a few more years and a lot of hard work to make penicillin into a drug that could be used. In 1940 two scientists, Howard Florey and Ernst Chain, began to experiment with penicillin at Oxford University in England. After many experiments, they found a way to make pure penicillin and they began to test it as a medicine. By this time World War II was raging in Europe. As bombs exploded overhead, Florey and Chain's team of workers rushed to find ways of making more and more penicillin.

By 1942 penicillin was being made in large amounts. Many soldiers wounded in battle developed infections that often became deadly. With penicillin, they could now be saved. People called penicillin the wonder drug because of the thousands of wonderful cures it made possible. Because of the many medical uses that were found for penicillin, Fleming was awarded the Nobel Prize.

At about the same time that Howard Florey and Ernst Chain were working on their molds of *Penicillium*, another scientist, René Dubos, discovered two more substances that kill bacteria. These are produced by bacteria that live in soil. Together with penicillin, these substances are known as *antibiotics.*

Antibiotics are given in an injection with a needle, or as a liquid or a pill that can be swallowed. Each antibiotic works by preventing bacteria from growing or dividing normally. Today there are many kinds of antibiotics. Perhaps you have taken penicillin, amoxycillin, or tetracycline. These are all antibiotics. Some of these drugs are now made in a factory *synthetically*—that is, without using mold or bacteria.

Antibiotics do not work against viruses. They kill only certain kinds of bacteria. Other kinds of bacteria are resistant to antibiotics. That means that these bacteria are not harmed by the antibiotics. Some scientists think that using antibiotics too often makes bacteria more resistant, so it is important to use these drugs with care and only when necessary. Although antibiotics are not perfect, they have helped conquer such once-deadly diseases as pneumonia, typhoid fever, and cholera. They have lived up to their name, wonder drugs.

Bits, Bytes, and Binary Numbers

WHAT DOES PLAYING A VIDEO GAME have in common with making a telephone call or adding numbers on an abacus? Each activity makes use of a computer. Computers are machines designed to handle information, or *data*. There are many different kinds of computers, but they all have one thing in common—whatever they are designed to do, they perform their tasks with numbers.

Many devices have computers built into them. For example, videocassette recorders, or VCRs, and microwave ovens have built-in computers. A pocket calculator is also a computer. Computers affect many parts of your life.

The earliest computers were used to add, subtract, multiply, and divide numbers. People have always looked for easier ways to do arithmetic. The abacus was invented thousands of years ago to help people do mathematical calculations. It was an early computer.

In the 1800's, Charles Babbage, an Englishman, set out to find an easier and faster way to do mathematical calculations. He began to build a machine he called his Analytical Engine. This machine had many wheels and gears and was steam-powered. Babbage had a vision that hundreds of mathematical problems could be solved with such a machine. Up until his time, many mechanical calculators had been invented before, but Babbage had come upon a new idea—a machine that could be given a set of instructions and then would perform them on its own. Babbage never completed his Analytical Engine, but others began to work on his idea.

In the 1930's, a German engineer named Konrad Zuse built a machine that could be given a set of step-by-step instructions, or *program,* that would enable it to solve any kind of mathematical problem. His calculator could do the computations, then display the answers or store them in a mechanical memory bank for later use. To give his calculator its set of instructions, Zuse punched holes in strips of old home movie film. The holes in the film would catch on certain parts of his calculator, programming the calculator to do such operations as adding or dividing two numbers.

Meanwhile, in the United States, several kinds of calculators were built that used small electric motors. Similar to Zuse's, these calculators got their instructions by reading a sequence of holes punched out on a long ribbon of paper.

In the 1940's, scientists were hard at work trying to design new computers that could solve complicated problems quickly. At the University of Pennsylvania, John W. Mauchly and Presper Eckert, Jr., proposed to build an *electronic computer* that would use circuits instead of electric motors or other moving parts. They borrowed some ideas from John V. Atanasoff, an engineer who believed that a computer could be built using vacuum tubes—the same devices that had made radio communication a great success about 20 years earlier. The electronic computer Mauchly proposed would be a

BITS, BYTES, AND BINARY NUMBERS

high-speed, all-purpose, programmable machine. It was named ENIAC, for electronic numerator, integrator, analyzer, and computer.

ENIAC was huge. It took up almost all of a large 30-by-50-foot room. It contained more than 17,000 vacuum tubes and 6000 switches. In one second it could add an amazing 5000 numbers together.

ENIAC was the world's first electronic computer. Each of ENIAC'S many panels stored one number and contained 20 vacuum tubes—two tubes for each of the ten possible numbers in the decimal numbering system. One pair stood for the number 0, another pair for the number 1, and so on, through the number 9. To make a calculation, the tubes were switched on and off—actually the electric current was switched higher or lower. This made the tubes act as electrical switches. The tubes were large and bulky and produced a great deal of heat. Fans had to be installed just to keep the computer from getting too hot. When a tube burned out, the calculations would come to a dead stop and the tube would have to be replaced.

A big problem with ENIAC was that it needed 20 vacuum tubes just to store one number. Some computer pioneers thought another numbering system, called the *binary system,* would work better. Instead of using the ten numbers 0 through 9, as the decimal system does, the binary system uses only two digits, 0 and 1.

In the decimal system, any number up to the number 9 can be written using only one digit. To write a larger number, a second column of numbers—the tens column—must be used. For example, the decimal number 14 really means one ten plus four ones. To write a number larger than 99, another column—the hundreds column—must be added. In the decimal system, each column to the left is multiplied in value by ten.

In the binary system, the first column can contain only the numbers 0 and 1. The next column to the left is the twos column. The next column is the fours column, and the next is the eights column. Each column to the left is multiplied in value by two.

172

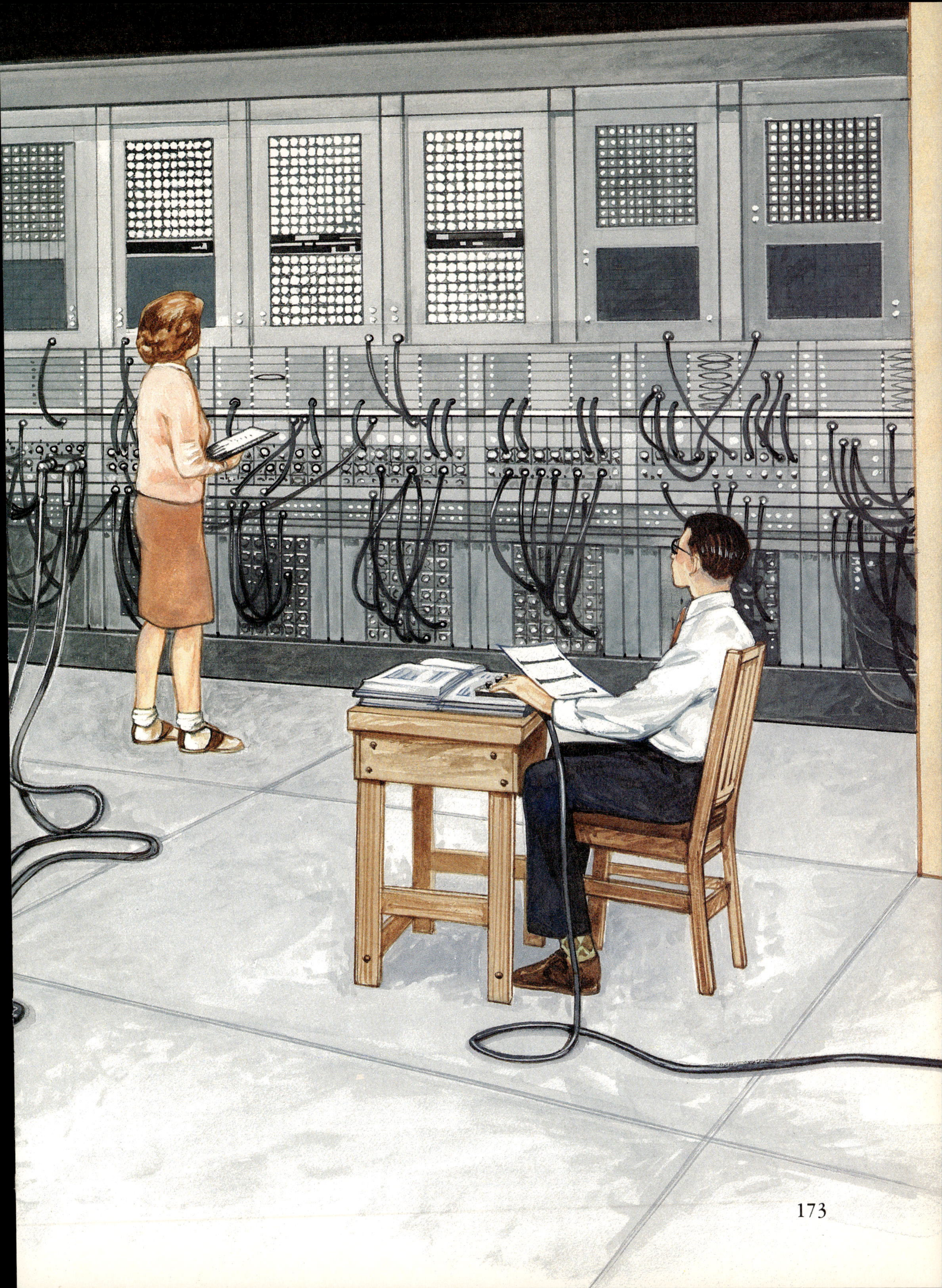

BITS, BYTES, AND BINARY NUMBERS

Eights	Fours	Twos	Ones
1	1	1	0

8 + 4 + 2 + 0 = 14

Any decimal number can be written as a binary number. For example, the decimal number 14 can be written as the binary number 1110, which means one in the eights column, one in the fours column, one in the twos column, and zero in the ones column. In others words, 8 + 4 + 2 + 0 = 14.

Computer scientists saw that any number could be written in the binary system using only two digits—0 and 1. A computer circuit could be switched on to represent the digit 1 and off to represent the digit 0. This meant computers could be built using fewer parts, making them simpler, faster, more reliable, and less expensive than ENIAC. In 1952 a new computer, EDVAC, was completed. It was the first major computer built in the United States to use binary numbers.

By the early 1950's, a number of computers were operating in the United States and England. The first general-use computer to become popular in business was UNIVAC—the *univ*ersal *a*utomatic *c*omputer.

All of these early computers were very large because of all the vacuum tubes they used. In 1947 scientists made an important breakthrough with the invention of the *transistor.* A transistor works like a vacuum tube but it is much smaller, uses much less power, and produces little or no heat. A transistor is made from several thin layers of a solid material called a *semiconductor.* Germanium and silicon are two semiconductor elements that are used to make transistors.

integrated circuit chip

About ten years later, scientists began putting several transistors and other electronic parts on the same piece, or *chip,* of silicon. This helped make electronic circuits smaller and simpler, and it was the beginning of the *integrated circuit.* By the 1960's integrated circuit chips were being used to build faster, more powerful computers. Soon scientists found ways to pack more and more transistors onto a single chip. Today a chip less than the size of a postage stamp may easily contain many thousands of transistors and other electronic parts. One tiny chip can store as much data as an early vacuum tube computer that took up a whole room.

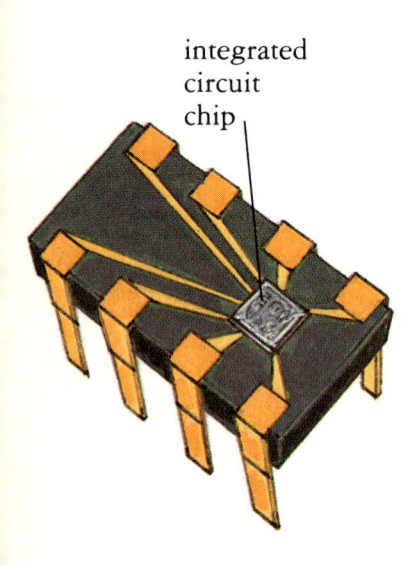

BITS, BYTES, AND BINARY NUMBERS

By the 1970's computer hobbyists were forming computer clubs and starting to put together their own computers. Some small computer companies began selling computers to people for their own personal use. Up to this time, only schools and businesses could afford to buy computers. Now anyone could buy and use one of these smaller *personal computers,* or PCs.

Whether it is a large *mainframe* computer, a smaller *minicomputer,* or a still smaller personal computer, every computer has the same basic parts. The "brain" of a computer is called the central processing unit, or *CPU.* The CPU carries out the instructions of the computer program and processes the information that is put into the computer—the *input.* The computer can receive its input from a keyboard, for example, or from an electronic file stored on a magnetic disk.

While the computer is running the program and processing the information, or data, fed into it, it keeps both the program and data in its electronic *memory.* When the computer has finished all the instructions in the program, it sends the processed data back out to the computer user. This is called the *output.* A computer can send its output to a computer monitor, a printer, or a magnetic disk or tape. Magnetic disks and tapes make it much easier to store and reuse programs and data.

175

BITS, BYTES, AND BINARY NUMBERS

Each piece of information fed into a computer is in the form of a binary digit, or a *bit,* and each bit is either a 1 or a 0. Eight bits together make up a *byte.* A byte is actually a binary number that a computer uses to represent a single letter, number, or other character. Because a byte is an eight-digit binary number, it can contain any one of 256 different combinations of 1 and 0—more than enough combinations to represent the numbers 0 through 9, all the letters of the alphabet, and many special characters, such as punctuation and mathematical signs.

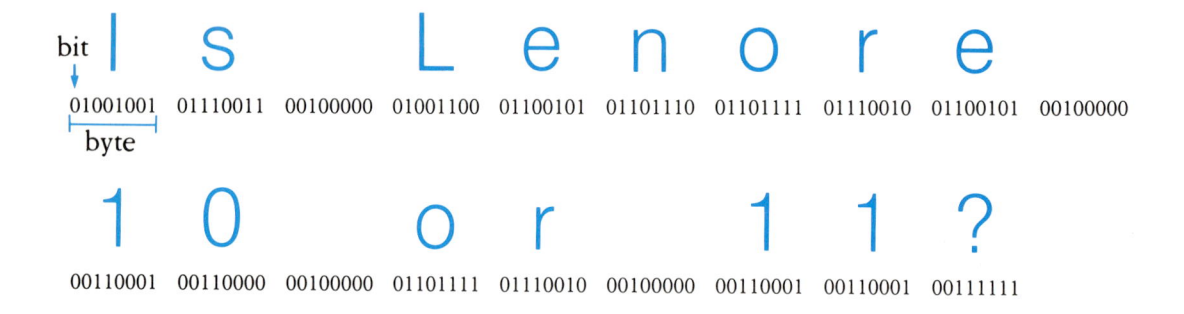

bit ↓
I   s   L   e   n   o   r   e
01001001 01110011 00100000 01001100 01100101 01101110 01101111 01110010 01100101 00100000
 └─byte─┘

1   0   o   r   1   1   ?
00110001 00110000 00100000 01101111 01110010 00100000 00110001 00110001 00111111

Today computers and computer chips are found in many appliances and in many places. Digital watches and pocket calculators have computer chips, and so do automobiles, dishwashers, televisions, compact disc players, gasoline pumps, and electronic cash registers.

Many medical devices use computers also. Sensitive machines such as the CAT scanner and magnetic resonance imager, or MRI, use computers to make detailed pictures of the organs and tissues inside a patient's body.

Computers are used in businesses, schools, hospitals, and homes. They are in stores, on ships, in planes, and even in satellites far out in space. No matter where they are or what they are used for, all of these computers use bits, bytes, and binary numbers.

The Magic Helix

JAMES WATSON, an American scientist living in England, awoke from his dream with a start. He had been dreaming of a spiral staircase. The idea of a spiral had been on his mind for a while now. He and his English partner, Francis Crick, had been working to unlock one of nature's secrets. They had been trying for months to learn the correct shape of the DNA molecule—the molecule of life. Perhaps the DNA molecule is shaped like a spiral, Watson thought. With the image of the spiral staircase fresh in his mind, Watson rushed to the telephone to tell Crick about his dream.

Every part of the human body is made up of tiny living units called *cells.* Within each cell is a special molecule that contains all the information your body needs to make you the person you are. This amazing molecule is made up of a substance called *deoxyribonucleic acid*—or DNA for short. DNA is what gives you your personal traits—your eye and hair color, for instance, your height, and your sex, or gender.

THE MAGIC HELIX

The DNA in your body's cells records millions of facts about you from the way in which the tiny parts of the DNA molecule are arranged. Even though the molecule is small enough to fit inside a cell, if it were uncoiled and stretched out it, would be about six feet long. The DNA molecule can also make exact copies of itself. DNA makes it possible for new cells to replace old ones and for new people to be born.

When Watson had his dream, scientists knew that the DNA molecule is made of smaller molecules arranged like building blocks. These molecules are called nitrogen bases, sugar molecules, and phosphate molecules. Watson and Crick knew that finding out the way in which these molecules are linked together would be a big breakthrough in learning about how people inherit their traits.

Watson's spiral staircase is similar to what scientists call a *double helix.* A double helix is like a ladder that has been twisted into a spiral. The rungs of the DNA ladder are made of paired molecules of nitrogen bases. These bases are attached to sugar and phosphate molecules, which form the long outer sides of the DNA ladder. It was the exact arrangement of these molecules that Watson and Crick were attempting to find.

How can you figure out what a molecule is made of if molecules are too small to be seen even with a microscope? Watson and Crick looked at pictures of DNA made by another team of scientists, Rosalind Franklin and Maurice Wilkins, using a special x-ray microscope. This microscope sent a beam of x-rays through the DNA molecule. The x-rays bounced off the molecule and were recorded on a photograph. The picture that resulted helped Watson and Crick to see how the molecule was constructed.

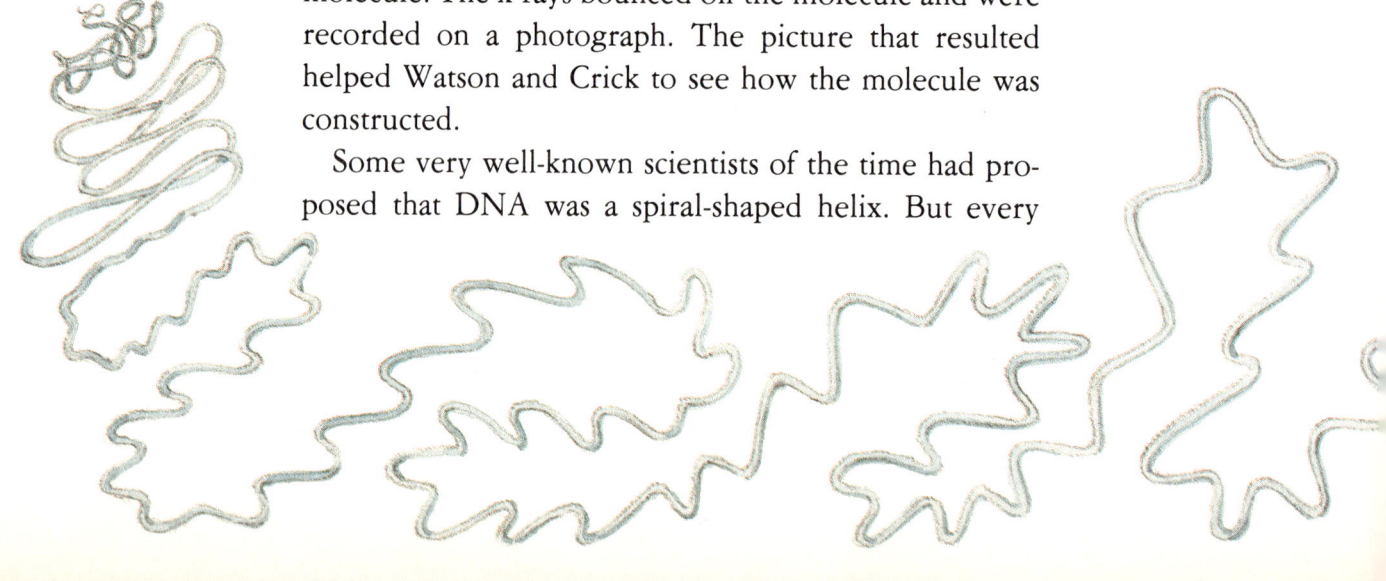

Some very well-known scientists of the time had proposed that DNA was a spiral-shaped helix. But every time a model was made to show how the rungs of the ladder were connected, it was found to be incorrect. In England and the United States several scientists were working on finding the structure of DNA.

Watson and Crick made many models of what they thought the DNA molecule might look like. They used cardboard cutouts or pieces of metal and studied the x-ray pictures taken by Rosalind Franklin. Franklin herself did not think that the DNA was a helix. But Watson and Crick were able to put their theory and the pictures together to make the correct model.

In 1953, after many months of working on the problem, Watson and Crick presented their model of the DNA molecule. Their work revolutionized science. Ten years later, in 1963, they and Maurice Wilkins were awarded the Nobel Prize. Rosalind Franklin had died several years before. Since the time of their award, the field of genetics has become the fastest growing in all of biology.

After finding out that DNA is made of a double helix, scientists began working on the problem of the DNA code. The exact way in which the pairs of nitrogen bases make up the rungs of the DNA ladder is how the DNA molecule stores its information. The body's cells read this code in order to produce each person's special characteristics. Each characteristic is controlled by a section of the DNA molecule called a *gene.* Genes can contain from about a thousand to several million nitrogen base pairs. All the genes are arranged in an exact order along the DNA molecule. Scientists believe human DNA has from 50,000 to 100,000 genes.

In cracking the DNA code, or genetic code, scientists learned that three pairs of nitrogen bases in the DNA rungs work together to make one piece of the code. A gene is made up of many of these three-rung bits of code linked together.

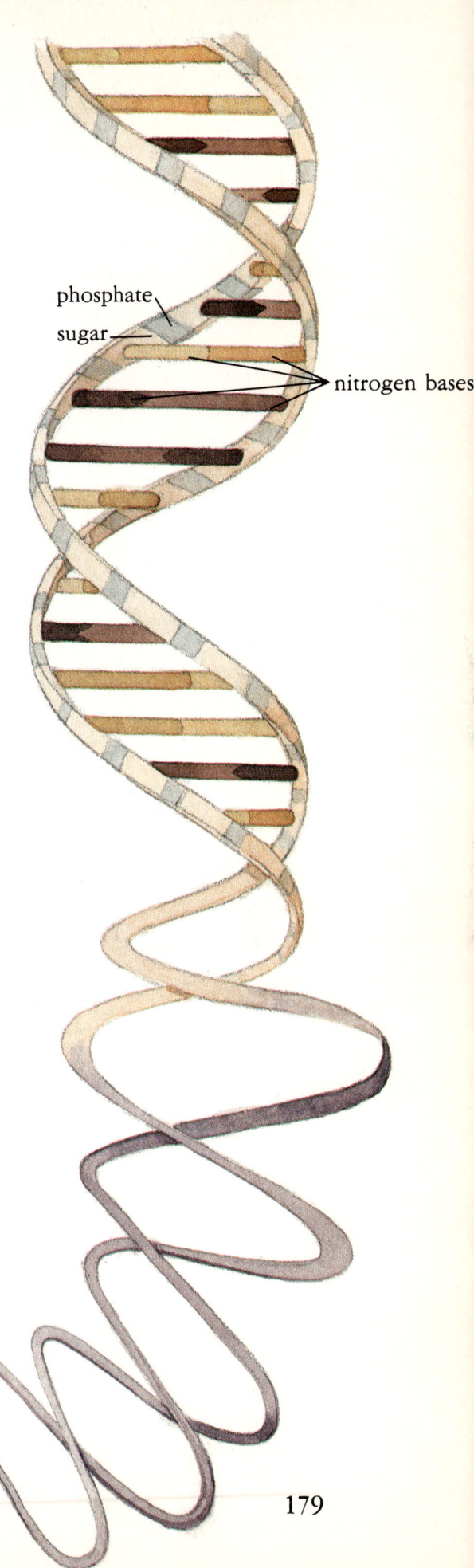

DNA is found in a small part of the cell called the *nucleus.* Inside the nucleus the DNA is divided into smaller units called *chromosomes.* The chromosomes are linked up two by two, in identical pairs. Most human cells have 23 pairs of chromosomes. All the genes that control a person's traits are contained within these 23 pairs of chromosomes.

Knowing the exact gene and chromosome that is responsible for a particular trait has made possible a new field of science called *genetic engineering.* In genetic engineering, scientists remove parts of chromosomes from one organism and transplant them into the chromosomes of another organism. For example, scientists know what genetic code is needed for the human body to make an important substance called insulin. Scientists can snip off this part of the DNA code and transplant it into the DNA of bacteria. The bacteria are then able to make insulin. The bacteria reproduce very fast and soon there are billions of insulin-producing bacteria. The insulin is collected for use by people whose bodies cannot make insulin.

Genetic engineering is also being used to produce more nutritious food crops that are resistant to disease and to improve animal breeds for health and vigor.

An ambitious project is under way to learn the function of every part of the DNA in human chromosomes. Even though no two people have exactly the same DNA, the genes for certain traits are always located in the same place on the same chromosome.

Sometimes the DNA in a gene is not arranged the way it should be. A person having such a faulty gene may develop a genetic disease. Such a disease is hemophilia, in which a person's blood is unable to clot properly to stop bleeding and help heal a wound. For some of these diseases, scientists have learned which genes to look at for faulty DNA codes. Researchers hope someday to be able to replace the defective parts of genes with good DNA. Then they will be able to cure genetic diseases even before a person shows the first signs of sickness.

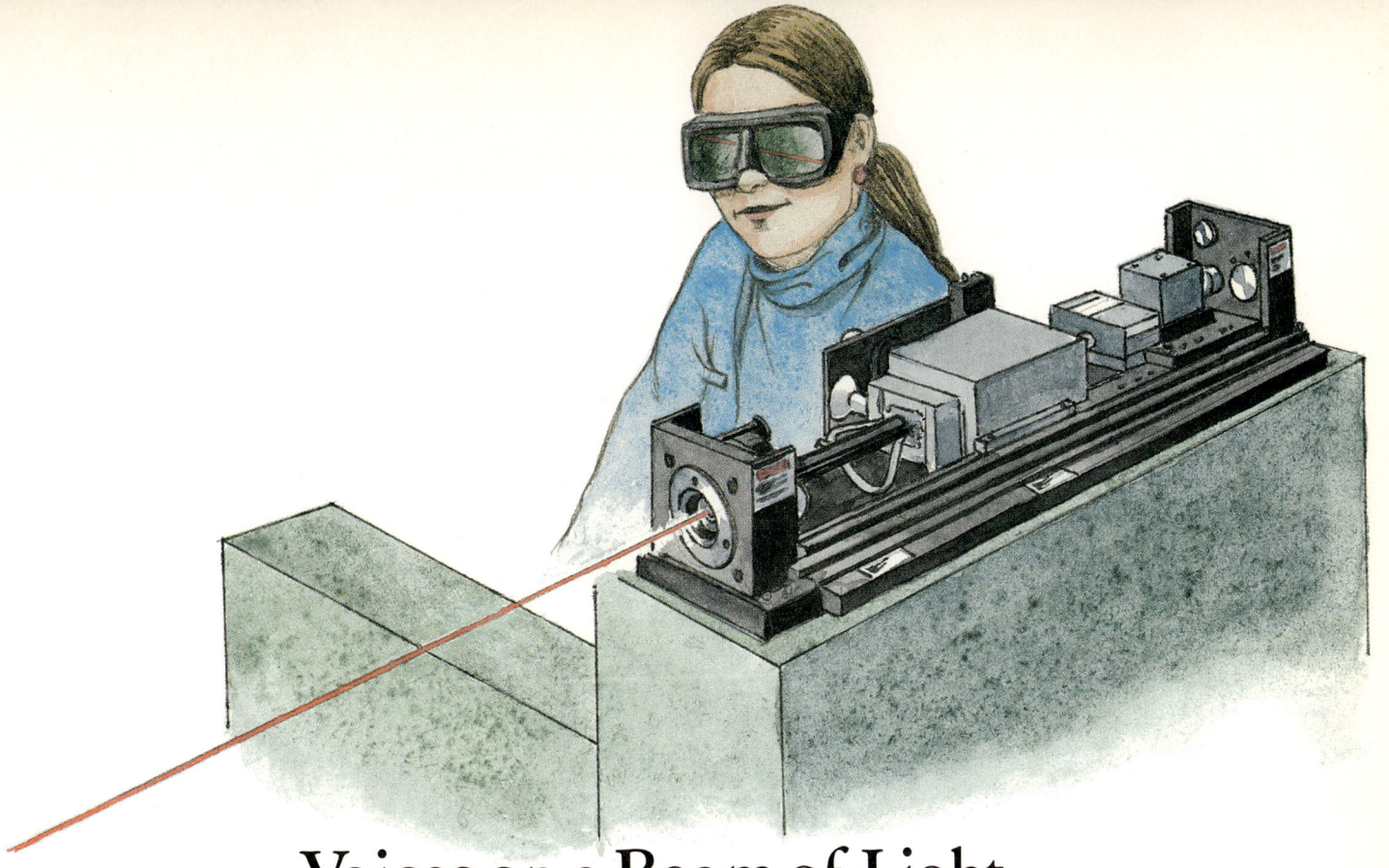

Voices on a Beam of Light

YOU ANSWER THE TELEPHONE. The caller is a friend who is calling long distance. Your friend's voice sounds loud and clear. Your conversation, along with a thousand others, is being carried hundreds of miles by beams of light moving through specially designed glass fibers. Carrying a long-distance telephone call is just one use of beams of light called *lasers.*

You may have seen the ruby-colored light of a laser in the scanner that reads bar codes at the supermarket checkout. You probably know that lasers can also cut through a hard diamond or read the music on a compact disc. How can a laser do all these things?

Ordinary light, such as sunlight, usually contains a mixture of all the colors of the rainbow. In contrast, a laser beam contains only one color, or wavelength, of light. Light ordinarily spreads out in all directions. In a laser beam, the light waves all travel in the same direction. Because of these properties, a laser beam is a concentrated source of energy. This energy can be used to do different jobs.

VOICES ON A BEAM OF LIGHT

The word laser comes from the first letters of five words—*l*ight *a*mplification by *s*timulated *e*mission of *r*adiation. A laser uses light to *stimulate,* or energize, the electrons in a substance. The energized electrons give off, or *emit,* energy, or *radiation,* in the form of light. In turn, this light radiation stimulates more electrons, which then give off even more light energy. In this way the original light energy is boosted, or *amplified,* many times. Because the atoms of the substance are all exactly the same, the light emitted by their electrons is exactly the same wavelength and can be focused into a very narrow beam.

The idea for a laser began in the 1950's. Charles H. Townes was experimenting with ways to amplify radio waves. His idea was that energy waves of one kind can trigger, or stimulate, other energy waves. Although he and another scientist, Arthur Schawlow, never made a laser themselves, their ideas encouraged other scientists to perform further experiments.

In 1960 Theodore Maiman made the first working laser, using a ruby crystal. The ends of a ruby rod were cut flat, highly polished, and coated with mirrors to reflect light. When a powerful light was sent into the rod, the atoms of the ruby crystal began to emit a bright ruby-colored light. This light was bounced back and forth inside the crystal rod by the mirrors at each end. This stimulated the ruby crystal to produce even more light.

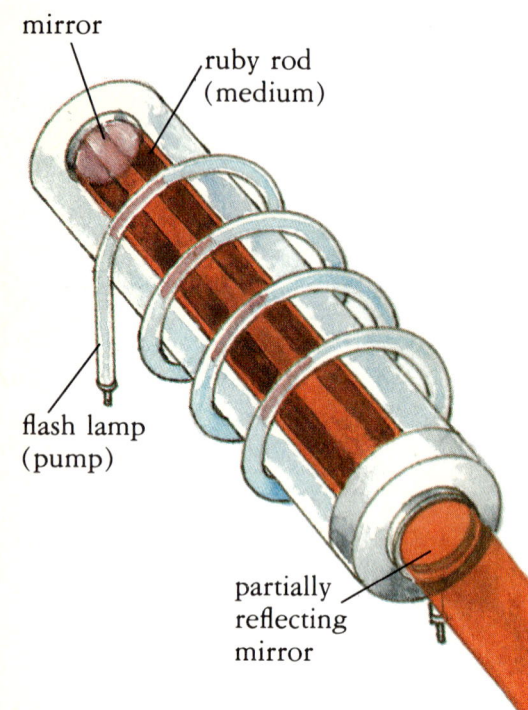

Other scientists soon built lasers using different materials. All lasers have the same three basic parts as the first laser did. A laser must have a substance that can be stimulated to produce light. This is called the *medium.* The medium in the first laser was the rod of ruby crystal. A laser medium can also be a liquid or a gas. Every laser must also have an energy source to stimulate the medium. This part is called the *pump.* In the ruby laser, a lamp was the pump. Finally, every laser must have a way of controlling the direction of the laser beam. This is usually done with two mirrors that face each other. One of the mirrors does not reflect the light as completely as the other, and the laser beam is able to escape from the medium through it. In the ruby laser the mirrors were on the ends of the rod.

In a liquid laser, the ruby rod is replaced by a glass container filled with liquid. Some liquid lasers can be "tuned" to produce a particular color, or wavelength, of light.

In some lasers the medium is a gas. A glass or quartz crystal tube is filled with one or more gases, such as helium, neon, argon, or carbon dioxide. Each gas produces a different wavelength of light.

Gas lasers are often used in light shows at concerts, stadiums, planetariums, and fireworks displays. Several gas lasers can be used together along with prisms, light filters, and mirrors to produce a variety of colored light beams and patterns. Even images, including faces and intricate designs, can be projected by lasers. In films and videos, lasers are sometimes used to light up stages and scenery.

Lasers are also used to carry telephone calls through tiny, hollow glass tubes called *optical fibers.* The inside of the optical fiber reflects the laser light almost completely. This means the light can travel for great distances without losing its energy. One pair of optical fibers can carry more than 1000 conversations at once. Lasers have helped make telephone communications better, more reliable, and less costly.

Some lasers are designed to emit a strong beam of light that contains a great amount of energy. Such lasers are used in industry to cut, melt, or even vaporize metals and other materials. These powerful lasers are employed for jobs such as welding and making parts fit together perfectly.

Drilling with lasers is used where precise holes are needed in materials that are either too hard or too soft for other drills. For example, lasers have been used to drill tiny holes in watch parts and even in the rubber nipples in babies' bottles.

A laser cutting tool is very precise and can do the same job over and over again in very little time. Lasers are used for cutting cloth, plastic, glass, and wood. One laser can cut cloth for more than 40 suits of clothing in one hour.

Lasers are used not only to manufacture products, but to sell them as well. In stores and supermarkets, *optical scanners* contain lasers that are used to read the bar code labels on products. As the laser beam moves over the pattern of lines in the bar code, its light is absorbed by the black bars and reflected back into the scanner by the white spaces between the bars. This absorbing, or reflecting, of the light is read by the scanner as a series of "on" and "off" signals. Then a computer identifies the signals, and from them the type of product and its price.

Optical scanning devices can also be used to feed information, such as the words on a page, directly into a computer. In this way, the words do not have to be typed on the computer's keyboard, speeding up the process of getting information into the computer.

Lasers are also used in compact disc players to read the information stored on the disc. The compact disc is actually a very highly polished metal disc inside a layer of plastic. The metal disc has a spiral of very tiny dots, or pits, burned into its surface. The player spins the disc just as a record player spins a record. The laser beam is aimed at the surface of the disc and follows the spiral track. Whenever the beam strikes the polished part of the spiral, it is reflected back and read by the player as an electrical "on" signal. Whenever the beam hits a pit, it is scattered in all directions, and the player reads this as an electrical "off" signal. The computerized circuitry inside the player reads this stream of on-off signals and changes it into sound signals.

Lasers are used by earth scientists to help them learn about—and perhaps predict—earthquakes. Pulses of laser light are beamed up to a satellite and reflected back to Earth. The returning pulses are carefully timed and compared with previous measurements. In this way, very small movements in Earth's crust can be detected.

In medicine, lasers are used in delicate surgery, as in repairing damaged parts of the eye or removing kidney stones. The advantage of laser surgery is that a laser beam can be aimed very accurately to destroy bad tissue without damaging surrounding good tissue. There is very little bleeding because the laser beam seals the blood vessels with its heat. A laser can also be used to open up clogged blood veins and arteries, or to remove scar tissue or birthmarks.

In a very short time, lasers have moved from the laboratory into our lives. From measuring movements in Earth's crust to carrying long-distance calls, from welding airplane parts to delicate surgery, lasers are helping to improve the quality of our lives.

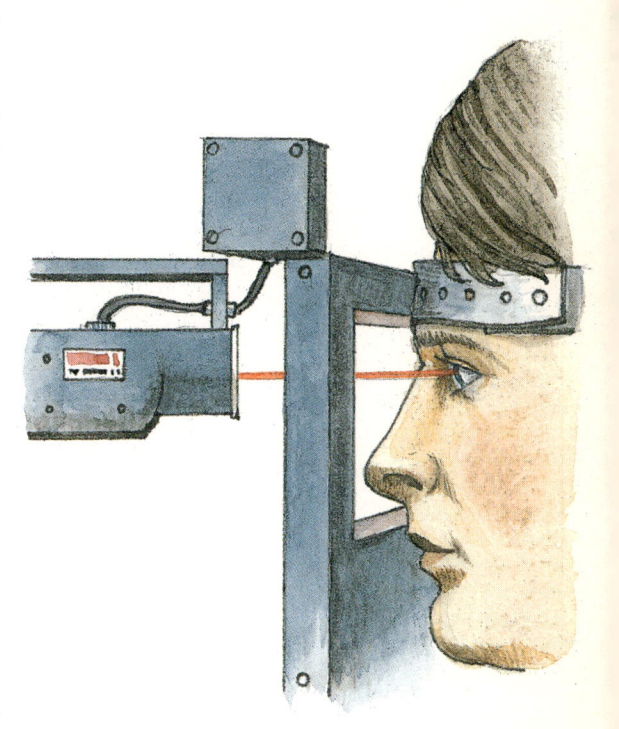

You, Scientist

A MARINE SCIENTIST DIVES from his deep-sea vessel to search the dark ocean floor for a special kind of living sponge. Back in a laboratory, another scientist will test the sponge. The scientist is looking for a substance with a remarkable property—the ability to build up the disease-fighting power of the human body. Perhaps in the future the sponge will be the source of a powerful drug that will help cure disease.

Thousands of miles away in a Central American rain forest, a biologist carefully lifts herself up onto a high platform. There, strapped in a harness, she can study the rain forest plants, which are in danger of becoming extinct. On the jungle floor below, another biologist tracks animals that have been fitted with radio collars. The signals emitted by the collars help the scientist study the movement and population of the animals. Together the scientists will report their findings to an international group of scientists studying the effects of cutting down the rain forest.

YOU, SCIENTIST

Elsewhere, in another laboratory, a physicist tests a piece of experimental ceramic for its ability to conduct electricity. The scientist is looking for a material that can conduct electricity without losing any of the electric energy as heat. Such a material, called a *superconductor,* has yet to be found, but scientists think they are getting close.

What do all of these scientists have in common? They are trained observers using modern technologies to help them solve some of the important problems of today. You have read about some famous people and their important scientific discoveries. Their work provided a foundation for today's scientists, perhaps even you, to build upon. There are many areas of scientific research that are still in their infancy. The key to your future may lie in one of these new fields.

You can start thinking like a scientist by trying to solve a problem where you live. That is the idea that some students from the state of Washington had several years ago. The stream near their school had become polluted by wastes from a paper manufacturing plant. Salmon, which used to be common in the stream, had not been seen for years. The students got the plant owners to stop dumping the harmful wastes. Then they started a campaign to clean up other streams and rivers and got other people in their state to "adopt a stream."

The students studied the science of streams and learned all they could about salmon. They used an aquarium to raise salmon from eggs, then released the young salmon into the stream. Within a year salmon were breeding in the stream again. The students had studied and solved a serious scientific problem—pollution.

There are many ways of seeing how scientists work and learning about the many different fields of science. Some research laboratories have summer tours and programs that enable visitors to see scientists at work. Many cities have natural history museums full of "hands-on" scientific exhibits. Even big power companies have exhibits with exciting demonstrations of how electricity works. Large companies often sponsor science fairs.

187

The science of genetic engineering is a rapidly growing field. Genetic engineers have learned how to change the DNA molecule, the "blueprint" that gives living things all the countless traits that make them what they are. Through genetic engineering, scientists have created new strains of bacteria that can produce lifesaving drugs. Other bacteria have been changed genetically so they can produce a kind of plastic. Still others have been developed that can eat and digest oil or toxic wastes. Genetic engineering has produced new varieties of disease-resistant plants and stronger, healthier animals.

Gene therapy is another exciting area of genetic research. In this experimental way of treating disease, doctors remove some white blood cells from patients who lack the ability to fight a disease. Then they carefully insert tiny pieces of DNA into the cells to help boost their disease-fighting ability. The patients are then injected with the boosted white blood cells. Scientists hope these white blood cells will help wake up the patient's own defenses against disease.

Other scientists are working to develop new artificial materials that can be used inside the body without triggering the body's natural defenses or causing an infection. Scientists use such materials to make replacements for damaged or diseased bones and joints, to devise *pacemakers* to help patients' hearts beat properly, and even to create special pumps that help prevent dangerous blood clots. Someday they may even be able to implant in patients' bodies special medicinal capsules that will dissolve and release their medicines very slowly, perhaps over months or years.

Are you interested in space? Many young people have learned about astronomy and space travel by going to "space camps." Maybe you would like to learn more about what lies beyond our planet. Astronomers have learned much about the shape of our galaxy, the Milky Way, and other stars and galaxies. One group of astronomers is trying to map the universe. They will need a lot of help, for they have only just begun this enormous job.

Many physicists and engineers work in the area of robotics. Robots are mechanical devices. They can be designed to do just about any kind of work. Most robots are computer controlled, so they are more than just machines. Many can be reprogrammed to do different tasks. Others are designed to do just one task very well. One kind of robot is a vehicle designed to go over harsh terrain. It looks a lot like a big insect—it has six legs for movement and a laser "eye" for seeing.

Another important area of research is in earth and atmospheric science. Changes that occur in the blanket of air that surrounds our planet affect everyone. You may have learned that a rise in the level of carbon dioxide gas in the atmosphere is causing a warming of Earth's climate. This global warming, called the greenhouse effect, could cause ice at the poles to melt, raise the level of the oceans, and flood the land near our shores.

Scientists are also studying the ozone layer, a layer of gas in the atmosphere that protects us from the sun's harmful ultraviolet radiation. The ozone layer is being damaged by chemical compounds called *chlorofluorocarbons,* or CFCs. CFCs are used in refrigerators, air conditioners, and other appliances, and also in many industries. Scientists are trying to develop new chemical compounds that will work in the same way as CFCs but will not damage Earth's precious ozone layer.

Scientists study information about our planet from pictures taken by satellites in orbit high above Earth. They also use computers to help them predict the effects of global warming. Computers and other electronic devices aid scientists in predicting earthquakes, volcanic eruptions, and severe storms. This helps to reduce the damage that might be done by these natural disasters.

Another growing field is *particle physics*—the science of the particles that make up atoms. To study these particles, scientists use large underground tracks, sometimes several miles long, called particle accelerators. In an accelerator, atomic particles such as protons or electrons are speeded up, or accelerated, to very high levels. Often they are sent crashing into other particles or atoms. These collisions release even more kinds of particles. The paths of these particles can be detected and photographed; they have told scientists a great deal about how atoms are put together.

Particle accelerators use electromagnetic fields to speed up atomic particles. Scientists are experimenting with ways to use magnetism to power trains to speeds of 300 miles per hour. Others are looking for ways to build efficient electric cars. Still others are working to produce energy from the sun, the wind, the heat deep within Earth, and even the ocean. Scientists are trying to unlock the secret of *nuclear fusion,* the process by which the energy of the sun is produced.

These are just a few of the exciting areas that scientists are researching. Perhaps someday you will bring your own way of looking at things to one of these fields and help make the world a better place. Fresh ideas, imagination, and invention are all part of the adventure of science.

Fact Book

Facts About Our Earth

WHETHER OUR EARTH is a big or small place depends on how you look at it. It is only one of nine planets revolving around the sun (our star). Our star is only one of trillions of stars in the universe. Our Earth, just a speck in the vast universe, seems like a very tiny place.

Yet it is a pretty big place, too—over 24,000 miles around, which is equal to almost 200,000 city blocks. There are great mountains and rivers, continents covering millions of square miles, and oceans even larger than the continents. This section tells about the largest, longest, tallest, and greatest natural wonders of our Earth.

FACTS ABOUT OUR EARTH

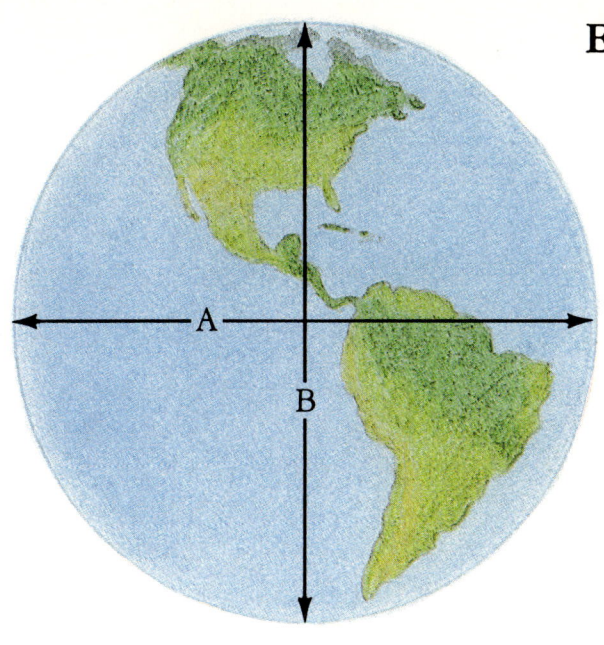

Earth

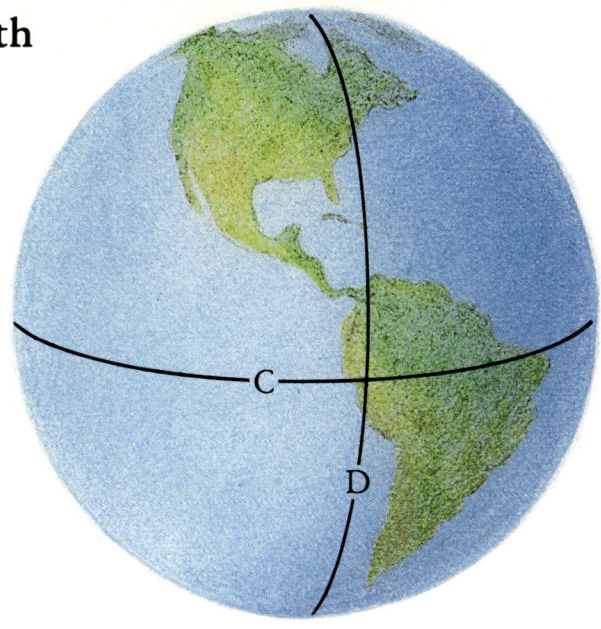

Diameter
A. equatorial diameter   7926 miles
B. polar diameter   7900 miles

Circumference
C. equatorial circumference   24,902 miles
D. polar circumference   24,860 miles

Earth's surface is approximately 71 percent water and 29 percent land.

area of land   57,470,000 square miles
area of water   139,480,000 square miles

FACTS ABOUT OUR EARTH

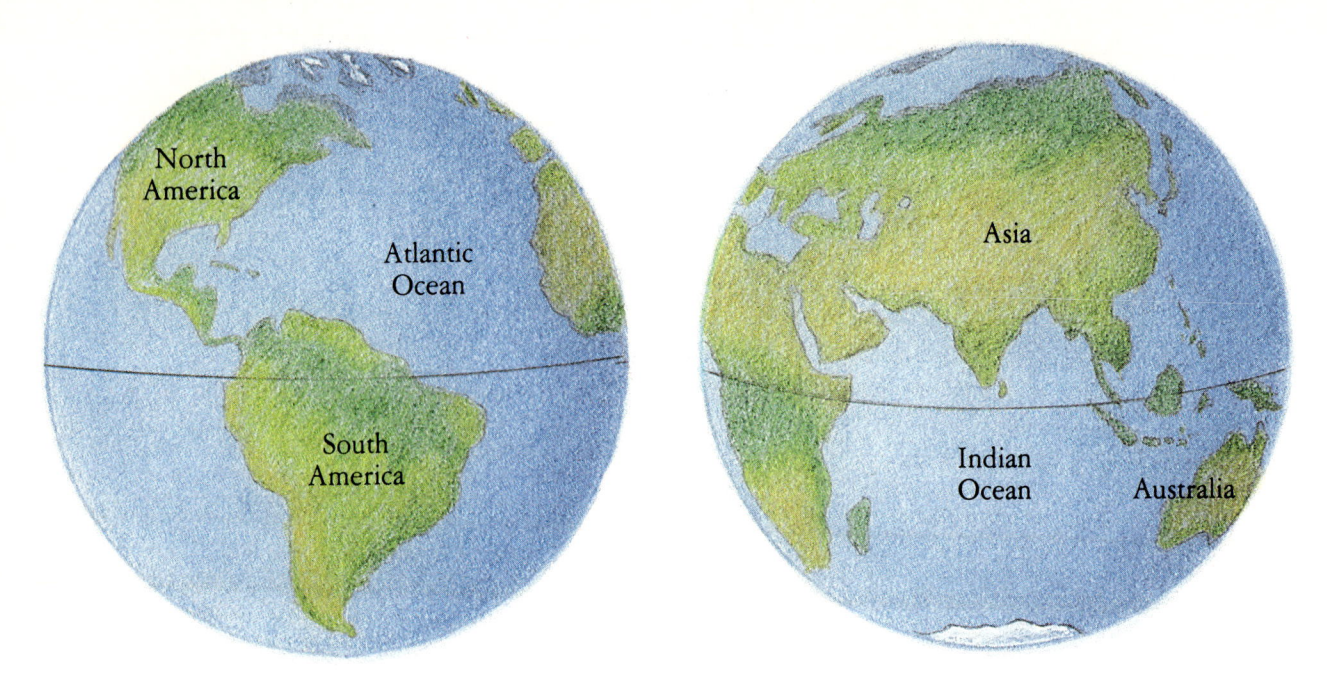

The Seven Continents

CONTINENT	AREA	RANK IN AREA	RANK IN POPULATION
Africa	11,500,000 square miles	2	3
Antarctica	5,300,000 square miles	5	7
Asia	16,900,000 square miles	1	1
Australia	2,968,000 square miles	7	6
Europe	3,750,000 square miles	6	2
North America	9,300,000 square miles	3	4
South America	6,800,000 square miles	4	5

The deepest mankind has ever gone into the earth's crust is at a gold mine in Carletonville, South Africa. The mine has reached a depth of 12,391 feet (almost 2½ miles), and it is planned to reach a depth of 12,730 feet.

FACTS ABOUT OUR EARTH

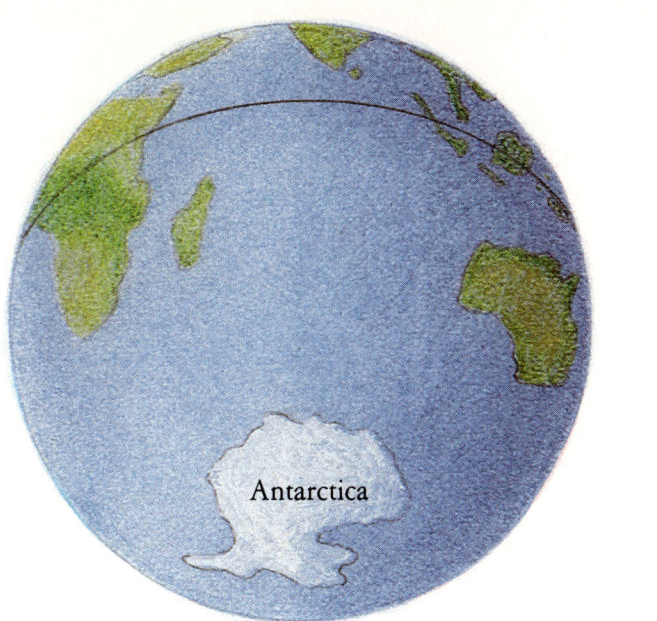

The Four Oceans

OCEAN	AREA	AVERAGE DEPTH	DEEPEST POINT
Arctic Ocean	5,440,000 square miles	3,953 feet	18,456 feet
Atlantic Ocean	31,839,000 square miles	12,880 feet	30,246 feet
Indian Ocean	28,356,000 square miles	13,002 feet	24,460 feet
Pacific Ocean	63,802,000 square miles	14,048 feet	36,198 feet

The deepest mankind has ever gone in an ocean is 35,802 feet (over 6¾ miles). Dr. Jacques Piccard and Lt. Donald Walsh made the descent in the U.S. Navy's bathyscaphe *Trieste.* The descent was into the Mariana Trench in the Pacific Ocean.

The Great Deserts of the World

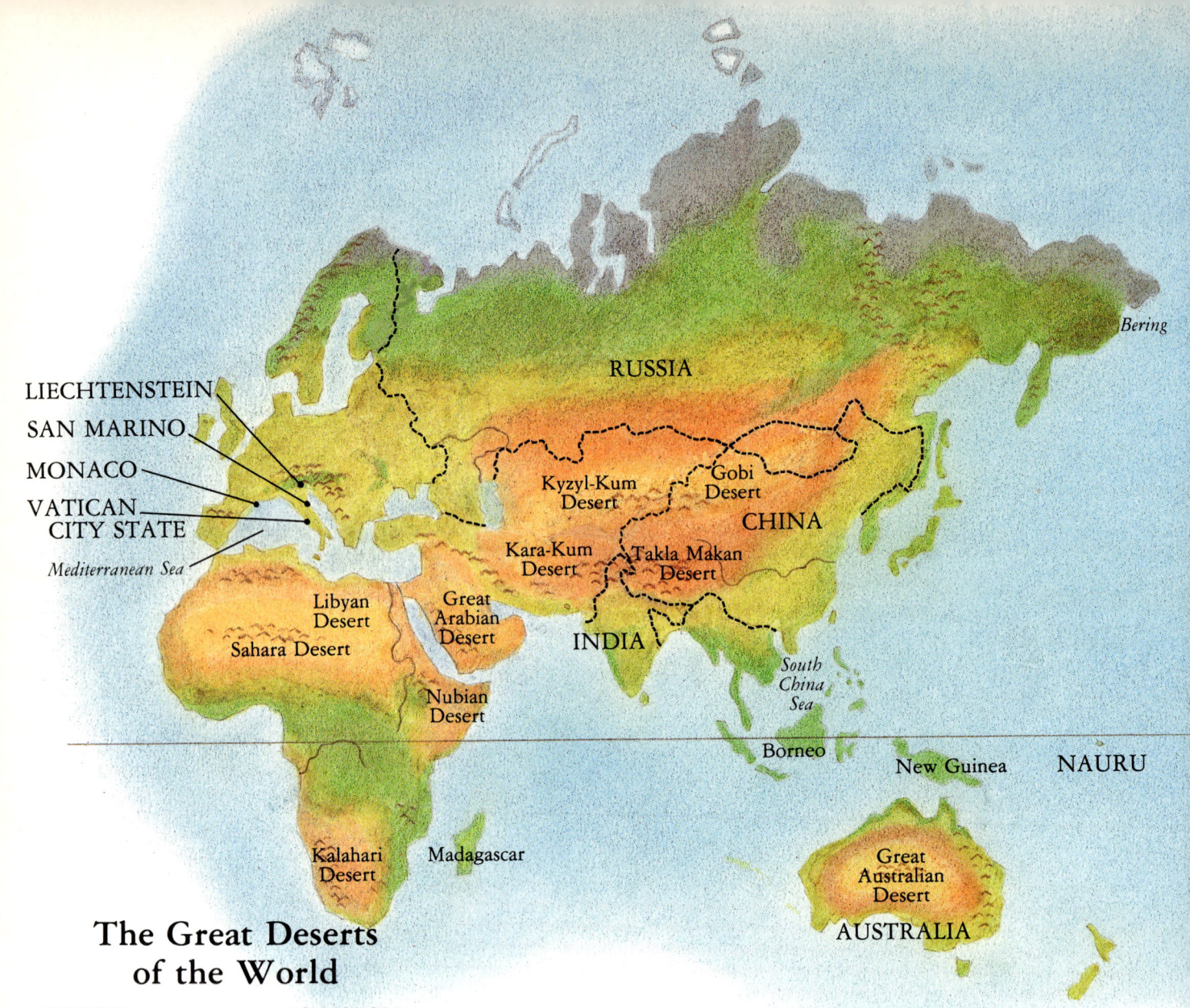

DESERT	LOCATION
Sahara	Africa
Great Australian	Australia
Libyan	Africa
Gobi	Asia
Kalahari	Africa
Takla Makan	Asia
Nubian	Africa
Kara-Kum	Asia
Kyzyl-Kum	Asia
Great Arabian	Saudi Arabia

The Five Largest Seas in the World

SEA	AREA	AVERAGE DEPTH
South China Sea	1,146,000 square miles	5400 feet
Caribbean Sea	1,063,000 square miles	8685 feet
Mediterranean Sea	966,750 square miles	4878 feet
Bering Sea	875,750 square miles	4714 feet
Gulf of Mexico	582,000 square miles	5300 feet

FACTS ABOUT OUR EARTH

The Largest Countries in the World

COUNTRY	AREA
Russia	6,592,700 square miles
Canada	3,852,000 square miles
China	3,705,000 square miles
United States	3,615,000 square miles
Brazil	3,287,000 square miles
Australia	2,968,000 square miles
India	1,176,000 square miles
Argentina	1,068,000 square miles

The Smallest Countries in the World

COUNTRY	AREA
Vatican City State	.17 square mile
Monaco	.58 square mile
Nauru	8.20 square miles
San Marino	23.60 square miles
Liechtenstein	61.00 square miles

The Four Largest Islands in the World

ISLAND	AREA	LOCATION
Greenland	840,000 square miles	Atlantic Ocean
New Guinea	316,600 square miles	Pacific Ocean
Borneo	286,900 square miles	Pacific Ocean
Madagascar	226,650 square miles	Indian Ocean

FACTS ABOUT OUR EARTH

The Highest Mountains

In The World

MOUNTAIN	HEIGHT	COUNTRY
Everest	29,028 feet	Nepal/Tibet
Godwin Austen	28,250 feet	India/Kashmir
Kanchenjunga	28,208 feet	Nepal/Sikkim
Lhotse	27,923 feet	Nepal/Tibet
Makalu	27,824 feet	Nepal/Tibet

On Each Continent

CONTINENT	MOUNTAIN	HEIGHT	COUNTRY
Asia	**Everest**	29,028 feet	Nepal/Tibet
South America	**Aconcagua**	22,831 feet	Argentina
North America	**McKinley**	20,320 feet	United States
Africa	**Kilimanjaro**	19,340 feet	Tanzania
Europe	**El'brus**	18,510 feet	Russia
Antarctica	**Vinson Massif**	16,864 feet	
Australia	**Kosciusko**	7,310 feet	

Lowest Areas in the World

In Each Continent

CONTINENT	AREA	FEET BELOW SEA LEVEL
Asia	**Dead Sea**-Israel/Jordan	1296
Africa	**Lake Assal**-Ethiopia	512
North America	**Death Valley**-United States	282
South America	**Salinas Grandes**-Argentina	131
Europe	**Caspian Sea**-Eastern Europe	96
Australia	**Lake Eyre**	39
Antarctica		0

The Great Lakes

The Great Lakes in North America together form the largest body of fresh water in the world.

LAKE	AREA	DEEPEST POINT
Lake Superior	31,820 square miles	1333 feet
Lake Huron	23,010 square miles	750 feet
Lake Michigan	22,400 square miles	923 feet
Lake Erie	9,930 square miles	210 feet
Lake Ontario	7,520 square miles	778 feet

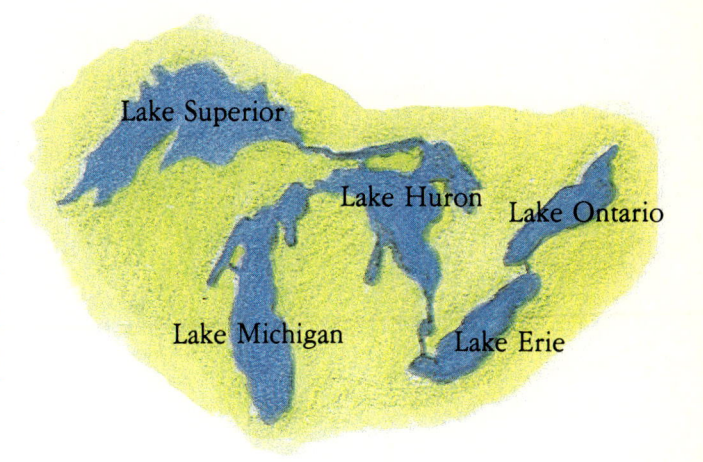

Waterfalls

The Highest

WATERFALL	HEIGHT	COUNTRY
Angel	3212 feet	Venezuela
Tugela	3110 feet	South Africa
Yosemite	2425 feet	United States
Cuquenán	2000 feet	Venezuela
Sutherland	1904 feet	New Zealand

The Largest

WATERFALL	COUNTRY
Sete Quedas	Brazil-Paraguay

(The Sete Quedas dumps an average of 470,000 cubic feet of water each second. The largest flow of the Sete Quedas is more than 1,750,000 cubic feet of water each second.)

The Five Longest Rivers in the World

RIVER	LOCATION	FLOWS INTO	LENGTH
Nile	Africa	Mediterranean Sea	4180 miles
Amazon	South America	Atlantic Ocean	3912 miles
Mississippi-Missouri-Red Rock	North America	Gulf of Mexico	3880 miles
Yangtze	Asia	China Sea	3602 miles
Ob-Irtish	Europe/Asia	Gulf of Ob	3459 miles

FACTS ABOUT OUR EARTH

Temperature

Highest Recorded

In the World	136 degrees Fahrenheit at Azizia, Libya
In the United States	134 degrees Fahrenheit at Death Valley, California

Lowest Recorded

In the World	−128.6 degrees (below zero) Fahrenheit at Vostok, Antarctica
In the United States	−79.8 degrees (below zero) Fahrenheit at Prospect Creek, Alaska

Rainfall

Most in the World
Tutunendo, Colombia
averaging 468.4 inches of rain per year

Least in the World
Calama, Atacama Desert, Chile
no rain has ever been recorded

200

People and Their Ways

THOUSANDS OF YEARS AGO, people's lives were very different from what they are today. As time went by, people traveled across Earth—learning new things, beginning new civilizations, and gradually creating the modern world as we know it today.

Today, more than 5 billion people live on Earth in large cities, towns, and farm areas. All of these men, women, and children live in a world with many different ways of life. In this section is an outline of important events in the history of people, facts about world populations and languages, and information on organizations for young people.

PEOPLE AND THEIR WAYS

The Story of Man

The story of man is full of events, discoveries, wars, great movements, and the rise and fall of civilizations. By studying the great events of the past we can understand better how the world of today came to be the way it is.

Important events of history are listed here in *chronological* order, that is, in the order in which they happened. Within each time period these events are further organized by region.

5000–3000 B.C. **Middle East**	Tigris-Euphrates Valley (Iraq) is settled (5000). Cities in Sumer (Iran) are built (3700). Sumerians develop *cuneiform* writing (3100).
Africa	Civilized settlements appear in Nile Valley (Egypt-5000). Egyptians develop *hieroglyphic* writing (3100).
Asia	People from the Asian mainland migrate to Japan (4000). Civilized settlements begin in the Indus Valley, India (3100).
Europe	Minoan settlements begin on the island of Crete (4000).
3000–1000 B.C. **Middle East**	Babylonian Empire begins (2600). Phoenicians settle on the coast of Syria (2500). Babylonian King Hammurabi writes code of laws to govern his empire (2050). Trading begins on the Mediterranean Sea (1825). Hittite Empire in Turkey and Syria develops (1700). Abraham leads the Hebrews (1550). Hittites develop iron weapons (1400). Hittite Empire falls (1100).
Africa	Egypt is unified by King Menes (3000). The great pyramids of Egypt are built (2400). Hebrews flee from Egypt *(exodus)* (1290).
Asia	Hsia dynasty appears in China (2200–1700). Shang dynasty appears in China (1700–1050). Chou dynasty begins in China (1050).

PEOPLE AND THEIR WAYS

Europe	Asians migrate to Greece (2900). Minoan culture exists on Crete; Minoans develop hieroglyphic writing (2000–1400). Greeks conquer Troy in Trojan War (1200). Crete falls to the Greek Dorian invasion (1100).
North America	Pueblo Indian culture begins (1450).

1000–500 B.C.

Middle East	David becomes King of Israel (1000). Solomon succeeds David as leader of the Hebrews (950). Assyrian Empire begins (900). New Assyrian Empire begins with the conquering of Babylon (745). Greeks settle in part of Italy (735). Zoroaster, a Persian, preaches the religion of the Magi (660). Chaldean Empire begins with the capture of Nineveh (606). Cyrus the Great establishes the Persian Empire (539).
Africa	Carthage (Tunisia) is founded (800). Carthaginian Empire begins (575). Egypt is conquered by Persia (525).
Asia	Hindu religion develops in India (950). Caste system develops in India (775). Buddha establishes his religion in India (526). Confucius forms his philosophy in China (510).
Europe	Greek city-states come into being (900). In Greece, Homer writes *The Iliad* and *The Odyssey* (875). Rome is founded (753).
South America and Central America	Mayas settle in Central America (1000). Indian settlements are made in the Andes Mountains (550).

PEOPLE AND THEIR WAYS

500–1 B.C. **Middle East**	Persia controls the Middle East and Egypt (500–400). Persia falls to the Greek armies of Alexander the Great; the Persian Empire collapses (331). Middle East is invaded by Rome (75). Jesus Christ is born in Judea (4).
Africa	Egypt gains its freedom from Persia (410). Egypt falls to Alexander the Great (332). Punic Wars between Carthage and Rome begin (264). Hannibal leads the Carthaginians (221). Carthage is destroyed by Rome (146). Cleopatra is queen of Egypt (60).
	Maurya Empire exists in India (320–190). Asoka the Great is ruler of India (274). Great Wall of China is built (214). Han dynasty begins in China (202). Andhra Empire in India begins (180). Buddhism is brought to China (100).
Europe	The Golden Age of Greece flourishes (500–400). Persian Wars are fought between Greece and Persia (490–479). First Peloponnesian War between Athens and Sparta is fought (460–445). Alexander the Great's empire stretches from Persia to Egypt to India (336–323). Hannibal crosses the Alps into Italy (216). Rome ends the Punic Wars by defeating Carthage (201). Germanic tribes begin to form (150). Julius Caesar conquers Gaul (58–51). Roman Empire is established under Augustus Caesar (27).
1 A.D.–400 A.D. **Middle East**	Jesus Christ is crucified, and the age of Christianity begins (30). Jerusalem is destroyed by the Romans (70). Sassanian Empire begins in Persia (226). Axumite kingdom rules Arabia (350).

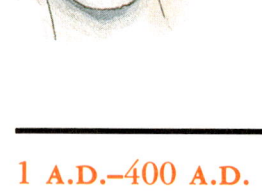

Asia	Paper is invented in China (110).
	Religion of Taoism is introduced in China (150).
	Polynesians migrate to the Pacific Islands (200).
	Gupta Empire is established in India (300).
	Hun and Mongol empires begin in China (350).
Europe	Romans control the largest empire in the history of the world (27–400).
	Britain is conquered by Rome (50).
	Nero rules Rome (54).
	Great Plague devastates Europe and Asia (164–180).
	Constantine rules the Roman Empire (306).
	Roman Empire is divided (395).
North America	Mayan settlements appear in Mexico (120).
South America and Central America	Mayan Empire begins in Central America (350).

400–800 A.D.	Muhammad develops the religion of Islam (570–632).
Middle East	Muslim Empire begins (622).
	Muslims conquer Jerusalem (637).
	Muslims conquer Alexandria, Egypt (641).
	Muslims conquer Spain and North Africa (725).
Asia	Attila leads the Hun invasion of Europe (450).
	Buddhism is introduced in Japan (552).
	Tang dynasty begins in China (618).
	Muslims invade India (700).
	Kyoto becomes the capital of Japan (800).
Europe	Visigoths under Alaric sack Rome (410).
	Germanic tribes (Franks, Goths, Visigoths, Vandals, and Burgundians) settle Europe (425).
	Rome falls and Middle Ages begin (476).
	Britain is invaded by the Angles, Saxons, and Jutes (500).
	Franks are united by Clovis I (500).
	Lombard Empire rules Italy (566).
	Carolingian dynasty is begun in France by Pepin (630).
	Charles Martel rules the Frankish Empire (721).

PEOPLE AND THEIR WAYS

800–1200 A.D.
Middle East
Muslim Empire is invaded by Charlemagne (800).
Jerusalem is captured by the First Crusade (1099).
Omar Khayyam writes poetry in Persia (1100).
Saladin is sultan of Egypt (1169).
The crusaders invade the Middle East (1200).

Asia
Angkor (in Cambodia) becomes Khmer capital (890).
Tang dynasty in China ends (907).

Europe
Charlemagne becomes emperor of the Frankish Empire (800).
Alfred the Great unites England (871–899).
Holy Roman Empire is founded by Otto I (962).
Normans, under William the Conqueror, rule England after the Battle of Hastings (1066).
El Cid leads the forces of Spain (1094).
First Crusade sets out (1095).
Frederick Barbarossa is crowned holy Roman emperor (1152).

North America
Vikings explore the east coast of North America (1000).
Aztec Indians begin settlements in Mexico (1100).

1200–1600 A.D.
Middle East
Ottoman Empire begins in Turkey (1299).
Ottoman Turks take Constantinople (Istanbul) and Byzantine Empire falls (1453).
Suleiman the Magnificent expands the Ottoman Empire (1525).

Africa
Portuguese migrate to Africa (1475).
North Africa is ruled by Ottoman Turks (1525).

Asia
Genghis Khan captures Peking, China (1214).
Kublai Khan rules the Mongols (1260).
Mongol Empire begins (1280).
Marco Polo visits China (1290).
Ming dynasty appears in China (1368–1644).
Khmers fall from power in Southeast Asia (1431).
Vasco Da Gama sails around Africa to India (1498).
Sikh religion is established in India (1520).
Magellan reaches the South Pacific (1520).

PEOPLE AND THEIR WAYS

Europe

Children's Crusade begins; armies of boys join the Fourth Crusade to the Holy Land (1212).
Magna Carta is signed in England (1215).
Inquisition begins in Italy (1215).
Dante writes the *Divine Comedy* in Italy (1310).
Hundred Years' War between France and England is fought (1337–1453).
Great Plague (Black Death) spreads through Europe (1348).
Chaucer writes poetry in England (1375).
Joan of Arc leads the French armies (1429).
Leonardo Da Vinci, artist and inventor, is born in Italy (1452).
The Renaissance begins in Europe (1453).
Wars of the Roses begin in England (1455).
Copernicus shows that Earth moves around the sun (1473–1543).
Michelangelo, painter and sculptor, lives in Italy (1475–1564).
Martin Luther founds the Lutheran religion in Germany (1521).
The Reformation begins in Europe (1525).
Henry VIII, king of England, founds the Church of England (1530).
Shakespeare writes in England (1564–1616).
Galileo proves Copernicus's theory of the solar system (1564–1642).
Peter Paul Rubens paints in Europe (1577–1640).
England defeats the Spanish Armada (1588).

207

PEOPLE AND THEIR WAYS

North America	Mexico City is founded by the Aztec Indians (1325). Columbus crosses the Atlantic Ocean and lands in America (1492). Mexico falls to Cortez (1520). Sir Walter Raleigh sends an expedition to Virginia (1584).
South America	Inca Indian civilization begins in Peru (1250). Brazil is settled by the Portuguese (1530). Pizarro conquers the Incas (1535).

1600–1800 A.D.

Asia	Japan is closed to Europeans; Tokyo becomes the capital (1638). Ming dynasty in China ends; Manchu dynasty begins (1644).
Australia	English settlement is made at Sydney (1787).
Europe	Rembrandt paints in Holland (1606–1669). John Milton, poet, lives in England (1608–1674). King James Bible is printed in England (1611). Thirty Years' War involves all of Europe (1618–1648). Isaac Newton, scientist and mathematician, works in England (1642–1727). Oliver Cromwell governs England after King Charles I is beheaded (1650). Johann Sebastian Bach composes music in Germany (1685–1750). Peter the Great rules Russia (1689–1725). England, Scotland, and Wales are joined to form the United Kingdom of Great Britain (1707). Mozart composes music in Austria (1756–1791). Catherine the Great rules Russia (1762–1796). Ludwig van Beethoven composes music in Germany (1770–1827). Industrial Revolution begins in England (1770). England goes to war with the American colonies (1775). French Revolution begins (1789). France becomes a republic (1792).

PEOPLE AND THEIR WAYS

North America
First English settlement is made at Jamestown, Virginia (1607).
Pilgrims land at Plymouth Rock (1620).
North America is explored (1625–1700).
French and Indian Wars are fought (1754–1763).
English General James Wolfe captures Quebec (1759).
Canada is ceded to the British (1763).
Declaration of Independence is signed (1776).
Revolutionary War ends (1783).
U.S. Constitution is ratified (1789).

1800–Present
Middle East
Suez Canal is built (1869).
Oil is discovered and developed (1915).
Saudi Arabia becomes independent (1922).
Israel wins independence (1948).
Suez Canal closed in Arab-Israeli war (1967).
Jordan defeats and expells Palestinian guerrilla forces (1970).
United Nations negotiates Arab-Israeli cease-fire (1970).
Arab states subsidize Egypt to keep Suez Canal closed (1972).
Arab-Israeli conflict triggers world energy crisis (1973).
Friction between Christians and Muslims in Lebanon leads to civil war (1975).
Anwar el-Sadat of Egypt makes bold peace gesture by visiting Jerusalem to meet with Menachem Begin of Israel (1977).
Middle East Peace accord agreed upon in historic meeting between Anwar el-Sadat of Egypt, Menachem Begin of Israel, and U.S. President Jimmy Carter at Camp David, Maryland (1978).
Shah of Iran is overthrown (1979).
U.S. Embassy in Teheran, Iran, is seized by Islamic militants, who hold 52 Americans hostage for 444 days (1979–1981).
Anwar el-Sadat is assassinated (1980).

PEOPLE AND THEIR WAYS

War between Iraq and Iran begins (1980).
Israel invades Lebanon, forcing Palestine Liberation Organization (PLO) forces to withdraw (1982).
U.S. Marine and French army headquarters in Beirut, Lebanon, are bombed by terrorists (1983).
Iran and Iraq agree to cease-fire, halting an eight-year war that has claimed some million lives (1988).
Iraq invades Kuwait, causing UN to approve use of force against Iraq (1990).
After six weeks of fighting, an international coalition forces Iraqi soldiers out of Kuwait (1991).
Israel and PLO sign accord to establish Palestinian self-rule in the Gaza Strip and in and around the city of Jericho (1993).

Africa

French control of Algeria begins (1848).
European colonies are established (1885).
Union of South Africa is established (1910).
African nations gain independence: Libya (1951), Sudan (1955), Morocco and Tunisia (1956), Ghana (1957), Nigeria (1960), Tanzania, Malawi, and Zambia (1964), and Rhodesia (1965).
Biafra secedes from Nigeria; civil war begins (1967).
Biafra is defeated by Nigeria (1970).
Drought and famine devastate sub-Saharan Africa (1985–1986).
South African government signs agreement with African National Congress (ANC) to grant equal rights to country's black majority (1993).

Asia

Opium wars exist in China (1839).
Japan is opened to world (1865).
Japanese war is fought with China (1894–1895).
Boxer Rebellion begins in China (1900).
Korea is annexed to Japan (1910).
Republic of China is established (1912).
Gandhi uses passive resistance to gain reforms and freedom for India (1919–1948).
Japan attacks United States at Pearl Harbor (1941).

PEOPLE AND THEIR WAYS

Atom bombs cause Japanese surrender in World War II (1945).
India and Pakistan gain their independence from England (1947).
China becomes a Communist state (1949).
Korean War is fought (1950–1953).
Vietnamese forces overthrow French rule (1954).
United States begins aid to South Vietnam (1955).
Federation of Malaysia is formed (1963).
Vietnam peace talks begin in Paris (1968).
Communist China replaces Nationalist China in United Nations (1971).
East Pakistan gains freedom from Pakistan and becomes Bangladesh (1971).
Vietnam truce signed (1973).
India tests its first nuclear bomb (1974).
North and South Vietnam become one nation (1976).
Red China and the United States establish diplomatic relations (1978).
Soviet Union sends military force into Afghanistan, sparking guerrilla warfare (1979).
Philippine President Ferdinand Marcos is deposed in a bloodless popular revolution (1986).
Agreement is reached on the withdrawal of Soviet troops from Afghanistan (1988).
Democratic movement in China is crushed by massacre of demonstrators at Tiananmen Square, Beijing (1989).

Australia

Confederation of Australia is established (1900).
World War I is fought with Allies (1918).
World War II is fought with Allies (1939).
First satellite for weather research is launched (1967).
Continuing cooperation with United States shown by Prime Minister John Frazer's visit to President Gerald Ford in Washington, D.C. (1977).
Treaty of friendship and cooperation signed with Japan (1977).
America's Cup won by yacht *Australia II* (1983).

PEOPLE AND THEIR WAYS

Europe

Napoleon becomes emperor of France (1804).
Napoleon's empire collapses after defeat at Waterloo (1815).
Queen Victoria rules England (1837–1901).
England and France oppose Russia in Crimean War (1854–1856).
Charles Darwin publishes theory of evolution (1859).
Impressionism, the first movement of modern painting, is developed in France (1862–1880).
Albert Einstein publishes relativity theory (1905).
World War I engulfs all of Europe (1914–1918).
Bolshevik Revolution succeeds in Russia (1917).
Germany and Austria surrender at Versailles, France, to end World War I (1918).
Mussolini rules Italy (1921).
Union of Soviet Socialist Republics (U.S.S.R.) is formed (1922).
Republic of Spain is established (1931).
Hitler comes to power in Germany (1933).
Spanish Civil War is fought (1936–1939).
World War II involves all of Europe (1939–1945).
Germany is defeated to end World War II (1945).
North Atlantic Treaty Organization (NATO) is formed (1949).
U.S.S.R. becomes the second country to develop nuclear weapons (1949).
Uprising in Hungary is crushed by Soviet troops (1956).
European Economic Community (Common Market) is formed (1957).
U.S.S.R. launches Sputnik I, the first satellite to orbit Earth (1957).
East Germany constructs wall between East and West Berlin (1961).
U.S.S.R. sends the first man into orbit around Earth (1961).
Czechoslovakia is invaded by Warsaw Pact forces, ending reform movement (1968).

PEOPLE AND THEIR WAYS

Big Four allies of World War II, East and West Germany sign pact for free traffic between West Germany and West Berlin (1971).
Free elections are held in Spain (1977).
Strikes in Poland are instigated by Solidarity movement (1980).
Mikhail Gorbachev becomes leader of U.S.S.R. (1985).
Nuclear reactor accident at Chernobyl, U.S.S.R, releases dangerous amount of radiation (1986).
Mikhail Gorbachev begins program of reform in U.S.S.R. (1987).
Political and economic reforms are begun in Eastern Europe (1989).
East and West Germany are reunited (1990).
The Soviet Union is dismantled. The Commonwealth of Independent States is formed in its absence (1991).

South America and Central America

Statesman-soldier Simon Bolivar helps liberate Venezuela (1811), Colombia (1821), Ecuador (1822) and Peru (1825).
Pan-American Union established (1889).
Panama Canal is completed (1914).
Organization of American States (OAS) is formed (1948).
Chile becomes first country to publicly elect a Communist government (1970).
Chile's leftist government ousted by coup (1973).
Military takes over in Argentina (1976).
U.S. signs two treaties with Panama regarding the function of the Panama Canal until 1999 and the neutrality of the waterway thereafter (1978).
Civil war erupts in El Salvador after coup (1979).
Sandinistas take over in Nicaragua (1979).
U.S. forces invade Grenada (1983).
Civilian rule returns to several Latin American countries, notably Argentina (1983), Brazil (1985), and Nicaragua (1990).

213

PEOPLE AND THEIR WAYS

North America

Louisiana Purchase expands the United States (1803).
United States fights England in War of 1812.
Exploration and settlement of western lands sweeps United States (1826–1900).
Mark Twain, U.S. writer and humorist, lives (1835–1910).
United States Civil War is fought (1861–1865).
Abraham Lincoln issues Emancipation Proclamation (1863).
Maximillian rules Mexico (1864–1867).
Spanish-American War is fought (1898).
United States enters World War I (1917).
Dominion of Canada is formed (1926).
Charles Lindbergh makes first nonstop flight across Atlantic (1927).
Great Depression begins in United States (1929).
United States enters World War II (1941).
United Nations is formed (1945).
World War II ends with the surrender of Germany and Japan (1945).
United States enters Korean War (1950).
Korean truce is signed (1953).
First U.S. manned satellite is launched (1962).
President John F. Kennedy is assassinated (1963).
United States lands first men on moon (1969).
Apollo moon probe program completed (1972).
President Nixon visits China (1972).
Nixon becomes first U.S. President to resign office (1974).
Final U.S. troops removed from South Vietnam (1975).
United States celebrates Bicentennial (1976).
First artificial heart implantation is performed in United States (1982).
Queen Elizabeth II signs the Canada Act, enabling Canada to amend its own constitution (1984).
Space shuttle *Challenger* explodes after takeoff, killing crew of seven (1986).

Populations

The World   5,506,000,000

The Continents

CONTINENT	NUMBER OF PEOPLE
Asia	3,257,000,000
Europe	513,000,000
Africa	677,000,000
North America	443,000,000
South America	305,000,000
Australia	17,800,000
Antarctica	0

The Five Largest Countries

COUNTRY	NUMBER OF PEOPLE
China	1,178,000,000
India	903,000,000
United States	258,000,000
Indonesia	197,000,000
Brazil	157,000,000

The World's Ten Largest Metro Areas

CITY	NUMBER OF PEOPLE
Tokyo–Yokohama, Japan	27,540,000
Mexico City, Mexico	21,615,000
Sao Paulo, Brazil	19,373,000
Seoul, South Korea	17,334,000
New York, United States	14,628,000
Osaka–Kobe–Kyoto, Japan	13,919,000
Bombay, India	12,450,000
Calcutta, India	12,137,000
Rio de Janeiro, Brazil	12,009,000
Buenos Aires, Argentina	11,743,000

The Ten Largest Metro Areas in the U.S.

CITY	NUMBER OF PEOPLE
New York, New York	14,628,000
Los Angeles, California	10,072,000
Chicago, Illinois	6,493,000
San Francisco, California	4,005,000
Philadelphia, Pennsylvania	3,970,000
Miami, Florida	3,522,000
Detroit, Michigan	2,890,000
Dallas, Texas	2,856,000
Washington, D.C.	2,572,000
Boston, Massachusetts	2,460,000

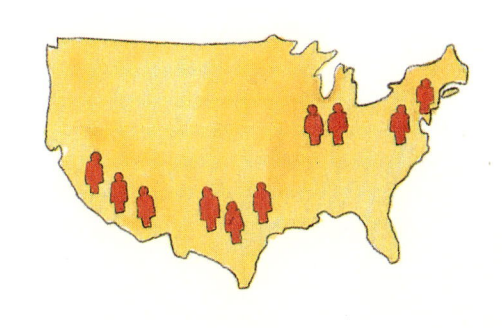

PEOPLE AND THEIR WAYS

The Ten Languages Most Often Spoken

LANGUAGE	AREAS WHERE SPOKEN	NUMBER OF PEOPLE SPEAKING IT	= 100 million people
Mandarin	China	806,000,000	
English	United Kingdom, British Commonwealth, Ireland, United States	426,000,000	
Hindustani	India, Pakistan	398,000,000	
Spanish	Spain, Latin America	308,000,000	
Russian	Russia, Ukraine	287,000,000	
Arabic	Middle East	182,000,000	
Bengali	Bangladesh, India	175,000,000	
Portuguese	Portugal, Brazil	166,000,000	
Malay-Indonesian	Malaysia, Indonesia	132,000,000	
Japanese	Japan	123,000,000	

This Is "Hello" in Each of These Languages

LANGUAGE	HOW TO WRITE IT	HOW TO SAY IT
Mandarin	好	HOW
English	Hello	heh-LO
Hindustani	नमस्ते	nah-mah-STAY
Spanish	Qué tal	kay-TAHL
Russian	Здравствуйте	zh-DRAHV-zhvoo-yeh-cheh
Arabic	آهلاً وسهلاً / السلام عليكم	ah-lahn wahs-ah-lahn / ahl sahl-am ah-LAY koom
Bengali	নমস্কার	nay-may-SKAHR
Portuguese	Como vai	ko-mo VAH-ee
Malay-Indonesian	Selamat datang	seh-lah-MAHT dah-TAHNG
Japanese	今日わ	ko-NEE chee-WAH

216

Ten Outstanding Organizations for Young People

ORGANIZATION	ACTIVITIES	AGE LIMIT	ADDRESS
Boys Clubs of America Magazine: *Connections*	sports, arts and crafts, social functions, vocational training	6–18	771 First Avenue New York, NY 10017
Boy Scouts of America Magazine: *Boy's Life*	outdoor education, physical fitness, crafts, nature study, citizenship	Cub Scouts (8–10) Boy Scouts (11–17) Explorer Scouts (15–20)	1325 Walnut Hill Lane Irving, TX 75038-3096
Camp Fire, Inc.	homemaking, arts and crafts, outdoor education, community service	up to 21	4601 Madison Avenue Kansas City, MO 64112
4-H Clubs	farming, livestock raising, community service, homemaking	9–19	Room 3860-S Federal Extension Service U.S. Department of Agriculture Washington, DC 20250
Girls' Clubs of America Magazine: *Voice for Girls*	arts and crafts, homemaking, sports and games	6–18	30 East 33rd Street New York, NY 10016
Girl Scouts of the U.S.A. Magazine: *GSUSA News*	arts and crafts, homemaking, nature study, citizenship	Daisies (5–6) Brownies (6–8) Junior Girl Scouts (8–11) Cadette Girl Scouts (11–14) Senior Girl Scouts (14–17)	830 Third Avenue New York, NY 10022
Little League Baseball	organized baseball leagues	Little League (6–12) Senior Division (13–15) Big League (16–18)	P.O. Box 3486 Williamsport, PA 17701
World Pen Pals	exchanging letters with children in other parts of the world		1690 Como Avenue St. Paul, MN 55108
Young Men's Christian Association (YMCA)	sports, arts and crafts, physical fitness, social functions, community service		101 North Wacker Drive Chicago, IL 60606
Young Women's Christian Association (YWCA)	arts and crafts, social functions, sports, outdoor education		726 Broadway, New York, NY 10003

What Mankind Has Done

PEOPLE HAVE DEVELOPED many wonderful things—airplanes, automobiles, electricity, television, highways, bridges, huge buildings, and fine schools. They have made rockets to go to the moon, produced beautiful works of art, and made great discoveries in medicine.

Mankind also has waged bloody wars and constructed weapons powerful enough to destroy the world. With all the knowledge and power people have gained, we now have the choice of working to improve life on Earth or completely destroying it. This section lists many of the great things people have already accomplished in our world.

Lighthouse of Alexandria

Statue of Zeus (Jupiter)

Pyramids of Egypt*

Tomb at Halicarnassus

Hanging Gardens of Babylon

Temple of Artemis (Diana)

Colossus of Rhodes

The Seven Wonders of the World

WONDER	LOCATION	DATE BUILT (APPROXIMATELY)
Colossus of Rhodes	Island of Rhodes (off the coast of Turkey)	280 B.C.
Hanging Gardens of Babylon	Iraq	600 B.C.
Lighthouse of Alexandria	Island of Pharos (off the coast of Egypt)	300 B.C.
Pyramids of Egypt*	Giza, Egypt	2580 B.C.
Statue of Zeus (Jupiter)	Olympia, Greece	500 B.C.
Temple of Artemis (Diana)	Ephesus, Turkey	350 B.C.
Tomb at Halicarnassus	Bodrum, Turkey	325 B.C.

*The Pyramids of Egypt are the only one of the Seven Wonders of the World still in existence.

WHAT MANKIND HAS DONE

The Largest Buildings in the World

BUILDING	FLOOR AREA	STORIES	LOCATION	DATE BUILT
Pentagon	6,500,000 square feet	5	Arlington, Virginia	1943
Sears Tower	4,500,000 square feet	110	Chicago, Illinois	1974
Merchandise Mart	4,023,400 square feet	25	Chicago, Illinois	1931

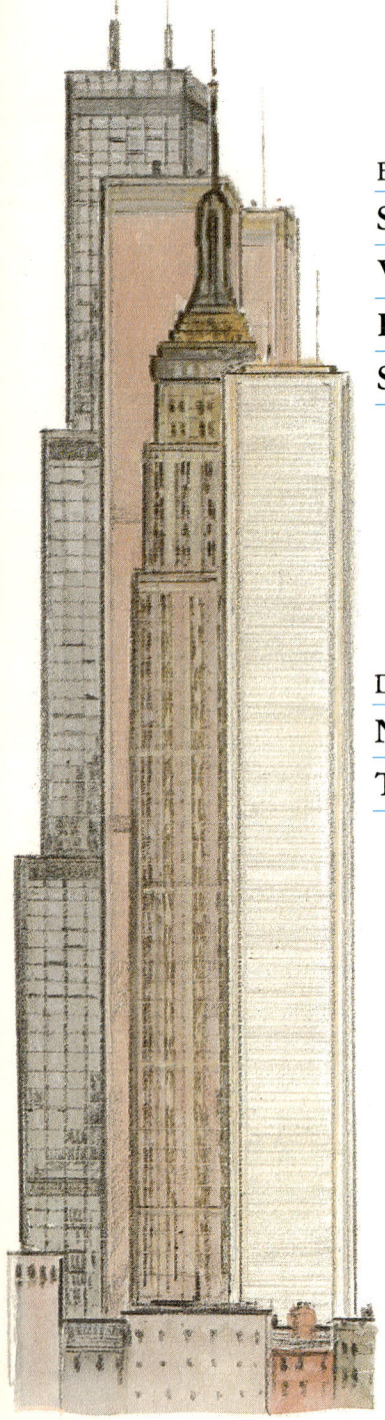

The Tallest Buildings in the World

BUILDING	HEIGHT	STORIES	CITY	COMPLETED
Sears Tower	1454 feet	110	Chicago	1974
World Trade Center	1353 feet	110	New York	1972
Empire State Building	1250 feet	102	New York	1931
Standard Oil Building	1136 feet	80	Chicago	1972

The Largest Dams in the World

DAM	LOCATION	CONSISTS OF
New Cornelia Tailings	Arizona	274,015,000 cubic yards (earth fill)
Tarbela	Pakistan	186,000,000 cubic yards (earth fill)

The Tallest Dams in the World

DAM	LOCATION	HEIGHT
Rogun	Tajikistan	1066 feet
Nurek	Tajikistan	984 feet
Grand Dixence	Switzerland	932 feet

WHAT MANKIND HAS DONE

The Longest Seaway in the World

CANAL	LOCATION	LENGTH
St. Lawrence Seaway	United States–Canada	189 miles

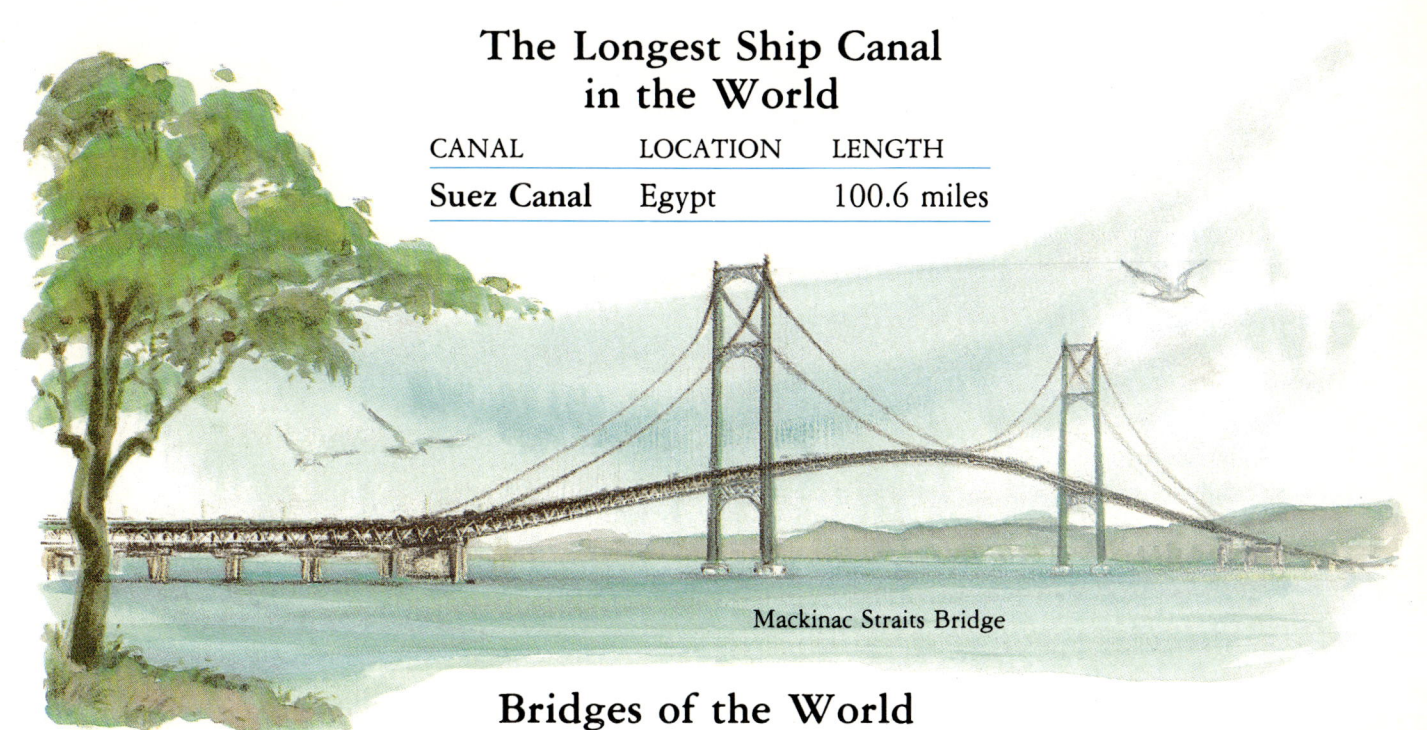

The Longest Ship Canal in the World

CANAL	LOCATION	LENGTH
Suez Canal	Egypt	100.6 miles

Mackinac Straits Bridge

Bridges of the World

TYPE OF BRIDGE	BRIDGE	LOCATION	LENGTH
longest **suspension** bridge	Mackinac Straits	Mackinaw City-St. Ignace, Michigan	7400-foot total span
longest **single span** bridge	Humber	Hull, Great Britain	4626-foot center span
longest **highway** bridge	Lake Pontchartrain Causeway	New Orleans	24 miles
longest **steel arch** bridge	New River Gorge	Fayetteville, West Virginia	1700-foot span
longest **cantilever** bridge	Quebec (Railway)	Quebec, Canada	1800-foot span
highest bridge	Royal Gorge	Arkansas River, Colorado	HEIGHT ABOVE WATER 1053 feet
oldest bridge (still in existence)	Meles River	Izmir (Smyrna), Turkey	DATE BUILT 850 B.C.

Man Has Created Many Earth Satellites

SATELLITE	COUNTRY	YEAR LAUNCHED	IMPORTANCE
Sputnik 1	U.S.S.R.	1957	first satellite launched
Vanguard 1	U.S.	1958	first to study Earth from orbit, revealing its "pear shape"
Echo 1	U.S.	1960	relayed first voice and television signals
Tiros 1	U.S.	1960	relayed first cloud-cover photos
Vostok 1	U.S.S.R.	1961	first manned satellite
OSO-1[1]	U.S.	1962	studied sun's effects on Earth
OGO-1[2]	U.S.	1964	studied interaction of Earth and sun
Voskhod 1	U.S.S.R.	1964	carried first three-man crew
Voskhod 2	U.S.S.R.	1965	first walk in space
Nimbus 2	U.S.	1966	telecast day and night cloud cover and measured Earth's heat balance
Explorer 38	U.S.	1968	huge antennas studied radio waves from distant parts of our galaxy
OAO-2[3]	U.S.	1968	outside Earth's atmosphere its 11 telescopes studied stars
Soyuz 4–Soyuz 5	U.S.S.R.	1969	first space transfer between crafts
NATOSAT-1	U.S.	1970	carried military communications
Salyut 1	U.S.S.R.	1971	first orbiting space station
ERTS-1[4]	U.S.	1972	reports air and water pollution, forest and crop conditions, ice movements, and ocean currents
Skylab	U.S.	1973	orbital laboratory was manned by three crews of three men for 171 days
Soyuz 19–Apollo 18	U.S.S.R. U.S.	1975	crews linked up in space and conducted joint experiments
Salyut 7	U.S.S.R.	1984	set manned space endurance record of 237 days
Mir	U.S.S.R.	1986	base unit for planned permanently operated space station; set new space endurance record of 326 days
TDRS-C	U.S.	1988	tracking and data relay satellite for better satellite-to-ground communications
Hubble telescope	U.S.	1990	photographed distant stars and galaxies, increasing our knowledge of the universe

[1] Orbiting Solar Observatory
[2] Orbiting Geophysical Observatory
[3] Orbiting Astronomical Observatory
[4] Earth Resources Technology Satellite

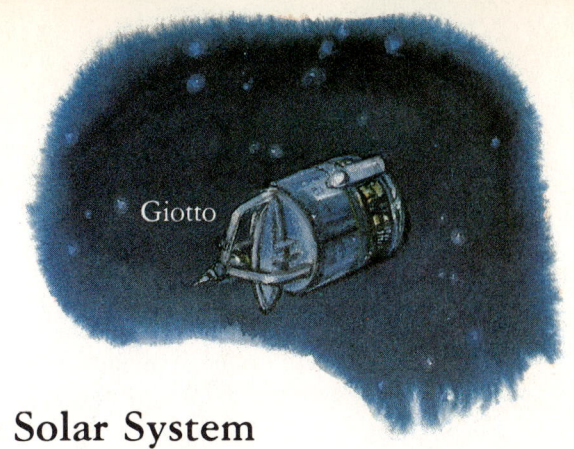

Man Has Explored the Solar System

PROBE	COUNTRY	YEAR LAUNCHED	IMPORTANCE
Pioneer 1	U.S.	1958	first moon shot
Luna 1	U.S.S.R.	1959	first probe to hit moon
Mariner 2	U.S.	1962	first successful flight past Venus
Mariner 4	U.S.	1964	returned first photos of Mars
Venera 3	U.S.S.R.	1965	first probe to land on a planet
Luna 9	U.S.S.R.	1966	first soft landing on moon
Lunar Orbiter 1	U.S.	1966	explored moon and its environment
Apollo 9	U.S.	1969	simulated, in Earth orbit, landing of lunar module, return to, and docking with command module
Apollo 11	U.S.	1969	first men land on moon
Apollo 15	U.S.	1971	first travel on moon in Lunar Roving Vehicle; first deep-space walk
Mariner 9	U.S.	1971	entered Mars orbit and returned 7000 photos of planet's surface
Mars 3	U.S.S.R.	1971	soft-landed space robot on Mars
Apollo 17	U.S.	1972	most successful moon probe, last in the Apollo program
Pioneer 10	U.S.	1972	near perfect launch of probe to study Jupiter and outer fringes of solar system
Voyager 1 and 2	U.S.	1977	highly successful probes to Jupiter, Saturn, Uranus, and Neptune
Vega 1 and 2	U.S.S.R.	1984	mission to Halley's comet
Giotto	European Space Agency	1985	mission to Halley's comet
Suisei and Sakigake	Japan	1985	missions to Halley's comet
Magellan	U.S.	1989	used radar to map surface of Venus
Galileo	U.S.	1989	mission to study Jupiter's atmosphere and moons

Nobel Peace Prize Awards

YEAR	WINNER	COUNTRY
1901	Jean Henry Dunant	Switzerland
	Frédéric Passy	France
1902	Elie Ducommun	Switzerland
	Charles Albert Gobat	Switzerland
1903	Sir William R. Cremer	England
1904	Institute of International Law	Belgium
1905	Baroness Bertha von Suttner	Austria
1906	Theodore Roosevelt	United States
1907	Ernesto Teodora Moneta	Italy
	Louis Renault	France
1908	Klas Pontus Arnoldson	Sweden
	Fredrik Bajer	Denmark
1909	Auguste Beernaert	Belgium
	Baron d'Estournelles de Constant	France
1910	International Peace Bureau	Switzerland
1911	Tobias Asser	Netherlands
	Alfred Fried	Austria
1912	Elihu Root	United States
1913	Henri La Fontaine	Belgium
1917	International Red Cross	Switzerland
1919	Woodrow Wilson	United States
1920	Léon Bourgeois	France
1921	Karl Hjalmar Branting	Sweden
	Christian Louis Lange	Norway
1922	Fridtjof Nansen	Norway
1925	Sir Joseph Austen Chamberlain	England
	Charles Gates Dawes	United States
1926	Aristide Briand	France
	Gustav Stresemann	Germany
1927	Ferdinand Buisson	France
	Ludwig Quidde	Germany
1929	Frank B. Kellogg	United States

(Missing dates indicate years in which Peace Prize was not awarded.)

Theodore Roosevelt

International Red Cross

YEAR	WINNER	COUNTRY
1930	Nathan Söderblom	Sweden
1931	Jane Addams	United States
	Nicholas Murray Butler	United States
1933	Sir Norman Angell	England
1934	Arthur Henderson	England
1935	Carl von Ossietzky	Germany
1936	Carlos Saavedra Lamas	Argentina
1937	Viscount Cecil of Chelwood	England
1938	Nansen International Office for Refugees	Switzerland
1944	International Red Cross	Switzerland
1945	Cordell Hull	United States
1946	Emily Greene Balch	United States
	John R. Mott	United States
1947	American Friends Service Committee	United States
	Friends Service Council	England
1949	Lord Boyd-Orr	England
1950	Ralph Bunche	United States
1951	Léon Jouhaux	France
1952	Albert Schweitzer	Africa
1953	George C. Marshall	United States
1954	Office of the United Nations High Commissioner for Refugees	
1957	Lester B. Pearson	Canada
1958	Dominique Georges Pire	Belgium
1959	Philip J. Noel-Baker	England
1960	Albert John Luthuli	South Africa
1961	Dag Hammarskjold	Sweden
1962	Linus C. Pauling	United States
1963	International Red Cross	Switzerland
	League of Red Cross Societies	Switzerland
1964	Dr. Martin Luther King	United States

Albert Schweitzer

Dr. Martin Luther King, Jr.

WHAT MANKIND HAS DONE

YEAR	WINNER	COUNTRY
1965	United Nations Children's Fund (UNICEF)	
1968	René Cassin	France
1969	International Labor Organization	
1970	Norman E. Borlaug	United States
1971	Willy Brandt	West Germany
1973	Henry Kissinger Le Duc Tho	United States North Vietnam
1974	Sean MacBride Eisaku Sato	Ireland Japan
1975	Andrei D. Sakharov	U.S.S.R.
1976	Mairead Corrigan Betty Williams	Northern Ireland Northern Ireland
1977	Amnesty International	England
1978	Anwar el-Sadat Menachem Begin	Egypt Israel
1979	Mother Teresa of Calcutta	India
1980	Adolfo Pérez Esquivel	Argentina
1981	Office of the United Nations High Commissioner for Refugees	
1982	Alfonso Garcia Robles Alva Myrdal	Mexico Sweden
1983	Lech Walesa	Poland
1984	Bishop Desmond Tutu	South Africa
1985	International Physicians for the Prevention of Nuclear War	
1986	Elie Wiesel	United States
1987	Oscar Arias Sánchez	Costa Rica
1988	United Nations Peacekeeping Forces	
1989	Dalai Lama	Tibet
1990	Mikhail Gorbachev	U.S.S.R.
1991	Daw Aung San Suu Kyi	Myanmar
1992	Rigoberta Menchu	Guatemala
1993	Frederick W. de Klerk Nelson Mandela	South Africa

Mother Teresa of Calcutta

United Nations Peacekeeping Forces

Numbers Tell Us Many Things

NUMBERS ARE A LANGUAGE all to themselves. They help describe to us how long something is, how heavy it is, how much space it takes up, and how much it costs. Numbers are important in everyone's daily life, whether they describe the 25 cents left over from someone's allowance or that the sun is 93 million miles away from Earth.

Listed here are the measurements commonly used in the United States (English system), those used in many different countries (metric system), and the different ways to measure temperature. There are also lists of the values of money in the United States and in many other countries.

NUMBERS TELL US MANY THINGS

Numerals

The most common numerals used throughout the world are the ones we see everyday. They are called

| Hindu-Arabic | 1 | 2 | 3 | 4 | 5 | 6 | 7 | 8 | 9 | 10 |

Other numerals that are used occasionally are

Roman numerals	I	II	III	IV	V	VI	VII	VIII	IX	X
	1	2	3	4	5	6	7	8	9	10

1 9 4 5 = MCMXLV = 1000 + 900 + 40 + 5

L	C	D	M
50	100	500	1000

There have been other sets of numerals used throughout history.

Egyptian	I	II	III	IIII	II / III	III / III	III / IIII	IIII / IIII	III / III / III	∩
	1	2	3	4	5	6	7	8	9	10

Greek	α′	β′	γ′	δ′	ε′	ϛ′	ζ′	η′	θ′	ι′
	1	2	3	4	5	6	7	8	9	10

Chinese	一	二	三	四	五	六	七	八	九	十
	1	2	3	4	5	6	7	8	9	10

Hindu	?	?	?	?	?	?	?	?	?	o
	1	2	3	4	5	6	7	8	9	10

Arabic	١	٢	٣	٤	٥	٦	٧	٨	٩	•
	1	2	3	4	5	6	7	8	9	10

Weights and Measures

Length

ENGLISH SYSTEM	EQUALS	EQUALS IN METRIC SYSTEM
inch		2.54 centimeters
foot	12 inches	.3048 meter
yard	3 feet	.9144 meter
rod	5½ yards	5.0292 meters
furlong	40 rods	201.1684 meters
mile	8 furlongs	1.6093 kilometers

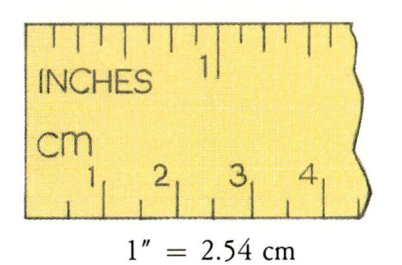

METRIC SYSTEM	EQUALS	EQUALS IN ENGLISH SYSTEM
millimeter		.03937 inch
centimeter	10 millimeters	.3937 inch
decimeter	10 centimeters	3.937 inches
meter	10 decimeters	1.0936 yards
kilometer	1000 meters	.62137 mile

1" = 2.54 cm

Area

ENGLISH SYSTEM	EQUALS	EQUALS IN METRIC SYSTEM
square inch		6.4516 square centimeters
square foot	144 square inches	.0929 square meter
square yard	9 square feet	.8361 square meter
square rod	30¼ square yards	25.293 square meters
acre	160 square rods	.4047 hectare
square mile	640 acres	2.59 square kilometers

1 square inch

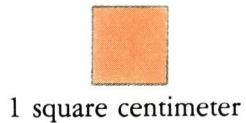

METRIC SYSTEM	EQUALS	EQUALS IN ENGLISH SYSTEM
square millimeter		.002 square inch
square centimeter	100 sq. millimeters	.155 square inch
square decimeter	100 sq. centimeters	15.5 square inches
square meter	100 sq. decimeters	10.7639 square feet
are	100 sq. meters	3.9537 square rods
hectare	100 ares	2.471 acres
square kilometer	100 hectares	.3861 square mile

1 square centimeter

NUMBERS TELL US MANY THINGS

Weight

ENGLISH SYSTEM (avoirdupois)	EQUALS	EQUALS IN METRIC SYSTEM
grain		.0648 gram
dram	27.3438 grains	1.7718 grams
ounce	16 drams	28.3495 grams
pound	16 ounces	.4536 kilogram
ton	2000 pounds	.9072 metric ton

Besides the *avoirdupois* measure of weights in the English system, there are also two different measures—*troy* and *apothecaries*. *Troy* weight is used for weighing gold and silver; *apothecaries'* weight is for measuring medical prescriptions.

METRIC SYSTEM	EQUALS	EQUALS IN ENGLISH SYSTEM (avoirdupois)
milligram		.0154 grain
centigram	10 milligrams	.1543 grain
decigram	10 centigrams	1.5432 grains
gram	10 decigrams	.0353 ounce
kilogram	1000 grams	2.2046 pounds
metric ton	1000 kilograms	1.1023 tons

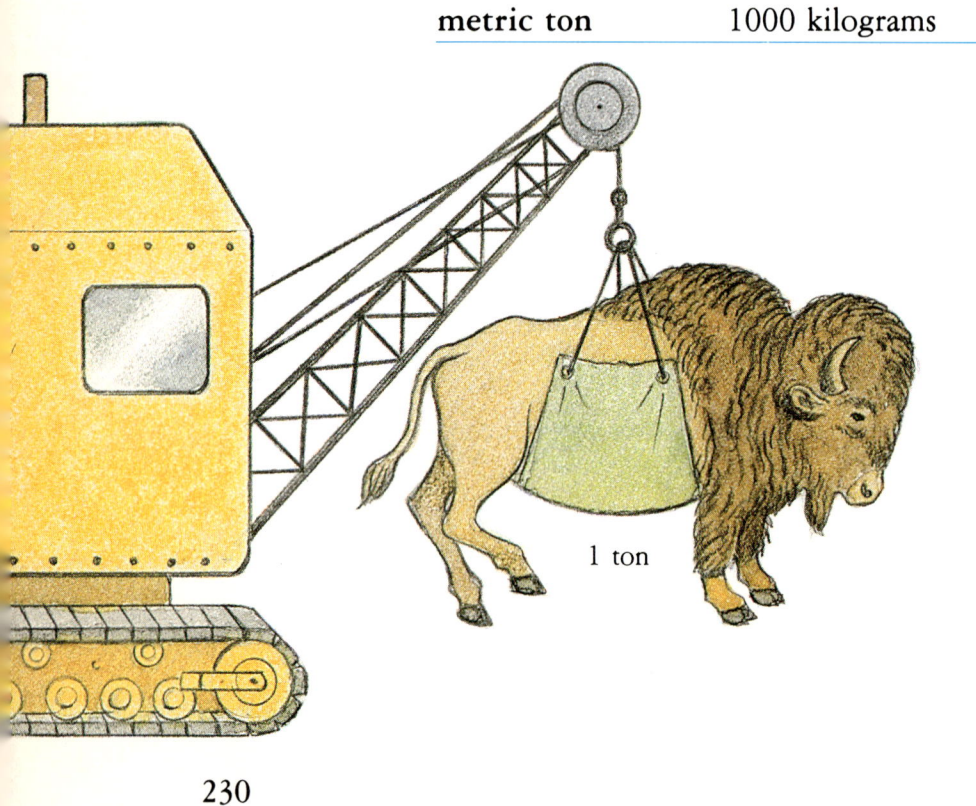

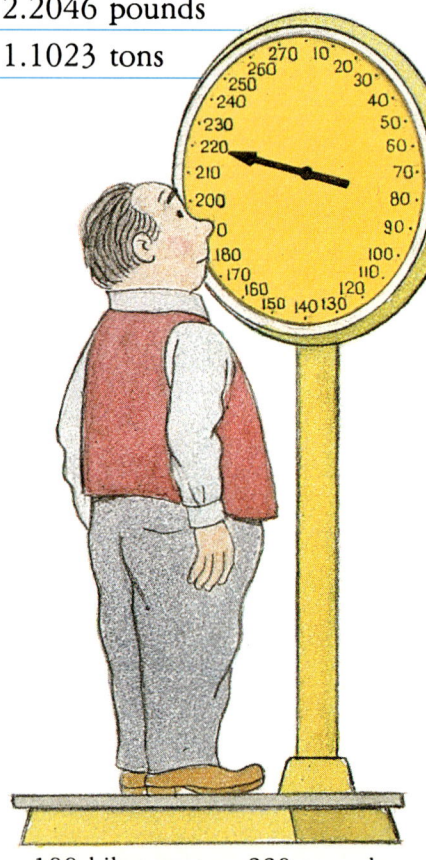

1 ton

230

100 kilograms = 220 pounds

NUMBERS TELL US MANY THINGS

Capacity In the United States there are both *liquid* and *dry* measures. In the metric system, there is only one measure for both liquid and dry units.

UNITED STATES LIQUID MEASURE	EQUALS	EQUALS IN METRIC SYSTEM
fluid ounce		29.574 milliliters
pint	16 fluid ounces	.4732 liter
quart	2 pints	.9463 liter
gallon	4 quarts	3.7853 liters

UNITED STATES DRY MEASURE	EQUALS	EQUALS IN METRIC SYSTEM
pint		.5506 liter
quart	2 pints	1.1012 liters
peck	8 quarts	8.8096 liters
bushel	4 pecks	35.2383 liters

METRIC SYSTEM	EQUALS	EQUAL TO U.S. LIQUID MEASURE	EQUAL TO U.S. DRY MEASURE
milliliter		.0338 fluid ounce	.0018 pint
centiliter	10 milliliters	.3381 fluid ounce	.0182 pint
deciliter	10 centiliters	3.3815 fluid ounces	.1816 pint
liter	10 deciliters	1.0567 quarts	.9081 quart

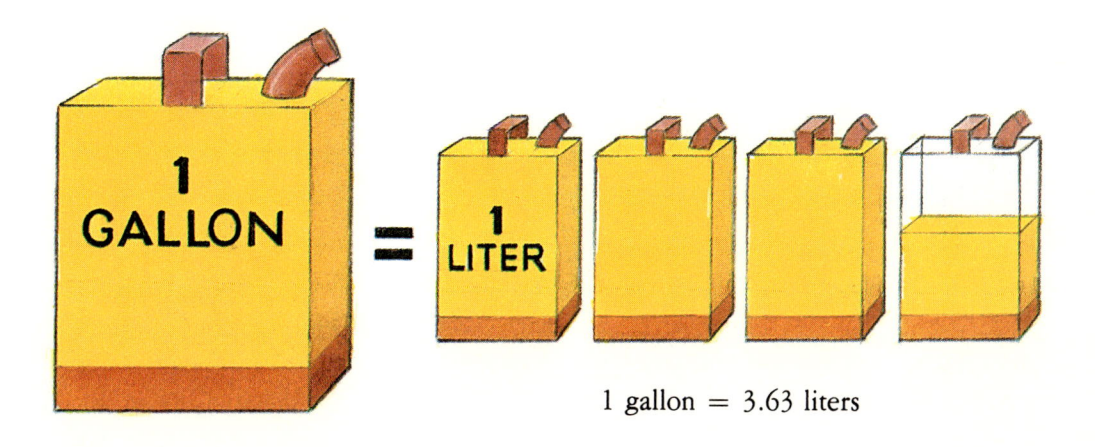

1 gallon = 3.63 liters

NUMBERS TELL US MANY THINGS

Volume

ENGLISH SYSTEM	EQUALS	EQUALS IN METRIC SYSTEM
cubic inch		16.3872 cubic centimeters
cubic foot	1728 cubic inches	.0283 cubic meter
cubic yard	27 cubic feet	.7646 cubic meter
cord	128 cubic feet	3.6246 cubic meters

1 cubic inch

1 cubic centimeter

METRIC SYSTEM	EQUALS	EQUALS IN ENGLISH SYSTEM
cubic millimeter		.00006 cubic inch
cubic centimeter	1000 cubic millimeters	.06102 cubic inch
cubic decimeter	1000 cubic centimeters	61.02374 cubic inches
cubic meter (stere)	1000 cubic decimeters	35.31467 cubic feet

Temperatures

There are two commonly used measures of temperature—*Fahrenheit* and *Celsius*. Fahrenheit is the measure most commonly used in the United States and England. The Celsius scale is used in many other parts of the world, and its use is becoming more widespread in the United States.

Boiling point of water

The average temperature of the human body is 98.6 degrees Fahrenheit (or 37 degrees Celsius).

Freezing point of water

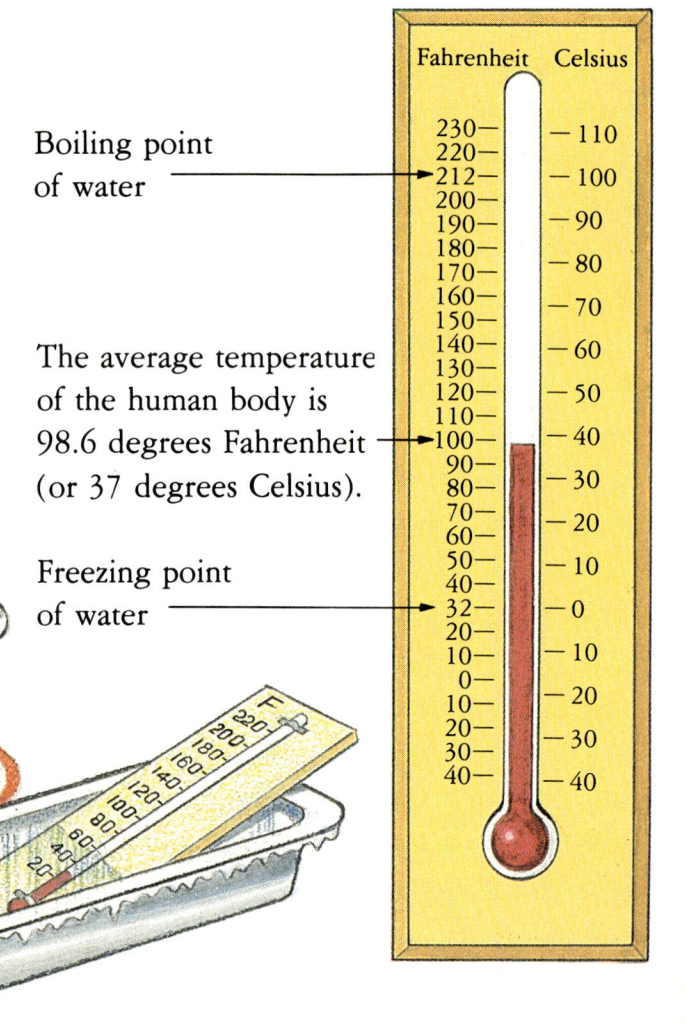

232

Coins and Currency in the United States

Coins

DENOMINATION		PORTRAIT ON COIN	DESIGN ON BACK
cent (penny)	$.01	Abraham Lincoln	Lincoln Memorial
nickel	.05	Thomas Jefferson	Monticello
dime	.10	Franklin D. Roosevelt	Liberty torch between oak and laurel branches
quarter	.25	George Washington	Eagle
half-dollar	.50	John F. Kennedy	Presidential seal surrounded by 50 stars

Nickel

Half-dollar

Twenty dollar bill

Currency (paper money or "bills")

DENOMINATION	PORTRAIT ON BILL	DESIGN ON BACK
$1	George Washington	Word "ONE" between front and back of Great Seal of U.S.
$2	Thomas Jefferson	Monticello
$5	Abraham Lincoln	Lincoln Memorial
$10	Alexander Hamilton	U.S. Treasury Building
$20	Andrew Jackson	White House
$50	Ulysses S. Grant	Capitol
$100	Benjamin Franklin	Independence Hall
$500	William McKinley	Words "FIVE HUNDRED"
$1,000	Grover Cleveland	Words "ONE THOUSAND"
$5,000	James Madison	Words "FIVE THOUSAND"
$10,000	Salmon P. Chase	Words "TEN THOUSAND"
$100,000	Woodrow Wilson	Words "ONE HUNDRED THOUSAND"

The largest denomination bill still being issued is the $100 bill, but the larger denomination bills are still legal currency.

Money from Different Countries

COUNTRY	MONETARY UNIT	COUNTRY	MONETARY UNIT
Australia	dollar	Japan	yen
Belgium	franc	Korea (both)	won
Brazil	cruzeiro	Mexico	peso
Canada	dollar	Netherlands	guilder
China	yuan	Pakistan	rupee
Denmark	krone	Portugal	escudo
Egypt	pound	Russia	ruble
France	franc	Saudi Arabia	riyal
Germany	Deutsche mark	Spain	peseta
Greece	drachma	Sweden	krona
Haiti	gourde	Taiwan	dollar
India	rupee	Turkey	lira
Ireland	pound	United Kingdom	pound
Israel	shekel	Vietnam	dong
Italy	lira	Yugoslavia	dinar

5 lira

1000 yen

Australian 5-dollar bill

British 5-pound note

5 rubles

Our United States

THE EXCITING STORY of the United States began with the Indians, the first Americans. The Indians lived with and sometimes fought with the people who came from Europe to settle in America. In the early days, most of these settlers lived in the 13 colonies. These colonies became the first 13 states of the United States of America.

The country grew to have 50 states, each separate but all united. Contained in this section are facts about the Indians, the colonies, the signers of the Declaration of Independence, the growth of the United States, the Civil War, our presidents, the 50 states, and the U.S. government today.

The Indians

- Chinook
- Tolowa
- Tillamook
- Coos
- Klamath
- Shasta
- Hupa
- Wintun
- Yuki
- Yokuts
- Salinan
- Diegueno

WASHINGTON
- Kalispel
- Wenatchee
- Nez Percé
- Cayuse
- Yakima
- Klikitay

OREGON

- Blackfoot
- Arapaho
- Pend D'Oreilles
- Flathead
- Bannock
- Kiowa

MONTANA

- Apache
- Comanche

IDAHO

WYOMING
- Shoshone

- Gosiute
- Paiute

NEVADA

- Ute

UTAH

COLORADO
- Ute

NORTH DAKOTA
- Dako
- Mandan
- Sic

SOUTH DAKOT
- Ponca
- Om

NEBRASKA

- Pawnee
- Ka

KANS

CALIFORNIA

ARIZONA
- Mohave
- Hopi
- Pima
- Maricopa
- Yuma
- Chiricahua
- Papago

- Navaho
- Pueblo
- Zuni
- Apache

NEW MEXICO
- White Mountain
- Mescalero Apache

Wich
OKLA

TEX
- Tonkawan Trib

Legend
- West Coast Indians
- High Plains Indians
- Southwest Indians
- Plains Indians
- Southeast Indians
- Woodlands Indians

The First Americans

The Men Who Signed the Declaration of Independence

SIGNER	STATE	SIGNER	STATE
John Adams	Massachusetts	**Thomas Lynch, Jr.**	South Carolina
Samuel Adams	Massachusetts	**Thomas McKean**	Delaware
Josiah Bartlett	New Hampshire	**Arthur Middleton**	South Carolina
Carter Braxton	Virginia	**Lewis Morris**	New York
Charles Carroll	Maryland	**Robert Morris**	Pennsylvania
Samuel Chase	Maryland	**John Morton**	Pennsylvania
Abraham Clark	New Jersey	**Thomas Nelson, Jr.**	Virginia
George Clymer	Pennsylvania	**William Paca**	Maryland
William Ellery	Rhode Island	**Robert Treat Paine**	Massachusetts
William Floyd	New York	**John Penn**	North Carolina
Benjamin Franklin	Pennsylvania	**George Read**	Delaware
Elbridge Gerry	Massachusetts	**Caesar Rodney**	Delaware
Button Gwinnett	Georgia	**George Ross**	Pennsylvania
Lyman Hall	Georgia	**Benjamin Rush**	Pennsylvania
John Hancock	Massachusetts	**Edward Rutledge**	South Carolina
Benjamin Harrison	Virginia	**Roger Sherman**	Connecticut
John Hart	New Jersey	**James Smith**	Pennsylvania
Joseph Hewes	North Carolina	**Richard Stockton**	New Jersey
Thomas Heyward, Jr.	South Carolina	**Thomas Stone**	Maryland
William Hooper	North Carolina	**George Taylor**	Pennsylvania
Stephen Hopkins	Rhode Island	**Matthew Thornton**	New Hampshire
Francis Hopkinson	New Jersey	**George Walton**	Georgia
Samuel Huntington	Connecticut	**William Whipple**	New Hampshire
Thomas Jefferson	Virginia	**William Williams**	Connecticut
Francis Lightfoot Lee	Virginia	**James Wilson**	Pennsylvania
Richard Henry Lee	Virginia	**John Witherspoon**	New Jersey
Francis Lewis	New York	**Oliver Wolcott**	Connecticut
Philip Livingston	New York	**George Wythe**	Virginia

The Original Thirteen Colonies

COLONY	FIRST PERMANENT SETTLEMENT	ENTERED UNION
Connecticut	Hartford (1635)	January 9, 1788
Delaware	Wilmington (1638)	December 7, 1787
Georgia	Savannah (1733)	January 2, 1788
Maryland	St. Mary's (1634)	April 28, 1788
Massachusetts	Plymouth (1620)	February 6, 1788
New Hampshire	Rye (1623)	June 21, 1788
New Jersey	Elizabeth (1664)	December 18, 1787
New York	New York City (1614)	July 26, 1788
North Carolina	Albemarle (1653)	November 21, 1789
Pennsylvania	Tinicum Island (1643)	December 12, 1787
Rhode Island	Providence (1636)	May 29, 1790
South Carolina	Albemarle Point (1670)	May 23, 1788
Virginia	Jamestown (1607)	June 25, 1788

How the United States Grew

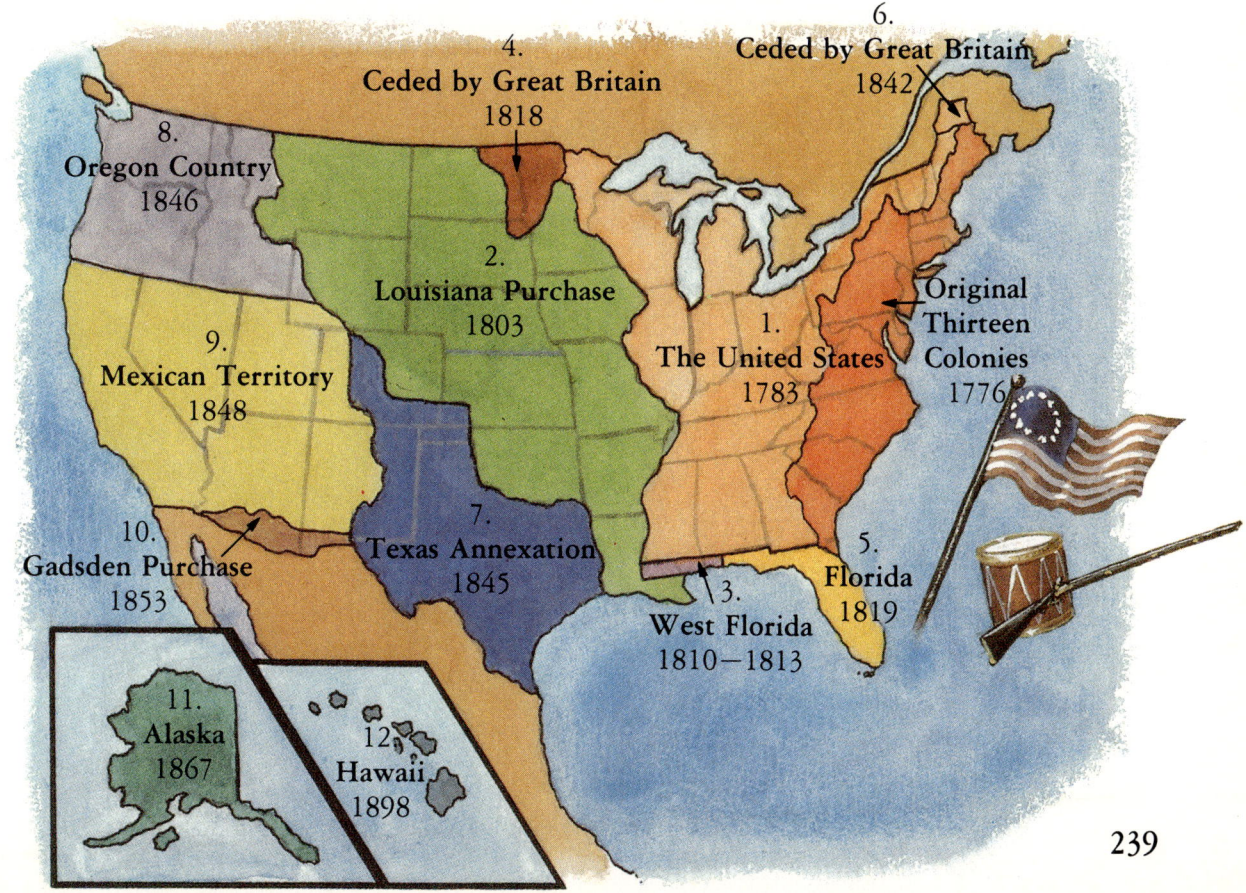

1. The United States 1783 — Original Thirteen Colonies 1776
2. Louisiana Purchase 1803
3. West Florida 1810–1813
4. Ceded by Great Britain 1818
5. Florida 1819
6. Ceded by Great Britain 1842
7. Texas Annexation 1845
8. Oregon Country 1846
9. Mexican Territory 1848
10. Gadsden Purchase 1853
11. Alaska 1867
12. Hawaii 1898

OUR UNITED STATES

The Civil War States (1861–1865)

UNION	CONFEDERACY	DATE OF SECESSION	READMITTED TO THE UNION
California	Alabama	January 11, 1861	June 25, 1868
Connecticut	Arkansas	May 6, 1861	June 22, 1868
Delaware	Florida	January 10, 1861	June 25, 1868
Illinois	Georgia	January 19, 1861	July 15, 1870
Indiana	Louisiana	January 26, 1861	June 25, 1868
Iowa	Mississippi	January 9, 1861	February 23, 1870
Kansas	North Carolina	May 20, 1861	June 25, 1868
Kentucky	South Carolina	December 20, 1860	June 25, 1868
Maine	Tennessee	June 8, 1861	July 24, 1866
Maryland	Texas	February 23, 1861	March 30, 1870
Massachusetts	Virginia	April 17, 1861	January 26, 1870
Michigan			
Minnesota			
Missouri			
Nevada			
New Hampshire			
New Jersey			
New York			
Ohio			
Oregon			
Pennsylvania			
Rhode Island			
Vermont			
West Virginia			
Wisconsin			

- Union States
- Confederate States
- Territories

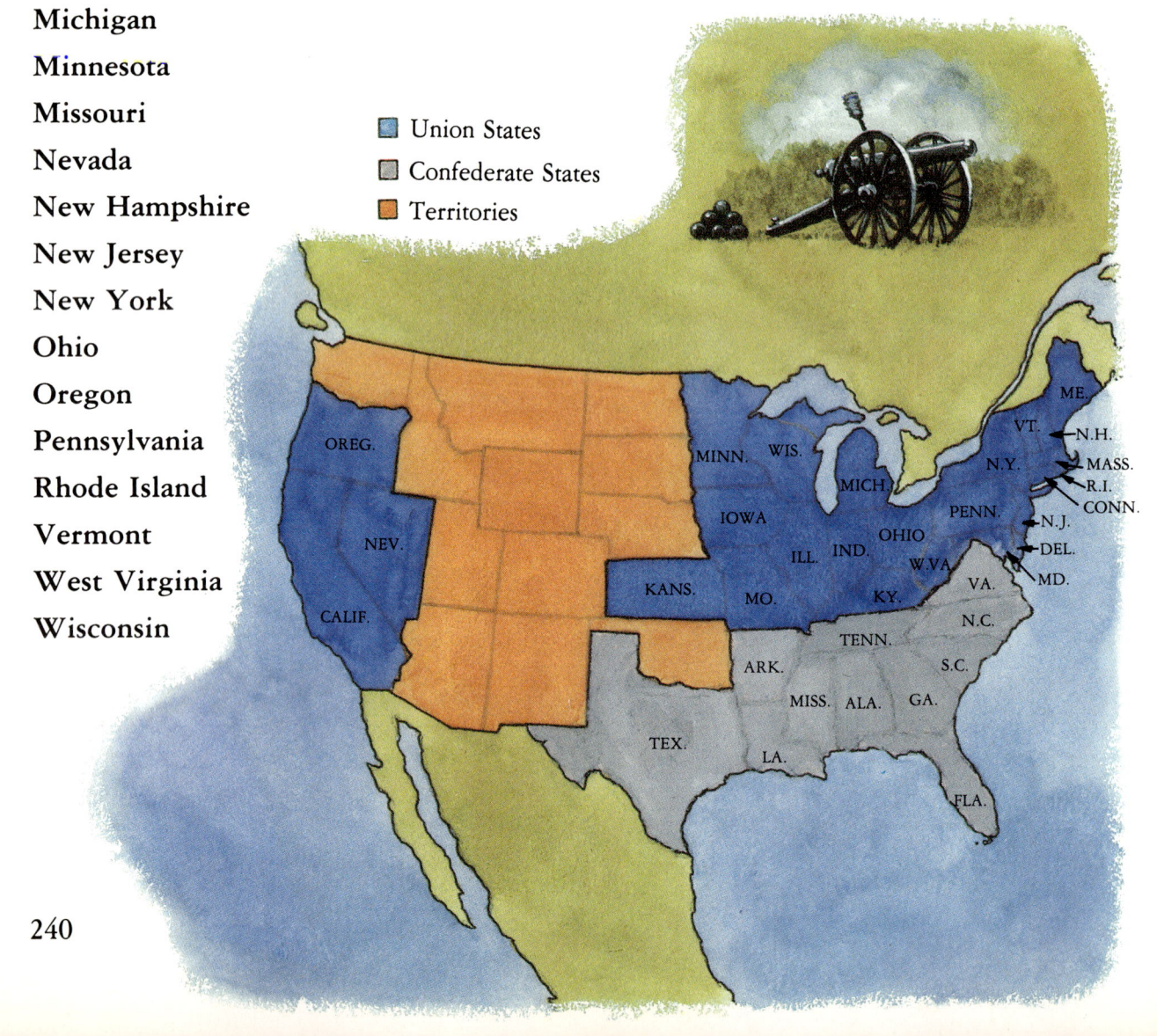

240

OUR UNITED STATES

The Growth of American Railroads

As the United States grew, so did American railroads, linking cities and towns from coast to coast. The coming of the automobile and the building of new roads and highways in the 20th century made the railroads less important as a means of transportation.

Main Rail Lines About 1900

- New York Central
- Erie
- Pennsylvania
- Baltimore & Ohio
- Southern
- Chesapeake & Ohio
- Illinois Central
- Atchison, Topeka & Santa Fe
- Great Northern
- Northern Pacific
- Southern Pacific
- Union Pacific

YEAR	TRACK MILEAGE
1830	23 miles
1840	2,808 miles
1850	9,021 miles
1860	30,626 miles
1870	52,922 miles
1880	93,267 miles
1890	163,597 miles
1900	193,346 miles
1910	240,439 miles
1920	**252,845 miles**
1930	249,052 miles
1940	233,670 miles
1950	223,779 miles
1960	217,552 miles
1970	206,000 miles
1975	199,000 miles
1980	179,000 miles
1985	155,000 miles

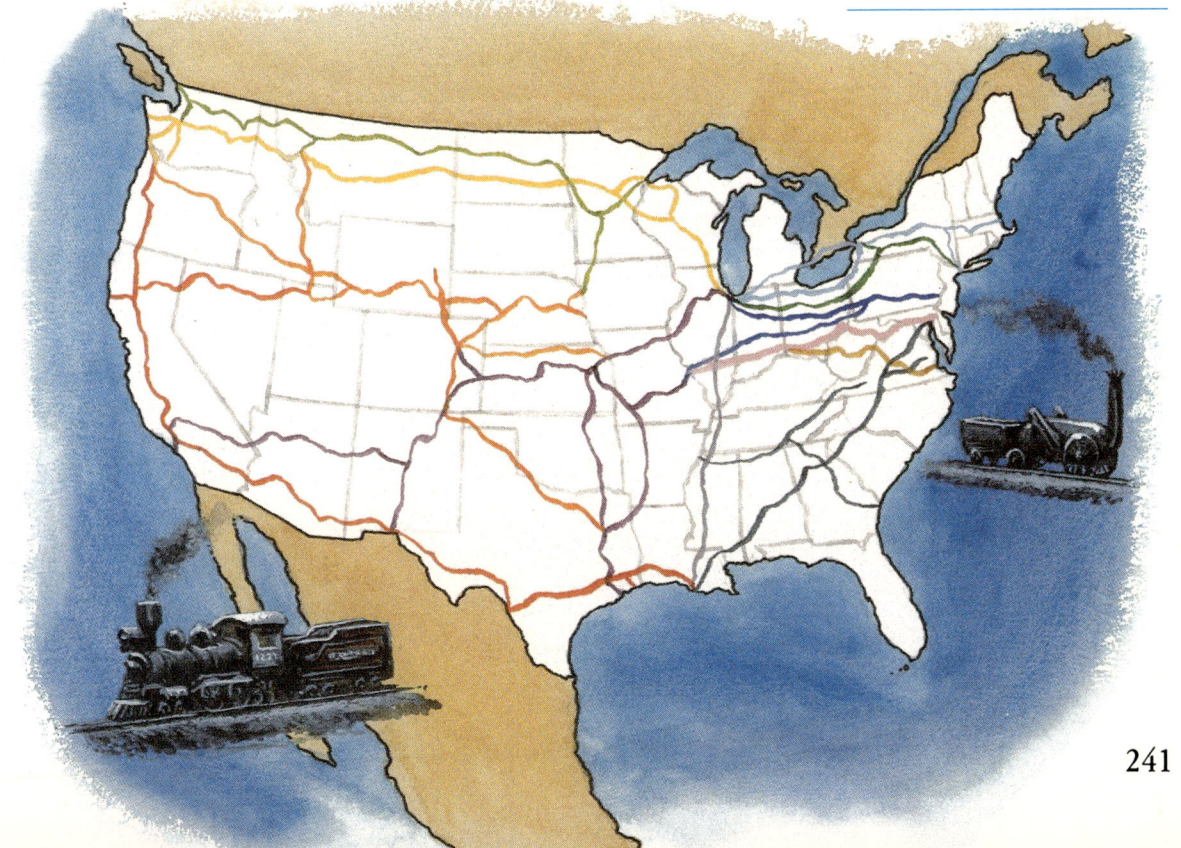

241

George Washington

Thomas Jefferson

Abraham Lincoln

Presidents of the United States

PRESIDENT	BIRTHPLACE	POLITICAL PARTY	OCCUPATION	TERM OF OFFICE
1 George Washington	Virginia	Federalist	planter, soldier	1789–1797
2 John Adams	Massachusetts	Federalist	lawyer	1797–1801
3 Thomas Jefferson	Virginia	Democratic Republican	lawyer	1801–1809
4 James Madison	Virginia	Democratic Republican	planter	1809–1817
5 James Monroe	Virginia	Democratic Republican	lawyer	1817–1825
6 John Quincy Adams	Massachusetts	Democratic Republican	lawyer	1825–1829
7 Andrew Jackson	South Carolina	Democratic	lawyer, soldier	1829–1837
8 Martin Van Buren	New York	Democratic	lawyer	1837–1841
9 William Henry Harrison	Virginia	Whig	soldier	1841
10 John Tyler	Virginia	Whig	lawyer	1841–1845
11 James K. Polk	North Carolina	Democratic	lawyer	1845–1849
12 Zachary Taylor	Virginia	Whig	soldier	1849–1850
13 Millard Fillmore	New York	Whig	lawyer	1850–1853
14 Franklin Pierce	New Hampshire	Democratic	lawyer	1853–1857
15 James Buchanan	Pennsylvania	Democratic	lawyer	1857–1861
16 Abraham Lincoln	Kentucky	Republican	lawyer	1861–1865
17 Andrew Johnson	North Carolina	Democratic	legislator	1865–1869
18 Ulysses S. Grant	Ohio	Republican	soldier	1869–1877
19 Rutherford B. Hayes	Ohio	Republican	lawyer	1877–1881
20 James A. Garfield	Ohio	Republican	educator, soldier	1881

Franklin D. Roosevelt

John F. Kennedy

George Bush

PRESIDENT	BIRTHPLACE	POLITICAL PARTY	OCCUPATION	TERM OF OFFICE
21 Chester A. Arthur	Vermont	Republican	lawyer	1881–1885
22 Grover Cleveland	New Jersey	Democratic	lawyer	1885–1889
23 Benjamin Harrison	Ohio	Republican	lawyer	1889–1893
24 Grover Cleveland	New Jersey	Democratic	lawyer	1893–1897
25 William McKinley	Ohio	Republican	lawyer, soldier	1897–1901
26 Theodore Roosevelt	New York	Republican	soldier	1901–1909
27 William Howard Taft	Ohio	Republican	lawyer	1909–1913
28 Woodrow Wilson	Virginia	Democratic	educator	1913–1921
29 Warren G. Harding	Ohio	Republican	newspaper publisher	1921–1923
30 Calvin Coolidge	Vermont	Republican	lawyer	1923–1929
31 Herbert C. Hoover	Iowa	Republican	mining engineer	1929–1933
32 Franklin D. Roosevelt	New York	Democratic	lawyer	1933–1945
33 Harry S. Truman	Missouri	Democratic	businessman, legislator	1945–1953
34 Dwight D. Eisenhower	Texas	Republican	soldier	1953–1961
35 John F. Kennedy	Massachusetts	Democratic	legislator	1961–1963
36 Lyndon B. Johnson	Texas	Democratic	legislator	1963–1969
37 Richard M. Nixon	California	Republican	lawyer	1969–1974
38 Gerald R. Ford	Nebraska	Republican	lawyer	1974–1977
39 James Earl Carter	Georgia	Democratic	businessman	1977–1981
40 Ronald Reagan	Illinois	Republican	actor	1981–1989
41 George Bush	Massachusetts	Republican	businessman	1989–1993
42 William J. Clinton	Arkansas	Democratic	lawyer	1993–

OUR UNITED STATES

The Fifty States

STATE	CAPITAL	ENTERED UNION	REPRESENTATIVES IN CONGRESS	NICKNAME
Alabama	Montgomery	1819	7	Yellowhammer State
Alaska	Juneau	1959	1	Land of the Midnight Sun
Arizona	Phoenix	1912	5	Grand Canyon State
Arkansas	Little Rock	1836	4	Land of Opportunity
California	Sacramento	1850	45	Golden State
Colorado	Denver	1876	6	Centennial State
Connecticut	Hartford	1788	6	Nutmeg State
Delaware	Dover	1787	1	Diamond State
Florida	Tallahassee	1845	19	Sunshine State
Georgia	Atlanta	1788	10	Peach State
Hawaii	Honolulu	1959	2	Aloha State
Idaho	Boise	1890	2	Gem State
Illinois	Springfield	1818	22	Prairie State
Indiana	Indianapolis	1816	10	Hoosier State
Iowa	Des Moines	1846	6	Hawkeye State
Kansas	Topeka	1861	5	Sunflower State
Kentucky	Frankfort	1792	7	Bluegrass State
Louisiana	Baton Rouge	1812	8	Pelican State
Maine	Augusta	1820	2	Pine Tree State
Maryland	Annapolis	1788	8	Free State
Massachusetts	Boston	1788	11	Bay State
Michigan	Lansing	1837	18	Wolverine State
Minnesota	St. Paul	1858	8	Gopher State
Mississippi	Jackson	1817	5	Magnolia State

Alaska

OUR UNITED STATES

FLOWER	BIRD	MOTTO
camellia	yellowhammer	We dare defend our rights
forget-me-not	willow ptarmigan	North to the future
saguaro	cactus wren	God enriches
apple blossom	mockingbird	The people rule
golden poppy	California valley quail	Eureka (I have found it)
Rocky Mountain columbine	lark bunting	Nothing without Providence
mountain laurel	robin	He who transplanted still sustains
peach blossom	blue hen chicken	Liberty and independence
orange blossom	mockingbird	In God we trust
Cherokee rose	brown thrasher	Wisdom, justice, and moderation
hibiscus	Hawaiian goose	The life of the land is perpetuated in righteousness
syringa	mountain bluebird	May you last forever
violet	cardinal	State sovereignty, national union
peony	cardinal	The crossroads of America
wild rose	Eastern goldfinch	Our liberties we prize and our rights we will maintain
sunflower	Western meadow lark	To the stars through difficulties
goldenrod	cardinal	United we stand, divided we fall
magnolia	Eastern brown pelican	Union, justice and confidence
white pine cone and tassel	chickadee	I direct
blackeyed Susan	Baltimore oriole	Manly deeds, womanly words
mayflower	chickadee	By the sword we seek peace but peace only under liberty
apple blossom	robin	If you seek a pleasant peninsula, look around you
showy lady's slipper	common loon	The star of the north
magnolia	mockingbird	By valor and arms

Nevada

STATE	CAPITAL	ENTERED UNION	REPRESENTATIVES IN CONGRESS	NICKNAME
Missouri	Jefferson City	1821	9	Show-Me State
Montana	Helena	1889	2	Treasure State
Nebraska	Lincoln	1867	3	Cornhusker State
Nevada	Carson City	1864	2	Sagebrush State
New Hampshire	Concord	1788	2	Granite State
New Jersey	Trenton	1787	14	Garden State
New Mexico	Santa Fe	1912	3	Land of Enchantment
New York	Albany	1788	34	Empire State
North Carolina	Raleigh	1789	11	Tar Heel State
North Dakota	Bismarck	1889	1	Sioux State
Ohio	Columbus	1803	21	Buckeye State
Oklahoma	Oklahoma City	1907	6	Sooner State
Oregon	Salem	1859	5	Beaver State
Pennsylvania	Harrisburg	1787	23	Keystone State
Rhode Island	Providence	1790	2	Ocean State
South Carolina	Columbia	1788	6	Palmetto State
South Dakota	Pierre	1889	1	Sunshine State
Tennessee	Nashville	1796	9	Volunteer State
Texas	Austin	1845	27	Lone Star State
Utah	Salt Lake City	1896	3	Beehive State
Vermont	Montpelier	1791	1	Green Mountain State
Virginia	Richmond	1788	10	Old Dominion State
Washington	Olympia	1889	8	Evergreen State
West Virginia	Charleston	1863	4	Mountain State
Wisconsin	Madison	1848	9	Badger State
Wyoming	Cheyenne	1890	1	Equality State

OUR UNITED STATES

FLOWER	BIRD	MOTTO
hawthorn	bluebird	The welfare of the people shall be the supreme law
bitter root	Western meadow lark	Gold and silver
goldenrod	Western meadow lark	Equality before the law
sagebrush	mountain bluebird	All for our country
purple lilac	purple finch	Live free or die
violet	Eastern goldfinch	Liberty and prosperity
yucca	roadrunner	It grows as it goes
rose	bluebird	Ever upward
dogwood	cardinal	To be rather than to seem
wild prairie rose	Western meadow lark	Liberty and union, now and forever, one and inseparable
scarlet carnation	cardinal	With God, all things are possible
mistletoe	scissor-tailed flycatcher	Labor conquers all things
Oregon grape	Western meadow lark	She flies with her own wings
mountain laurel	ruffed grouse	Virtue, liberty, and independence
violet	Rhode Island red	Hope
Carolina yellow jessamine	Carolina wren	Prepared in mind and resources
pasqueflower	ring-necked pheasant	Under God the people rule
iris	mockingbird	Tennessee—America at its best
bluebonnet	mockingbird	Friendship
sego lily	seagull	Industry
red clover	hermit thrush	Freedom and unity
dogwood	cardinal	Thus always to tyrants
coast rhododendron	willow goldfinch	By and by
rhododendron	cardinal	Mountaineers are always free
wood violet	robin	Forward
Indian paintbrush	meadow lark	Equal rights

247

OUR UNITED STATES

The United States Government Today

Executive Branch

President

Vice President

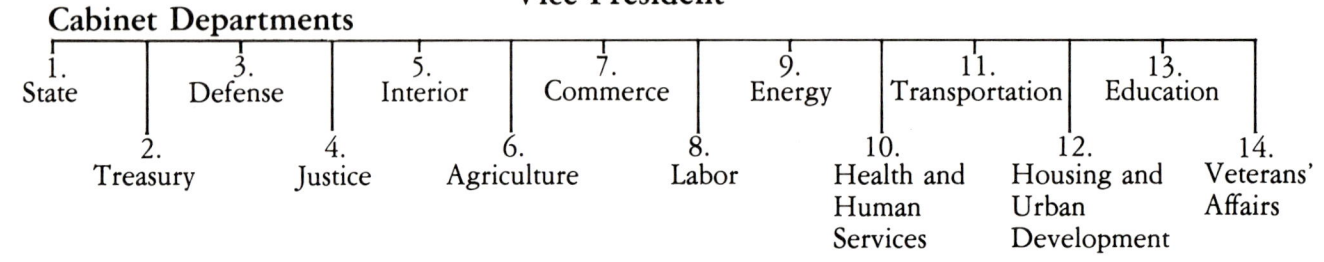

Cabinet Departments

1. State
2. Treasury
3. Defense
4. Justice
5. Interior
6. Agriculture
7. Commerce
8. Labor
9. Energy
10. Health and Human Services
11. Transportation
12. Housing and Urban Development
13. Education
14. Veterans' Affairs

Important Bureaus and Offices in Executive Branch
(numbers identify Cabinet departments, as shown above)

BUREAU/OFFICE	DEPARTMENT
Air Force	3
Alcohol, Drug Abuse, and Mental Health	10
Army	3
Bureau of Alcohol, Tobacco, and Firearms	2
Census	7
Centers for Disease Control	10
Coast Guard	11
Council of Economic Advisers	*
Customs	2
Defense Intelligence Agency	3
Drug Enforcement Administration	4
Federal Bureau of Investigation	4
Fish and Wildlife Service	5
Food and Drug Administration	10
Food and Nutrition Service	6
Foreign Service	1
Forest Service	6
Geological Survey	5
Health Care Financing Administration	10

BUREAU/OFFICE	DEPARTMENT
Immigration and Naturalization Service	4
Indian Affairs	5
Internal Revenue Service	2
Labor Statistics	8
Land Management	5
Marine Corps	3
Mine Safety and Health Administration	8
Bureau of Mines	5
National Bureau of Standards	7
National Institutes of Health	10
National Oceanic and Atmospheric Administration	7
National Parks Service	5
National Security Council	*
Navy	3
Office of Management and Budget	*
Patent and Trademark Office	7
Secret Service	2
Social Security Administration	10

*Executive office

OUR UNITED STATES

Legislative Branch

Congress
House of Representatives — Senate

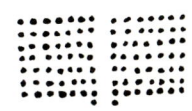

Speaker of the House

435 members
The number from each state is determined by the population of the state.
(See THE FIFTY STATES for number from each state.)

President of the Senate
(Vice President of the United States)

100 members
two from each state

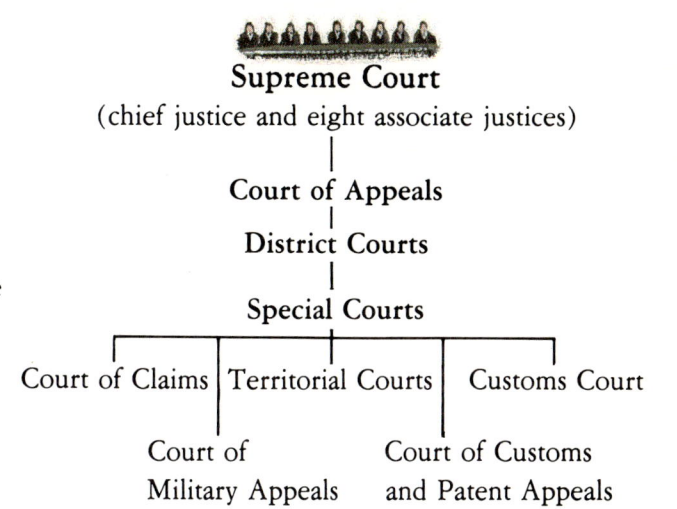

Judicial Branch

Supreme Court
(chief justice and eight associate justices)

Court of Appeals

District Courts

Special Courts

Court of Claims | Territorial Courts | Customs Court

Court of Military Appeals | Court of Customs and Patent Appeals

---

Independent Agencies in Executive Branch

ACTION
Agency for International Development
Arms Control and Disarmament Agency
Central Intelligence Agency
Consumer Product Safety Commission
Environmental Protection Agency
Equal Employment Opportunity Commission
Farm Credit Administration
Federal Communications Commission
Federal Deposit Insurance Corporation
Federal Election Commission
Federal Home Loan Bank Board
Federal Mediation and Conciliation Service
Federal Reserve System
Federal Trade Commission

General Services Administration
Interstate Commerce Commission
National Aeronautics and Space Administration
National Foundation on the Arts and Humanities
National Labor Relations Board
National Mediation Board
National Science Foundation
Nuclear Regulatory Commission
Securities and Exchange Commission
Selective Service System
Small Business Administration
Smithsonian Institution
Tennessee Valley Authority
United States Postal Service
Veterans Administration

Sports

SPORTS ARE FUN to watch, and it is exciting to cheer for favorite teams and athletes. But, most of all, sports are fun to play. Baseball, football, and basketball are probably the three most popular sports in America, for both the athletes and their fans. Soccer is growing rapidly in popularity, especially among young people. Other favorite sports include swimming, skiing, track and field events, tennis, golf, and volleyball.

Each sport has its own set of rules and equipment, but there is one ideal common to all sports: "It is not whether you win or lose, but how you play the game." Keep this in mind as you play, and you should always enjoy your favorite sports.

SPORTS

Baseball

Object The object of the game is to see which team can score more runs during the innings the teams have agreed to play. A team scores a run when a player, after reaching first, second, and third base, safely crosses home plate.

What You Need to Play In order to start a baseball game, you should have the following:

1. **Playing area**—An outdoor area on which a diamond can be laid out (see diagram).
2. **Bases**—Pieces of soft rubber or other flexible material that will not hurt a player sliding into base.
3. **Bat and ball**—The ball may be a regulation league baseball (9-inch), or a rubber ball the same size. Softball is played with a larger ball (either 12-inch or 16-inch). The playing area for softball is smaller than that for baseball (see diagram). A plain rubber ball is suggested for young people just learning to play baseball.
4. **Gloves**—When playing with a ball the size of a regulation league baseball or a 12-inch softball, all players in the field should wear gloves. The softball glove has a slightly larger pocket than the baseball glove. Gloves are not necessary if you are playing with a 16-inch softball.
5. **Players**—Enough players for two teams. A full team has nine players. "Choose-up" games can be played with as few as five players on a team.

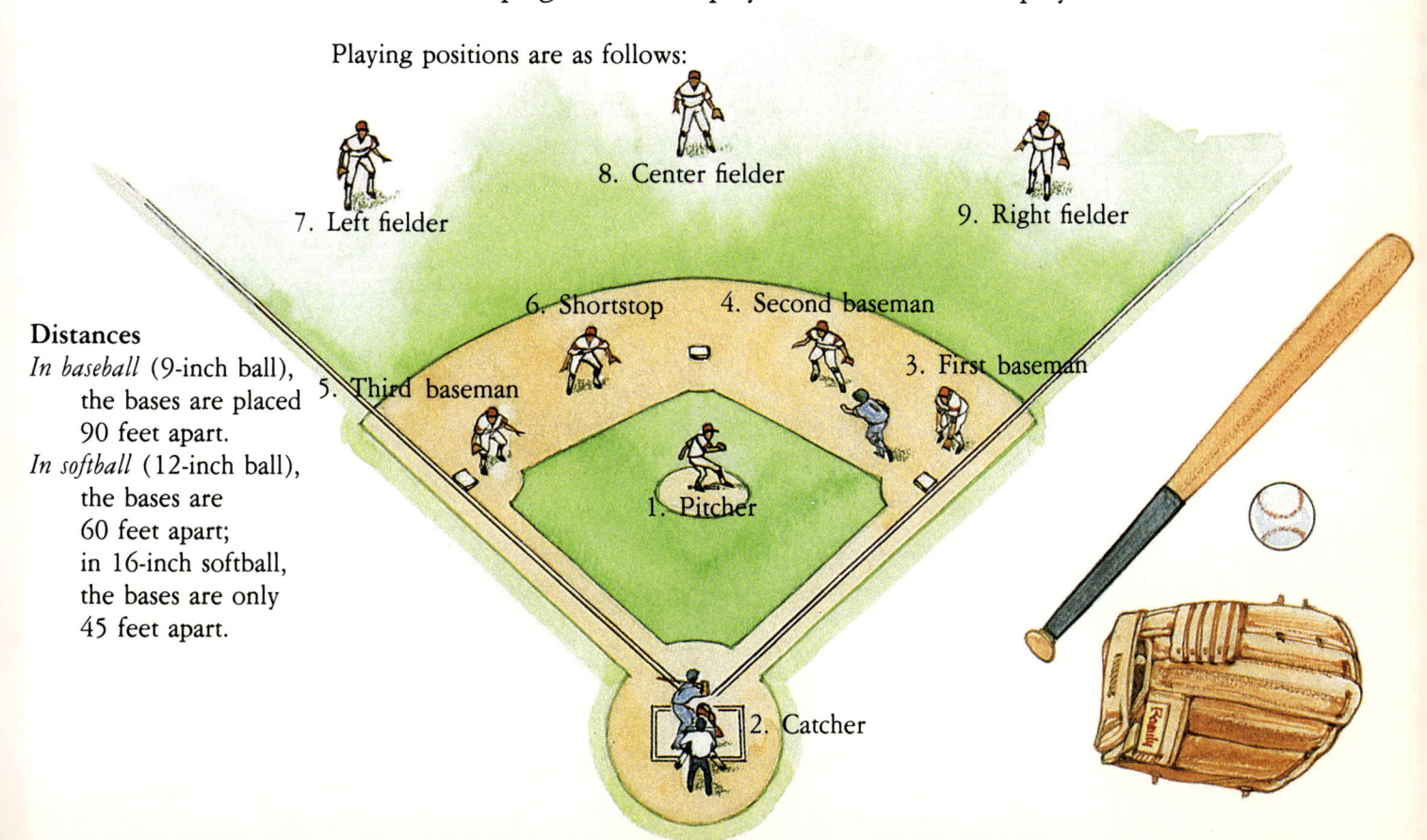

Playing positions are as follows:

7. Left fielder
8. Center fielder
9. Right fielder
6. Shortstop
4. Second baseman
5. Third baseman
3. First baseman
1. Pitcher
2. Catcher

Distances
In baseball (9-inch ball), the bases are placed 90 feet apart.
In softball (12-inch ball), the bases are 60 feet apart; in 16-inch softball, the bases are only 45 feet apart.

SPORTS

Baseball Terms

Players should understand the following baseball terms:

Inning—The period of time when both teams bat. Team 1 bats until it makes three outs. Then it takes the field and team 2 comes to bat. When team 2 makes three outs, the inning is over. Games are usually seven or nine innings. Players may decide to play fewer innings if they wish. More innings are played if the score is tied at the end of the game.

Pitch—The throwing of the ball over home plate by the pitcher of the team in the field. In hardball (9-inch ball), the pitch is thrown overhand. In softball (12-inch or 16-inch), it is thrown underhand.

Strike—If the batter does not swing at the ball when it is pitched, and the pitch is over home plate and between the knees and shoulders of the batter, the pitch is called a strike. It is also a strike if the batter swings at a pitched ball and misses. A ball hit into foul territory and not caught on the fly (before touching the ground) by the opposition is also called a strike. A foul ball hit on the *third* strike does not count unless it is caught. Then the batter is out.

Ball—If a pitched ball is not swung at, and if the ball does not come over home plate, or is over the plate but below the batter's knees or above the shoulders, it is called a ball.

Walk—The batter is allowed to go to first base if the pitcher throws four balls.

Strike out—The batter is out for having three strikes.

Fair ball—A batted ball that is hit somewhere between the first and third baselines. The team in the field must play this ball in order to get the batter out.

Foul ball—A batted ball outside either the first or third baselines. The batter is out only if a member of the opposition catches the ball on the fly.

252

How to Play

Remember the following when you are at bat:

1. Grip the bat in both hands above the knob at the bottom of the bat. If you are right-handed, your right hand should be above your left hand. The bottom of your right hand touches the top of your left hand.
2. Hold the bat in an upright position with your hands about chest high and away from your body. Do not let the bat rest on your shoulder as the pitcher prepares to pitch the ball.
3. When the pitcher throws the ball, watch the ball all the way until your bat hits it.
4. After hitting the ball, drop the bat. Do not throw it! Run to first base as fast as you can.

The team in the field tries to get each of the opposition batters out. A batter is out if:

1. He or she strikes out.
2. The batted ball is caught on the fly in fair or foul territory by a member of the opposition.
3. He or she hits a fair ball on the ground (a grounder), and a player in the field catches the ball and throws it to the first baseman, who tags first base before the batter touches first base. The first baseman need only tag first base with a foot. If the ball is hit to the first baseman, a teammate may cover first base.
4. After hitting a fair ball, arriving safely at first base, and continuing around the base path, the batter is tagged with the ball by a member of the opposition before he or she gets to second base, third base, or home plate.

The batter is safe at first base if:
1. He or she gets a walk.
2. A batted ball in fair territory is not caught on the fly, and the batter reaches first base before a member of the opposition with the ball tags first base.

The batter who has reached first base safely may try for second base if the batter thinks he or she can reach it before an opposing team member gets the ball and tags him or her with it. If the batter is tagged before reaching second base, he or she is out. The same is true if the batter tries for third base after reaching second base safely, or if the batter tries to get to home plate after reaching third base safely.

If a player is on first base and the next batter hits any fair ball that is not caught on the fly by the opposition, the base runner must advance to another base. He or she may only move *forward* (to second base to third base to home plate).

When the base runners advance on a batted ball, the opposition may get an out:
1. If a player in the field gets the ball and tags second base before the runner on first reaches second base (this type of an out is called a "force out").
2. If there are runners on first and second base and the team in the field forces them out at second or third base. If there are runners on all the bases, there are possible force outs at home plate, at third base, and at second base, in addition to the possible out at first base.
3. If a runner is tagged with the ball by a player in the field while the runner is off the base or between bases.

If a batted ball is caught on the fly by the team in the field, the batter is out, and a base runner cannot advance to the next base until after the ball has been caught. If the base runner leaves the base before the ball is caught, and the opposition tags the base the runner left, the base runner is out. Two outs would have been made on one play. This is called a "double play."

A base runner does not have to advance to the next base on a batted ball if he or she is on second or third base and there is no runner on first base. In this situation, the base runner should stay if he or she does not think the next base can be reached safely (without the base runner being tagged out). Remember, though, that when the ball is batted, base runners should try to advance as far as possible so as to score a run.

A base runner can never pass another base runner in front. A runner is out for passing another base runner.

Baseball or softball may be played "pitcher's-hands-out" rather than first-base-out. In pitcher's-hands-out, if a batter hits a grounder to an infielder, the infielder does *not* throw to the first baseman. He throws the ball to the pitcher, who must remain in the area of the pitcher's mound. If the pitcher catches the ball before the batter reaches first base, the batter is out.

Pitcher's-hands-out is not part of the official rules of baseball or softball, but it can be used to make a game more lively and more fun.

With young players, it often makes for a better game if balls and strikes are not called. The only strikes recorded would be foul balls or a swing and a miss. This system is not in the official rules, but it encourages players to swing at the ball and learn to hit. It is also practical because there often is no umpire in a choose-up game.

Since catching equipment (mask, chest protector, shin guards, cup) is usually available only in organized leagues, catchers in choose-up games should stand, not squat, far behind the batter.

Young players should also play in gym shoes rather than in spiked "baseball shoes."

SPORTS

Football

Object — The object of the game is to advance the football across your opponent's goal line and to prevent him from crossing your goal line.

What You Need to Play — In order to start a game, you must have:

1. **Playing area**—A regulation football field is 100 yards long (the goal lines are 100 yards apart). There is an additional 10 yards behind each goal line, which is called the end zone. A regulation field is 53⅓ yards wide (see diagram this page). Organized elementary school football is played on a regulation field; however, for a choose-up game, a smaller rectangular area may be used.

2. **Football**—A regulation-size football is difficult for young boys to handle. Smaller footballs may be used.

Distances *(for a regulation field)*
Goal line to goal line—100 yards
Goal line to goal post—10 yards
Sideline to sideline—53⅓ yards (160')
Goal post—at least 20' high, 23⅓' wide with a cross bar 10' high

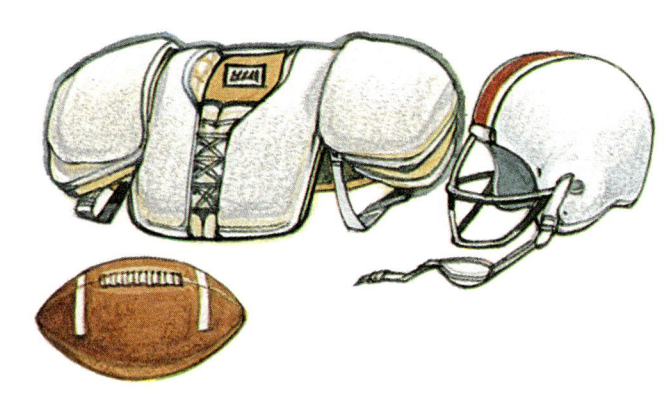

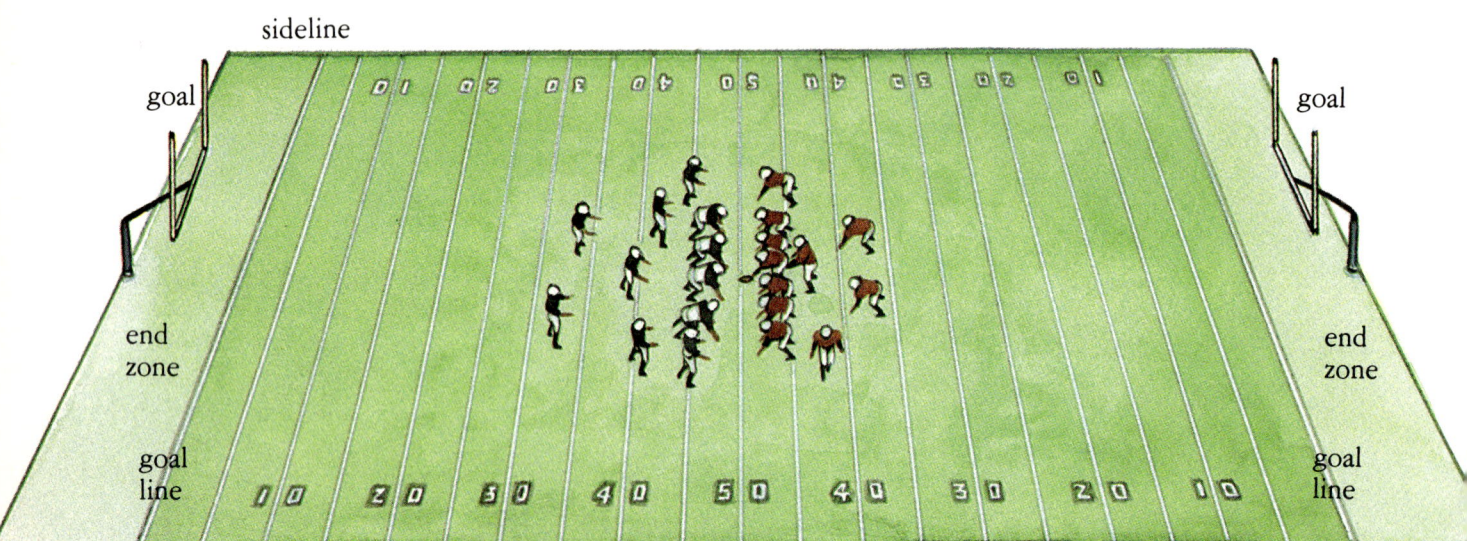

3. **Proper equipment**—Since football is essentially a body-contact sport, proper protective equipment is necessary. Such equipment should include:
   a. Head protector or helmet
   b. Face-mask, usually attached to the headgear
   c. Mouth guard
   d. Shoulder pads
   e. Thigh pads and kneepads, if the player has football pants
   f. Gym shoes (it is not necessary that young players wear cleated football shoes)
4. **Eleven players**—For one team:
   Center His job is to center the ball between his legs to the quarterback. The center also blocks.
   Guards (2) They block for the ball carrier.
   Tackles (2) They, too, block.
   Ends (2) They block and may also catch forward passes from the quarterback and run with the ball.
   Halfbacks (2) They may run with the ball, catch passes, throw passes, and block.
   Fullback He, too, may run, catch passes, throw passes, and block.
   Quarterback He gets the ball from the center, which starts the play. He may give the ball to another back, who will then run with it, or he may run with it himself. Or he may throw a forward pass to an end, halfback, or fullback.

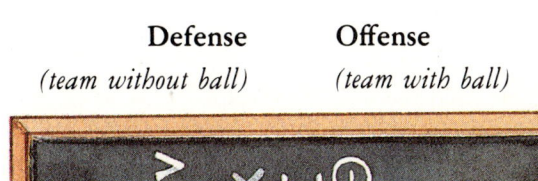

Defense
(team without ball)

Offense
(team with ball)

X—Defensive linemen
V—Linebackers
Z—Defensive backs

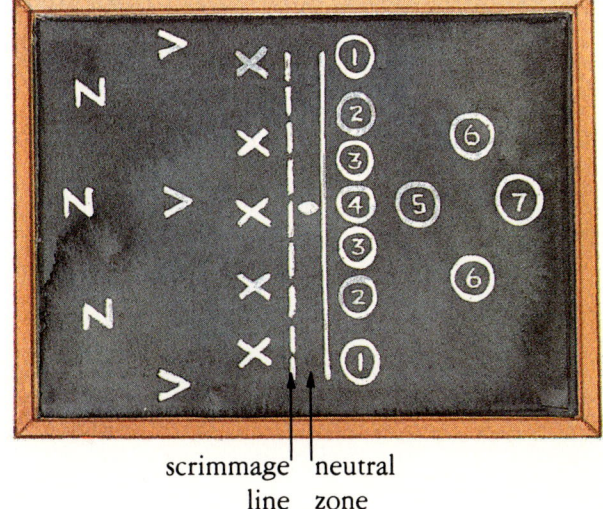

1—End
2—Tackle
3—Guard
4—Center
5—Quarterback
6—Halfback
7—Fullback

scrimmage line   neutral zone

SPORTS

How to Play

Players should know the following:

Blocking—Stopping an opponent by using your body. Members of the offensive team (the team with the ball) block. When blocking, you may not grab with your hands. Your hands must remain within the "framework" of your body—that is, within the area outlined by your body. You may use your hands to block but you may not reach out, and you may not grab. To block for a ball carrier, drive your shoulders into your opponent's stomach and leg area, or use your hands as described above. The object is to move him out of the way so the ball carrier can get through. The lower you block, the more effective your block will be. Never block with your head. Always avoid head contact in football.

You may also block by standing with your fists pressed against your chest, your elbows extended, and your feet wide apart. This block is used when your team is going to pass the ball.

Tackling—Stopping an opponent by using your shoulders, hands, and arms. Only the defensive team (the team that does not have the ball) may tackle, and they may only tackle the man with the ball. The best way to tackle is from a crouched position, with your head up so you can see. Drive your shoulder into the ball carrier's legs and lock your arms around his legs to bring him to the ground. Again, always avoid head contact—use only your shoulders, arms, and hands. On defense you may also use your hands to avoid blockers.

Kicking

a. *Place kick*—A kick used to start the game (kickoff), or for extra points and field goals. On a kickoff, one team kicks the ball to the other team. One player holds the ball in an upright position on the ground with his finger. If a kicking *tee* is available, a player will not have to hold the ball. Each time a team has scored a touchdown or field goal, it kicks off to the opponent. The place kick is also used for extra points and field goals (see Scoring).

b. *Punt*—A kick by a player on the offensive team, who drops the ball and kicks it before it touches the ground. Punting occurs when a team with the ball is giving up the ball to the opposition. The punt is used to put the ball back further from your goal line. The team that receives the punt may return it by catching it and running with it toward the goal line of the kicking team.

Running—The offensive team may run with the ball. Only the halfbacks, fullback, ends, and quarterback may run with the ball. The object is to run through the defense without being tackled and cross the goal line to score a *touchdown.*

Passing—Any backfield man may throw a forward pass, but it is usually the quarterback who throws passes. A forward pass must be thrown from *behind* the line of scrimmage. Only ends, halfbacks, the fullback, or the quarterback may catch a pass. If a pass is not caught, the ball is brought back to the line of scrimmage. If the pass is intercepted by a defensive player, he may run with it. On an intercepted pass, the defensive team takes control of the ball. A ball carrier may also throw an underhand pass, called a *lateral,* to another back or end. The lateral must be thrown to a man *behind* the ball carrier. It can never be passed to a player in front of the ball carrier. If a lateral is dropped, it is a free ball, the same as a fumble.

Fumbles—If the player with the ball drops it or has it knocked from his hands, it is a fumble. A fumble is a free ball, and the team that recovers it gains possession of the ball.

Beginning a Game

A football game starts with a kickoff by one team into the other team's half of the field. The team to kick off is determined before the game, usually by a toss of a coin. The team receiving the ball runs it back up the field as far as possible before its ball carrier is tackled. The line of scrimmage is set at the point the ball carrier is stopped.

The offensive and defensive teams line up across from each other. The action is started by the offensive team. When the center snaps the ball, the play starts. The play ends when the defense tackles the ball carrier or stops a pass.

Each team has four *downs* (or plays) to move the ball. If the team with the ball gains 10 yards, it is awarded a *first down.* The team then has four more downs to score or to make another first down. If the team with the ball does not score or make a first down in four downs, the ball is turned over to the opposing team.

SPORTS

Scoring

Touchdown—The team with the ball moves it across the goal line of the opposite team. A touchdown scores *6 points.*

Extra point—After a touchdown is made, the scoring team receives a bonus. The ball is placed 3 yards from the goal line. The team that has scored can either kick the ball between the goal posts and above the crossbar and receive *1 point;* or run or pass it over the goal and receive *2 points.*

Field goal—On a regular down, a team may kick the ball through the goal posts and above the crossbar instead of trying to make a touchdown. If the field goal is successful, it scores *3 points.*

Safety—If a player with the ball is tackled behind his own goal line, the opposite team is awarded *2 points.* The team that was caught behind its own goal must also kick off to the other team.

Penalties

When a penalty is called against a team, the opposite team can choose to accept the penalty or decline it. If the penalty is accepted, the yards are marked off by the referee and the down does not count. If the penalty is declined, however, the down counts. Sometimes it is better to decline a penalty because it is more of an advantage for the team that is fouled to have the down count. For example, a 5-yard penalty is called against the team with the ball. On the down, however, the team with the ball lost 10 yards. It would be better for the defensive team to decline the penalty and have the down count, because the loss was 10 yards and the penalty only 5 yards.

Off-sides—If either team moves across the line of scrimmage before the ball is centered or *snapped* to the quarterback, it is called off-sides; penalty—5 yards against the offending team.

Backfield in motion—If a backfield player on the team with the ball moves forward before the ball is centered, the team is penalized 5 yards.

Clipping—If a player blocks another player from behind, it is clipping; penalty—15 yards.

Holding—If a player on the offensive team grabs or holds a defensive player, he is called for holding; penalty—15 yards.

Unnecessary roughness—If a player is too rough in tackling or uses more force than necessary, his team is penalized 15 yards.

Pass interference—If a player interferes with another player going for a pass before either player has actually touched the ball, his team is guilty of interference. It is not interference, however, if both players are going for the ball and accidentally bump each other. Penalty—the pass is considered complete if the foul is against the defensive team. If the foul is called against the offensive team, it is a 15-yard penalty from the line of scrimmage.

Football games have four quarters of 15 minutes each. The team with the most points at the end of the game is the winner. There is no extra period if the game ends in a tie.

Touch Football   **Touch football** is played without tackling. Instead of tackling, the defensive team simply tags the ball carrier. It can be either a one-handed or two-handed tag. This should be decided before the game starts. None of the equipment described earlier is necessary for touch football. Touch football is the type usually played in schoolyards. As few as two or three players can play on a team, and in an area much smaller than on a regulation football field.

SPORTS

Basketball

Object The object of the game is to put the ball through the basket. This is the only way a team can score points. The team with the most points at the end of the game is the winner.

What You Need to Play

In order to start a game you must have:

1. **Basketball court**—Gymnasiums have regulation courts with baskets at both ends of the court (see diagram this page). Outdoor courts may have just one basket. Such courts are called half-courts. In a full-court game, each team shoots at a different basket. In a half-court game, both teams try to score at the same basket.
2. **Basketball**—Regulation or smaller size. The regulation-size ball for girls' basketball is slightly smaller than that used in boys' basketball.
3. **Players**—Enough players for two teams. There should be the same number on each team, and no more than five on each team; however, half-court games can be played with as few as two on a team.

Distances (fixed)
   Basket to free throw line—15'
   Free throw line—12' wide

Distances (changeable)
   Sideline to sideline—generally about 40'
   Basket to basket—generally at least 80'
   Three-point line—an arc drawn outside the free-throw circle, with an average distance from the basket of 19' 9"

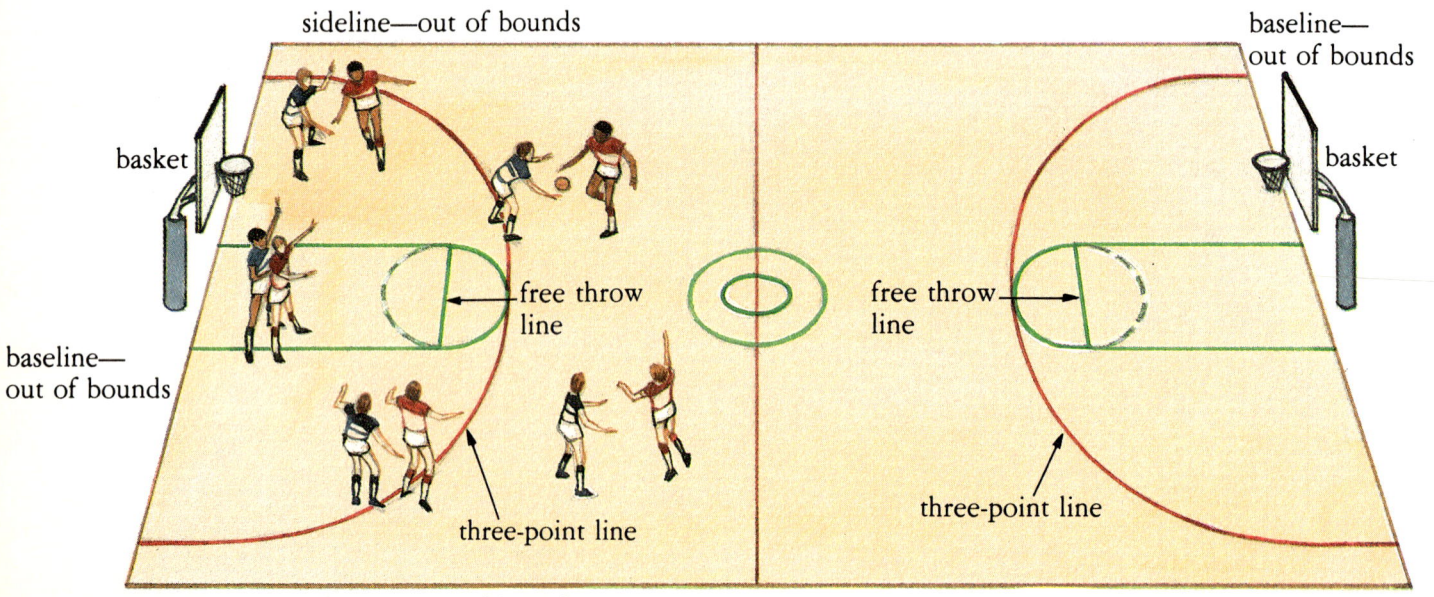

262

How to Play

All players interested in basketball should develop the following skills:

Shooting—Learn to make shots close to the basket. These shots are called lay-ups. A beginner (right-handed) can learn to shoot a lay-up as follows (a left-hander will use the opposite hand and foot):

a. With the basketball in both hands, stand 2 yards from the basket at an angle of 45 degrees to the backboard, feet parallel.

b. Take one full step forward with left foot.

c. As the left foot hits the ground, jump into the air with the right knee lifted high, and the left leg and ankle extended behind. The ball should be held high above the right shoulder.

d. At the peak of the jump, thrust the arms upward and push the ball with the right hand, aiming the ball above the rim. Usually there is a rectangular mark painted on the backboard. Aim for the right corner when approaching the basket from the right side and the left corner when approaching from the left side. The ball should bounce off the backboard and into the basket.

e. After mastering the one-step lay-up, move back 15 feet from the basket. Have someone pass the ball to you as you run toward the basket and shoot a lay-up after catching the pass. Be sure to jump off the left foot, raising the right knee into the air. You should also practice dribbling the ball to the basket for a lay-up.

Passing—Passing the ball is throwing it from one player to another. Because of the large size of the basketball, it is best to pass the ball with *two* hands. Both hands should be securely on the ball. As you pass, take a step in the direction of the teammate you are passing to.

Dribbling—A player can advance the ball by bouncing it with either the right or left hand; this is called dribbling the ball. You may dribble with one hand at a time only. Because it is easier to control the ball with your fingers, the ball should be bounced with your fingertips. To advance a ball, a player must dribble it. A player may not run while holding or carrying the ball. When a player stops dribbling, he or she must pass the ball to a teammate or shoot the ball at the basket.

Jumping—This is a vital skill in basketball. You must jump when you shoot a lay-up and to get rebounds (missed shots that bounce off the rim of the basket or the backboard).

Defense—When a team does not have the ball and is trying to stop the other team from scoring, it is said to be on defense. Since teams always have the same number of players, it is best to have each player on your team guard a player on the other team. When playing defense, *stay between your assigned player and the basket.* Try to block any passes to your assigned player, and try to keep the player from dribbling to the basket or passing to another opposing player.

Beginning a Game

A basketball game is begun with a *jump ball,* which determines which team has first possession of the ball.

Two players, one from each team, face off at the center circle at mid-court. Each player stands inside the circle, staying on the side of the half-court line that is in his or her team's half of the court. The referee throws the ball in the air between the two players, and each jumps and tries to tap the ball to a teammate. The team that gets control of the ball has first possession.

From this point on, whenever there is a struggle for control of the ball, or whenever it cannot be determined who last touched the ball before it went out of bounds, possession of the ball alternates between the teams.

Basketball is a fast-moving game. One minute your team may have the ball and be trying to score; an instant later you may be on defense because your team has lost the ball.

In addition to the jump ball rule, your team can lose the ball to the other team in the following ways:

1. The opposition may intercept a pass or steal the ball from someone dribbling.
2. The ball may be awarded by the referee to the opposition, who then put it back into play from out of bounds, as in the following situations—
   a. If the ball goes out of bounds and a player from your team touched it last, the ball is given to the opposition.
   b. If you or a teammate double-dribble when you have the ball. To double-dribble is to stop dribbling and then start again before passing to a teammate or taking a shot. It is also double-dribbling if you dribble with both hands at the same time.
   c. If you or a teammate *travel* (run) with the ball without dribbling.

Fouls

Players on both teams should avoid body contact. To foul an opposing player is to interfere with his or her action (shooting, passing, catching, dribbling, or playing defense) by body contact such as bumping, tripping, grabbing and holding, or pushing. When you foul a player, that player gets a free shot (called *free throw*) at the basket. If you foul while the player is trying to shoot at the basket, he or she gets two free throws.

The free throw line is 15 feet from the basket. It is marked on all regulation courts. There is a free throw line at both baskets. While the fouled player is shooting the free throw, members of both teams line up beside the free throw line in order to get the rebound if the free throw shooter misses the shot.

SPORTS

Scoring

1. A basket made during actual play is called a field goal and is worth two points if it is made from inside the three-point line, and three points if it is made from outside the three-point line.
2. A free throw is worth one point.

When a team scores a basket or a free throw, the ball is given to the opposition, who put the ball in play by passing it in from out of bounds behind the basket.

In girls' basketball, the team with the ball has a 30-second time limit in which to shoot for a basket. If the players do not shoot for a basket within that time, control of the ball goes to the other team. There is no time limit in boys' basketball.

In organized basketball, a game is divided into four periods or quarters. In elementary school basketball each quarter is six minutes. The team with the highest number of points at the end of four quarters is the winner. If the game ends in a tie, an extra period is played. This is called an overtime period.

Choose-up games, especially on outdoor courts, are very popular with young people. These games are usually half-court games—both teams try to score at the same basket. There are no referees in these games, so the players must be honest in admitting if they have double-dribbled, traveled, fouled, or touched the ball last before it went out of bounds.

When the ball changes hands in a half-court game, the team that has gotten the ball must take it back out past the free throw line before shooting at the basket. If someone is fouled, he or she does not shoot a free throw; rather, the player passes the ball in bounds for his or her team so they can try to make a field goal.

The winner of a half-court game is determined by setting a certain number of points as the end of the game. The first team to reach that number of points is the winner.

SPORTS

Soccer

Object The object of the game is to put the ball across the opposing team's goal line and into the goal. Players may use any part of their bodies to move the ball except their hands and arms. The team with the highest score at the end of the match is the winner.

What You Need to Play

1. **Playing area**—A regulation soccer field is 100 to 130 yards long and 50 to 100 yards wide. A standard football field (100 yards long and 53 1/3 yards wide) may be used. Corner flags are placed at the four corners of the field. The lines marking the sides of the field are called *touch lines*, and those marking the ends of the field are called *goal lines*.
2. **Ball**—A regulation-size soccer ball (27 to 28 inches in diameter). A smaller ball may be used by young players.
3. **Players' equipment**—Shin guards should be worn by all players. Gym shoes may be worn by young players. If shoes with studs are used, the studs must be less than three-quarters of an inch long and must not have sharp edges. Players may not wear anything that might hurt other players.
4. **Players**—A minimum of seven and a maximum of eleven per team.

Distances *(fixed)*
Goal—8 yards wide, 8 feet high
Goal area—20 yards wide, 6 yards deep
Penalty area—44 yards wide, 18 yards deep
Goal to penalty mark—12 yards
Penalty mark to penalty area arc—10 yards
Center spot to center circle—10 yards
Corner arc—1 yard radius

Distances *(changeable)*
Length of field—100 to 130 yards
Width of field—50 to 100 yards
Corner flag height—at least 5 feet

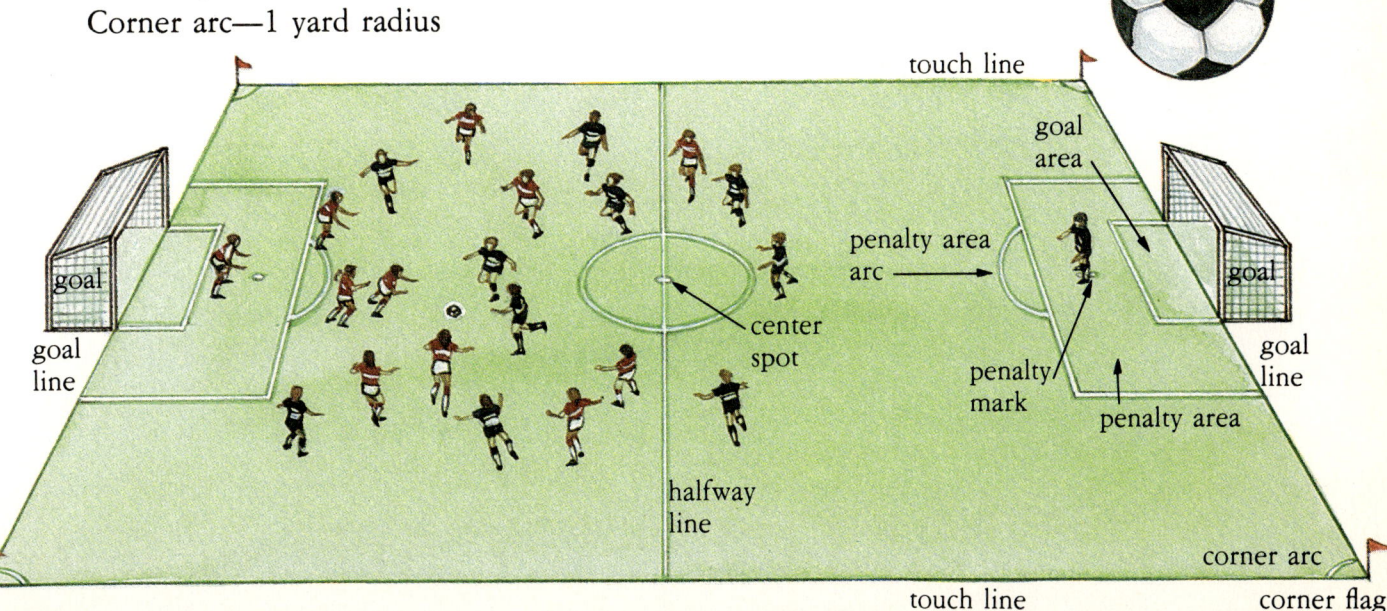

SPORTS

How to Play

Length of game—The game is divided into two halves. A regulation half is 45 minutes long, but young players may play 30-, 25-, or even 20-minute halves. There is a rest period of at least five minutes between halves.

Kickoff—The teams decide before the game, usually by a coin toss, which side will kick off. All players must be on their own half of the field, and players receiving the kickoff must be at least 10 yards from the ball. The ball is kicked off from the center spot at midfield. The ball must move forward into the defending team's half of the field. The player kicking off may not touch the ball again until it has been touched by another player.

A kickoff is used to start each half and any overtime period, and also to resume play after a goal is scored. To start the second half, the teams switch positions on the field and the team that received the ball at the beginning of the game kicks off.

Drop ball—If the referee stops play for any reason except a rules violation or to call the end of the first half or end of the game, play is resumed with a drop ball. The referee drops the ball where it was when play was stopped. The ball is not in play until it touches the ground. If a player touches the ball before it hits the ground, the referee must drop the ball again.

Ball out of play—The ball goes out of play when it crosses completely over the touch line or goal line, or at the moment the referee stops play.

Throw in—If the ball goes out of play past the touch line, it is put back into play by a throw-in, which is made by a player of the team that did not touch the ball last. The player must have part of both feet on or over the touch line. The player must throw with both hands, holding the ball up and behind the head, then throwing it smoothly over the player's head and onto the field.

If the throw-in is not made properly, or if the ball goes out of play again before another player touches it, the opposing team gets a throw-in. If the throw-in goes into the opposing team's goal, no goal is scored and the opposing team gets a goal kick (see below). If the player throws the ball into his or her own team's goal, the opposing team is given a corner kick (see below).

Goal kick—If the ball crosses completely over the goal line outside the goal posts, and it was last touched by an attacking player, the defending team is given a goal kick. The ball is placed anywhere in the half of the goal area on the side of the field where it went out of bounds. The kicker may ask that opposing players stand outside the penalty area. The ball must go into play outside the penalty area. The kicker may not touch the ball again until another player has touched it.

Corner kick—If the ball crosses completely over the goal line anywhere outside the goal posts and it was last touched by a defending player, the attacking team is given a corner kick. The ball is placed inside the corner arc on the side of the field where the ball went out of play. The kicker may ask that opposing players stand at least 10 yards from the ball.

The ball must be kicked a distance of at least one full turn of the ball, but the kicker may not touch the ball again until another player touches it. The kicker may score by kicking the ball directly into the defending team's goal.

Offside position—A player is in offside position when in the opposing team's half of the field and closer to the opposing goal than the ball is, and when there are fewer than two opposing players between the player and the goal line. Offside position is not against the rules, but being offside is (see below).

Offside—A player is offside when the player is in offside position and takes part in playing the ball, interferes with an opposing player, or tries in any way to benefit from being in offside position.

If the ball is played and a player who was not in offside position then moves into offside position to play the ball, the player may not be called offside.

The penalty for offside is an indirect free kick (see below) by the opposing team, made from the position of the offending player

Free kick—There are two kinds of free kicks in soccer:

a. Direct free kick—The ball is kicked directly into the opposing team's goal to score.

b. Indirect free kick—The ball must be touched by another player after it is put into play and before a goal is scored.

Substitutions—New players may be sent into the game to substitute for players on the field. Substitutions may be made only when the ball is out of play. Substitutes must wait until the players they replace have left the field, wait to receive the referee's signal, and enter at the halfway line.

Scoring

One point is scored for each goal. A goal is made when the ball goes completely across the goal line between the goal posts and under the connecting crossbar. The team that is scored against resumes play with a kickoff.

Fouls and Penalties

There are two types of fouls in soccer:

Penal foul—Players are charged with a penal foul if they intentionally do the following:

a. Kick or try to kick an opposing player
b. Hit or try to hit an opposing player
c. Hold an opposing player
d. Push an opposing player
e. Charge an opposing player in a dangerous way, from the front or from behind, or jump at an opposing player. A fair charge—charging an opponent using only shoulder-to-shoulder contact—is not a foul as long as the charge is safe for both players and both are within playing distance of the ball.
f. Touch the ball with hands or arms in an attempt to control the ball. If a player is only acting in self-protection or does not intentionally handle the ball, it is not a foul.

The penalty for a penal foul is a direct free kick or a penalty kick given to the opposing team.

A penalty kick is given when a defending player makes a penal foul inside the player's team's penalty area. The attacking team is given a kick from the penalty mark. The defending goalkeeper must stand in front of the goal, with both feet on the goal line, and must not move either foot until the ball is kicked. All other players except the kicker must stand outside the penalty area and the penalty arc area. The ball must move forward, and the kicker may not touch the ball again until another player has touched it.

Nonpenal foul—Players are charged with a nonpenal foul if they do the following:

a. Intentionally block an opposing player when not within playing distance of the ball
b. Put themselves or others in danger by their play
c. Charge the goalkeeper
d. Charge an opposing player when not within playing distance of the ball

Goalkeepers commit a nonpenal foul if they do any of the following:

a. Take more than four steps while in control of the ball
b. Delay play
c. Put the ball into play, then touch it before another player touches it outside the penalty area

The penalty for a nonpenal foul is an indirect free kick given to the opposing team.

Caution—The referee will caution a player who acts in an unsporting way, argues with the referee, enters or leaves the field without the referee's permission, or ignores the referee's warnings about bad behavior or rule violations. The referee marks a caution by raising a yellow card overhead. Players are permitted one caution per game. If a second caution is called against a player, the player is ejected.

Ejection—The referee will eject a player who acts violently, uses foul or threatening language, or receives a second caution. The referee indicates an ejection by raising a red card overhead. A substitute may not be sent into the game to replace an ejected player.

The game is stopped for a caution or an ejection. Play is resumed by the opposing team, with an indirect free kick if the offense did not involve a penal foul, or with a direct free kick or penalty kick if the offense did involve a penal foul.

SPORTS

Professional Sports Champions

Baseball

1993 Toronto Blue Jays (AL)
1992 Toronto Blue Jays (AL)
1991 Minnesota Twins (AL)
1990 Cincinnati Reds (NL)
1989 Oakland Athletics (AL)
1988 Los Angeles Dodgers (NL)
1987 Minnesota Twins (AL)
1986 New York Mets (NL)
1985 Kansas City Royals (AL)
1984 Detroit Tigers (AL)
1983 Baltimore Orioles (AL)
1982 St. Louis Cardinals (NL)
1981 Los Angeles Dodgers (NL)
1980 Philadelphia Phillies (NL)
1979 Pittsburgh Pirates (NL)
1978 New York Yankees (AL)
1977 New York Yankees (AL)
1976 Cincinnati Reds (NL)
1975 Cincinnati Reds (NL)
1974 Oakland Athletics (AL)
1973 Oakland Athletics (AL)
1972 Oakland Athletics (AL)
1971 Pittsburgh Pirates (NL)
1970 Baltimore Orioles (AL)
1969 New York Mets (NL)
1968 Detroit Tigers (AL)
1967 St. Louis Cardinals (NL)
1966 Baltimore Orioles (AL)
1965 Los Angeles Dodgers (NL)
1964 St. Louis Cardinals (NL)
1963 Los Angeles Dodgers (NL)
1962 New York Yankees (AL)
1961 New York Yankees (AL)

Football

1993–94 Dallas Cowboys
1992–93 Dallas Cowboys
1991–92 Washington Redskins
1990–91 New York Giants
1989–90 San Francisco 49ers
1988–89 San Francisco 49ers
1987–88 Washington Redskins
1986–87 New York Giants
1985–86 Chicago Bears
1984–85 San Francisco 49ers
1983–84 Los Angeles Raiders
1982–83 Washington Redskins
1981–82 San Francisco 49ers
1980–81 Oakland Raiders
1979–80 Pittsburgh Steelers
1978–79 Pittsburgh Steelers
1977–78 Dallas Cowboys
1976–77 Oakland Raiders
1975–76 Pittsburgh Steelers
1974–75 Pittsburgh Steelers
1973–74 Miami Dolphins
1972–73 Miami Dolphins
1971–72 Dallas Cowboys
1970–71 Baltimore Colts
1969–70 Kansas City Chiefs
1968–69 New York Jets
1967–68 Green Bay Packers
1966–67 Green Bay Packers

Basketball

1992–93 Chicago Bulls
1991–92 Chicago Bulls
1990–91 Chicago Bulls
1989–90 Detroit Pistons
1988–89 Detroit Pistons
1987–88 Los Angeles Lakers
1986–87 Los Angeles Lakers
1985–86 Boston Celtics
1984–85 Los Angeles Lakers
1983–84 Boston Celtics
1982–83 Philadelphia 76ers
1981–82 Los Angeles Lakers
1980–81 Boston Celtics
1979–80 Los Angeles Lakers
1978–79 Seattle Super Sonics
1977–78 Washington Bullets
1976–77 Portland Trail Blazers
1975–76 Boston Celtics
1974–75 Golden State Warriors
1973–74 Boston Celtics
1972–73 New York Knicks
1971–72 Los Angeles Lakers
1970–71 Milwaukee Bucks
1969–70 New York Knicks
1968–69 Boston Celtics
1967–68 Boston Celtics
1966–67 Philadelphia 76ers
1958–66 Boston Celtics
1957–58 St. Louis Hawks
1956–57 Boston Celtics
1955–56 Philadelphia Warriors
1954–55 Syracuse Nationals

272

Safety Tips

We live in a wonderful world, a world full of interesting things to see and do. But every day accidents happen and people are hurt.

Most of these accidents do not have to happen. If people take the time to do things safely, most accidents can be avoided.

This section includes tips on household safety, boating and swimming safety, bicycle and street safety, and automobile safety. Here too are important tips to help you when your parents are not with you—when *you* are in charge of your own safety.

SAFETY TIPS

Safety Around the House

1. **Keep the floors clear of toys** and other objects.
2. **Never play with the electric cords** of lamps, radios, or other electrical devices. Do not play with electrical outlets. If you see an electrical cord whose outer covering is cracked or worn, tell your parents right away. It should be replaced with a new cord.
3. **Do not play with electric devices,** such as a toaster, hair drier, stove or oven, washing machine, or clothes drier. Have your parents show you the right way to use them and get their permission before using them. Never use power tools unless your parents have given you permission. Make sure they or other adults are there to help you.
4. **Do not use electric devices near water,** and do not touch them if your hands are wet. If you are wet you can get a deadly shock from anything that plugs into the wall outlet—including hair driers, radios, and lamps. You can even get a shock from your telephone. Keep these items away from the bathtub, shower, and sink.

SAFETY TIPS

5. **Do not play with sharp or pointed things,** such as knives, scissors, handsaws, screwdrivers, or knitting needles.
6. **Never touch a firearm**—handgun, rifle, or shotgun—unless your mom or dad is with you and gives you permission. If you have been given permission, never point a gun at or near anyone, even if you *know* or have been *told* that the gun is not loaded. Never get in front of the barrel of a gun or turn the barrel toward you. Guns are not toys.
7. **Do not play with chemicals used around the house,** such as cleansers, bleach, insect sprays, furniture polish, floor wax, and lighter fluid. All such items should be kept in a cupboard or cabinet, away from heat and moisture. If the cabinet can be reached by small children, it should be locked.
8. **If you break something made of glass,** do not pick up the pieces with your hands. First, be sure to wear sturdy shoes to protect your feet, and keep pets away from the area. Then use a brush or broom and dustpan to pick up the glass. Look all around for little bits of glass—they may have fallen far from where you were when the glass broke. Then, if you are permitted to use the vacuum cleaner, vacuum the whole area well. Always tell your mom and dad about the accident so they can double-check the area.
9. **Do not play with plastic bags** (shopping bags, clothing covers, or trash bags); they can be dangerous. *Do not ever* put a plastic bag over your head. It could cut off your supply of fresh air and keep you from breathing. Keep all plastic bags out of the reach of small children.
10. **Do not light matches in the house** unless your parents or other adults are present and give you permission. Even if you have permission, do not light matches anywhere near loose papers, paint cans, household chemicals, curtains or drapes, a Christmas tree, or anything else that might catch fire. Matches should be kept in a drawer or cabinet away from heat and moisture and out of the reach of small children.
11. **Smoke detectors** should exist on every floor of your home—downstairs, upstairs, basement—and should be checked regularly to make sure they work properly. If a fire should start in the house, the smoke detector will sound an alarm, giving you time to get out of the house.
12. **Fire extinguishers** should be placed in the kitchen and in the basement or furnace room, near the furnace. They should be easy to get to and should be checked regularly.

SAFETY TIPS

13. **When playing outside,** stay in the yard. Do not play on the sidewalk or in the street. Check the yard for things that you might trip on, such as water sprinklers, garden hoses or garden tools, holes made by wild animals, and rocks sticking up out of the ground.
14. **Keep bicycles, skateboards, and other toys off the driveway** when you are not using them.
15. **Outdoor tools,** such as rakes, shovels, and clippers, should be cleaned and put away after they are used. If they are left out someone could trip and fall over them, or they might be struck by the blade of a lawnmower and cause a serious injury.
16. **Do not climb into an old refrigerator,** freezer, trunk, washing machine, clothes dryer, or the like when you are playing. It can be a deadly trap because you cannot reach the door handle from the inside. Once the door closes, you are trapped until someone lets you out. Tell your parents to remove the door latches and handles of such items that you find at home or nearby.

Safety and Falls

1. **Use a strong, sturdy stepladder** to reach high shelves and cupboards. Do not stand on a chair or stool to reach things high up. Make sure the stepladder is fully opened and that all four legs are resting flat on the floor. Never stand on the top step of the ladder. Always be sure of your footing. Never make motions that might throw you off balance.
2. **Keep floors free of toys,** clothing, books, and other things that could cause you to slip or trip.
3. **Watch out for slippery floors.** Step carefully on small rugs. They can slide out from under your feet, and you could have a bad fall.
4. **Do not run in the house.** You could slip and fall into the hard, sharp corners of tables or other furniture.
5. **Walk, do not run, on a stairway.** Keep your hand on the railing and watch where you step. Keep stairs clear of *everything.* Never put anything on a step.
6. **Never walk around in the dark.** There should be a lamp or a light switch within reach of every bed. If you have to get up in the night, turn on the light so you can see where you are going.
7. **Your bath or shower should have a shower mat,** or a nonskid surface, for you to stand on when showering or when stepping into or out of the tub. There should also be a strong, sturdy handbar attached to the wall.
8. **If there are toddlers** or very small children in the house, there should be gates at the bottom and top of staircases. It is easy for little ones to fall down stairs and get hurt.
9. **When using ladders outdoors,** make sure both feet of the ladder rest securely on the ground. Also make sure that the tops of the ladder are securely placed. The feet of the ladder should be placed away from the wall, so that your weight when climbing will keep the ladder steady against the wall. Here is a good rule of thumb. Place the bottom of the ladder 1 foot away from the wall for every 4 feet of height from the bottom of the wall to the top of the ladder. Always get permission before you climb ladders.
10. **Do not climb trees** when you are playing outside. You could easily slip and fall and be badly hurt. If you should get your kite or model plane or other toy caught in a tree, ask your mom or dad or another adult to help you get it down.

SAFETY TIPS

Street Safety

1. **Always cross streets at the street corner,** not in the middle of the block, whether in the city or in town. Cross the street when the traffic light facing you turns green, or when the WALK signal goes on. Whenever you cross the street, look all ways to make sure the traffic has stopped. Walk briskly, but do not run.
2. **Do not step out into the street from between or behind parked cars.** Always make sure drivers will be able to see you.
3. **Do not play in the street.** Do not ride bicycles on the sidewalk, and do not ride skateboards on the sidewalk or in the street. Ride skateboards only at skateboard rinks or other areas that have been set aside for skateboarders.
4. **When getting into or out of a car parked** on the street, always use the door on the curb side.
5. **Carry bags or packages in such a way** that they do not block your view of traffic. In bad weather, do not let your umbrella or the hood of your coat block your view.
6. **On roads where there are no sidewalks,** walk at the edge of the road, single file, and facing oncoming traffic. Wherever you can, walk on the ground beside the road, not on the road pavement. Always step away from the roadside when a car approaches you, and stop until it passes. This is especially important at night, when it is hard for drivers to see you, and when a car's bright lights can make it hard for you to see where you are going.
7. **When walking along the roadside at dusk** or at night, carry a flashlight or electric lantern so that cars can see you at a distance. Wear light-colored clothing—white and yellow are good. Light-colored clothing with reflective strips and bands is best for walking at night.

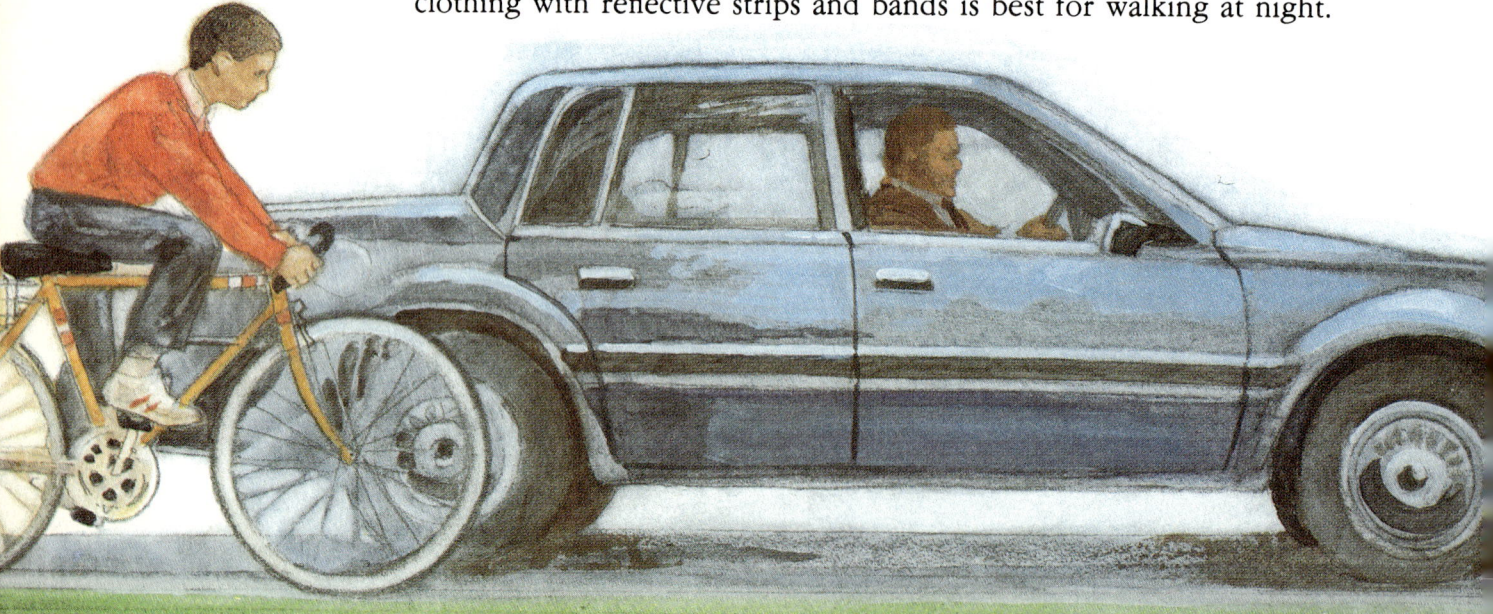

Bicycle Safety

1. **Keep your bicycle in good shape.** The tires should have good tread and the right amount of air in them. The brakes should work easily and stop the bike quickly and smoothly. Your bike should also have a good loud horn or bell. Mirrors mounted on the handlebars help you to see the traffic behind you.
2. **Ride after dusk or at night** only with your parents' permission. Your bike should have a headlamp, rear reflector, and reflector strips on the foot pedals. Reflectors that mount on the wheels also help others see you at night. Wear light-colored clothing, or clothing with reflective strips or bands.
3. **Always ride on the right-hand side of the road,** with, not against, the traffic. Ride close to the curb and in a straight line. Do not weave from side to side.
4. **When bicycling with others,** always ride single file, never side by side.
5. **Obey all traffic signs and signals.** Slow down and look both ways before crossing at an intersection, even if there is no stop sign or red light.
   At busy intersections or when crossing busy streets, get off your bike and walk it across. Walk briskly, but do not run.
6. **Always give the right of way to motorists** and people who are walking.
7. **Always signal when you are going to make a turn.** Hold your left arm out and bent up at the elbow to signal a right turn. Hold your left arm straight out to signal a left turn.
8. **Except when signaling turns or shifting gears** on your bicycle, keep both hands on the handlebars.
9. **Keep packages or other items in a basket** or carrier mounted on the bicycle.
10. **Do not carry passengers on your bicycle.** It was built to carry only one person—you! One more is one too many.

SAFETY TIPS

Automobile Safety

1. **Always wear your seat belt and shoulder harness.** Make sure the seat belt stretches snugly across your hips and that the shoulder belt stretches from your shoulder across your chest. Do not tuck the shoulder belt under your arm.
2. **Keep all doors locked** when the automobile is moving.
3. **Do not stick your arms or legs or head out** of the car window.
4. **Do not distract the driver** by yelling or shouting, playing the radio loudly, or moving about in the car. Do not poke or nudge the driver. Talk in a normal voice when you want to get the driver's attention.
5. **Do not block the driver's view** out of the side windows or rear window.
6. **Do not offer the driver something to eat or drink.** It is polite to offer food to others, but the driver of a car should never eat or drink while driving. He or she should keep both hands on the steering wheel and both eyes on the road.
7. **Do not throw anything out of an automobile,** not even a candy wrapper. Cups, paper, and other litter along the road can be a hazard to other cars. Put litter in a car litter bag and empty the bag at home.
8. **When the driver parks the car** on the street, get in and out of the car on the curb side, never on the street side.
9. **In parking lots,** make sure it is safe before you open your door and get out. Look to see if a car is coming into the space near your car. If so, wait for the car to park before opening your door.

    If there already is a car next to yours, open your car door carefully, so it does not hit the other car. Once out of the car, watch out for traffic, especially for cars that are pulling into or out of parking spaces.

Swimming Safety

1. **Learn how to swim well.** Many organizations offer swimming and water safety courses. The best way to have fun in the water is to be comfortable in the water. The best way to do that is to be a good swimmer.
2. **Always swim in regular swimming areas,** such as pools and beaches that have lifeguards on duty. Never swim in out-of-the-way spots, such as ponds or streams.
3. **Never swim alone.** Always swim with a buddy. If you should have any trouble, your buddy will be there to help you.
4. **If you cannot swim,** stay near the shore or at the shallow end of the pool. Do not use a floating chair, inner tube, air mattress, or the like to float in water that is over your head.
5. **Always obey the lifeguard—immediately.** Do not argue with or try to distract lifeguards. They have to watch everybody at once. Do not make their job even more difficult. Never call for help just for fun. Call for help when you need help.
6. **Never push or shove people** into the water. Never throw mud or rocks or other objects in a swimming area.
7. **Do not dive into water unless you know it is safe.** Check first to make sure the water is deep enough and that there are no hidden boulders, rock ledges, or other hazards. Do not fool around on a diving board. You could easily lose your footing and have a bad fall.
8. **Do not go swimming right after eating a meal.** Wait about an hour before going in the water.
9. **Stop swimming when you start to feel tired or cold.**
10. **Do not go into the water if you feel ill.**

Boating Safety

1. **Never go boating without your parents' permission.**
2. **Every boater should have a life jacket,** life vest, or seat cushion designed to help keep a person afloat in the water. Poor swimmers or nonswimmers should wear life jackets or vests at all times. In sailboats or canoes, everyone should wear life jackets or vests. There should be at least two jackets, vests, or floatable cushions in the boat at all times, even if only one person is using the boat.
3. **Wear sneakers** or deck shoes so you will have good footing on wet or slippery decks and floorboards.
4. **There should be one strong swimmer** for every weak swimmer or nonswimmer in the boat.
5. **Distribute the weight of the boaters evenly,** so that the boat rides as levelly as possible. Do not overload the boat. Check to see how many passengers the boat is designed to hold, and do not go over the limit.
6. **Stay in your seat in the boat.** Do not move around or stand up in the boat. If you have to change position in a small boat, move slowly and carefully in a crouched position. Try to stay close to the center of the boat. When changing places with another person, move so that the weight and motion of one person balances out the weight and motion of the other.

    In small canoes, paddle to shore or to a dock and switch positions there. Do not change positions in open water.

    Stay in your seat in a moving motorboat. Do not sit on the back of the seat or on the front, back, or sides of the boat.
7. **Never jump into a boat.** Step carefully into the center of the boat. At dockside, have someone hold the boat for you as you step into it, or make sure the boat is tied to the dock so that it will not start to float away from you as you get in. Once you are seated, you can help steady the boat for others to come aboard.
8. **If your boat becomes swamped**—filled with water—or if it capsizes—turns over completely—hang onto it and signal for help. Do not swim away from the boat unless you are very close to shore. The boat will remain afloat even if it is filled with water or overturned. If you are near shore, paddle the boat to it. Once ashore, you can right the boat and empty the water.

SAFETY TIPS

9. **At the first sign of bad weather,** head for shore. A boat is the wrong place to be during a storm, especially if there is lightning.
10. **All boats must have lights** to operate at night. Canoes, rowboats, and small sailboats can use a single white light, such as an electric lantern. The light should be clearly visible from all directions. Motorboats must have approved running lights.
11. **All boats should have a horn** or whistle so that distress signals can be heard. The horn or whistle should be able to give a four-second signal that can be heard at least half a mile away. Small boats can be equipped with an athletic-type whistle, but make sure it is attached by a string to the boat or to a life jacket. That way it will not get lost if the boat tips over.
12. **All boats should have a good anchor** and a bailing pump or can. Motorboats should also have a fire extinguisher, first aid kit, towline, and spare anchor. All gear should be stored out of the way, but should be easy to get to when needed.

Personal Safety Tips

Almost all the people you will meet in your life will be good, law-abiding, friendly people. But you cannot tell just by people's looks, or how they dress or act, what kind of people they are.

Here are some simple rules for keeping safe around people you do not know. It's a good idea to read these rules with your mom and dad. Do not try to read and remember them all at once. Read them over and then come back to them a number of times. Soon you will see that these rules make good sense.

1. **Stay out of the reach of people you do not know.** Think of how far they can reach with their arms. Then stand three or four feet farther away. If they move toward you, step back and away from them.

2. **Do not accept anything from people you do not know.** This includes candy, soda, food, pets, or gifts. And it also includes your own things.

    Let's say you are playing in your yard and a person you do not know comes up the driveway and picks up your favorite toy—a model car, or a doll, or a baseball bat. The man or woman holds out the toy to you. You cannot take the toy and still stay out of that person's reach. Instead of taking the toy, say politely, "Would you please put my toy down? I don't want it now, but I will want it later."

3. **Any time you are by yourself, you are in charge of your own safety.** When you are alone and find yourself in a situation that makes you uncomfortable or scared, it is all right to run away. It is always best to be safe, even if it means you are not being polite. If you are near your house, call loudly for your mom and dad and run inside. If you are not near home, call loudly for help and look for adults you know and can trust—a policeman, teacher, or shopkeeper, for example.

4. **Do not go anywhere with anyone you do not know,** no matter what that person tells you or who that man or woman claims to be.

   Suppose you are at school waiting for your mother to pick you up. A person you do not know drives up, calls you by your name, and says your mom has asked him to come get you.

   Let's say the person even has a badge and says he is a policeman, and that there will be trouble if you do not obey him.

   You do not know this person, so you should not go. If he really is a policeman, he will know that by refusing to go with him, you are only doing your job—taking charge of your own safety. Have the person prove to your teacher or principal that he is who he claims to be.

   Let's say your mom really did send a friend to pick you up. How could you know for sure? One good way is to get the person's name and then telephone your mom and get her permission to go.

   You and your parents may also decide to choose a special code word or saying to use as a password. It works this way: If the person who comes to get you at school tells you the code word, then you know that your mom asked him to pick you up. If that person does not know the code word, then you know your mom did not ask him to pick you up.

   If you and your parents decide to use a code word or saying, it should be something only your parents and you would know—it should be special enough that a stranger could not guess it or say it by accident.

5. **Do not go anywhere to meet someone you do not know,** unless your parents know the person well and have given you permission to go. If your parents do not know the person well, they should go with you or ask someone they know well to go with you. Follow this rule even if you are going to a public place like a gymnasium, shopping center, park, or playground.

6. **If a person you do not know stops his or her car and asks for directions,** you can help as long as you do not go near the car. If the person asks you to look at a map or list of directions, tell that person to ask an adult for help.

7. **Do not talk to people you do not know.** If you are alone and a person you do not know comes up to you and starts to talk to you or ask you questions, you can say, "I'm sorry, but I'm not allowed to talk with strangers."

   Suppose the person says, "Oh, I'm not a stranger," tells you his name, and says he knows your parents. It's all right for you to say, "I don't know you, so I'm still not allowed to talk to you."

SAFETY TIPS

8. **When you are alone at home, do not open the door** to anyone you do not know or let that person in the house. If you are outside, remember to stay out of the person's reach. If the person moves toward you, it is all right to go in the house and lock the door.

   Let's say the person has an envelope and says it is full of important papers for your mom or dad. You can say, "Please put it in the mailbox, or slide it under the door, or come back later." Or you can say, "Please take it next door." Your parents will be able to pick it up there. You do not have to open the door, even if the person gets angry.

   If your mom and dad are expecting something to be delivered to the house, they should tell you ahead of time and describe the item and the person who will deliver it.

9. **You are in charge of your own body.** This means that if anyone touches you in a way you do not like, you can tell that person to stop.

   Let's say your babysitter starts to tickle you, but you do not want to be tickled. You can say, "Please stop."

   Suppose a person wants you to give him or her a hug and you do not want to. It is all right for you to say so. If that person tries to give you a hug anyway, you can say, "Stop." If the person continues to bother you, let that person know you are going to tell your mom and dad.

10. **Always talk with your mom and dad whenever you have any problems,** especially problems with other adults.

    Your parents are there to help you with any problem you have, no matter how big or small it seems to be.

    Sometimes it is hard to get parents to understand that you have a problem and need their help. What should you do? Keep telling them about your problem, and do not stop until you get the help you need.

    Whenever you have a problem, always talk with your mom and dad first. But there are other adults who can help you, too. You could talk with your teacher or the school principal, and don't forget the head of your church or synagogue. All of these adults are there to help you.